Jan 2005

Dearest Michael,
  We are [...] to you for [...] prayers (se[...] on page xii [...] absolute "jewel".

Lots of love,
Manprit aka
Bibi. Bibi.

A STATE OF INJUSTICE

Dear Michael,
  I cannot express the extent to which we have been lifted up and encouraged by all your support + prayers. It's good to know that you are as famous in Australia as you must be in London.

Much love Bob—

This book is dedicated to Ranjit

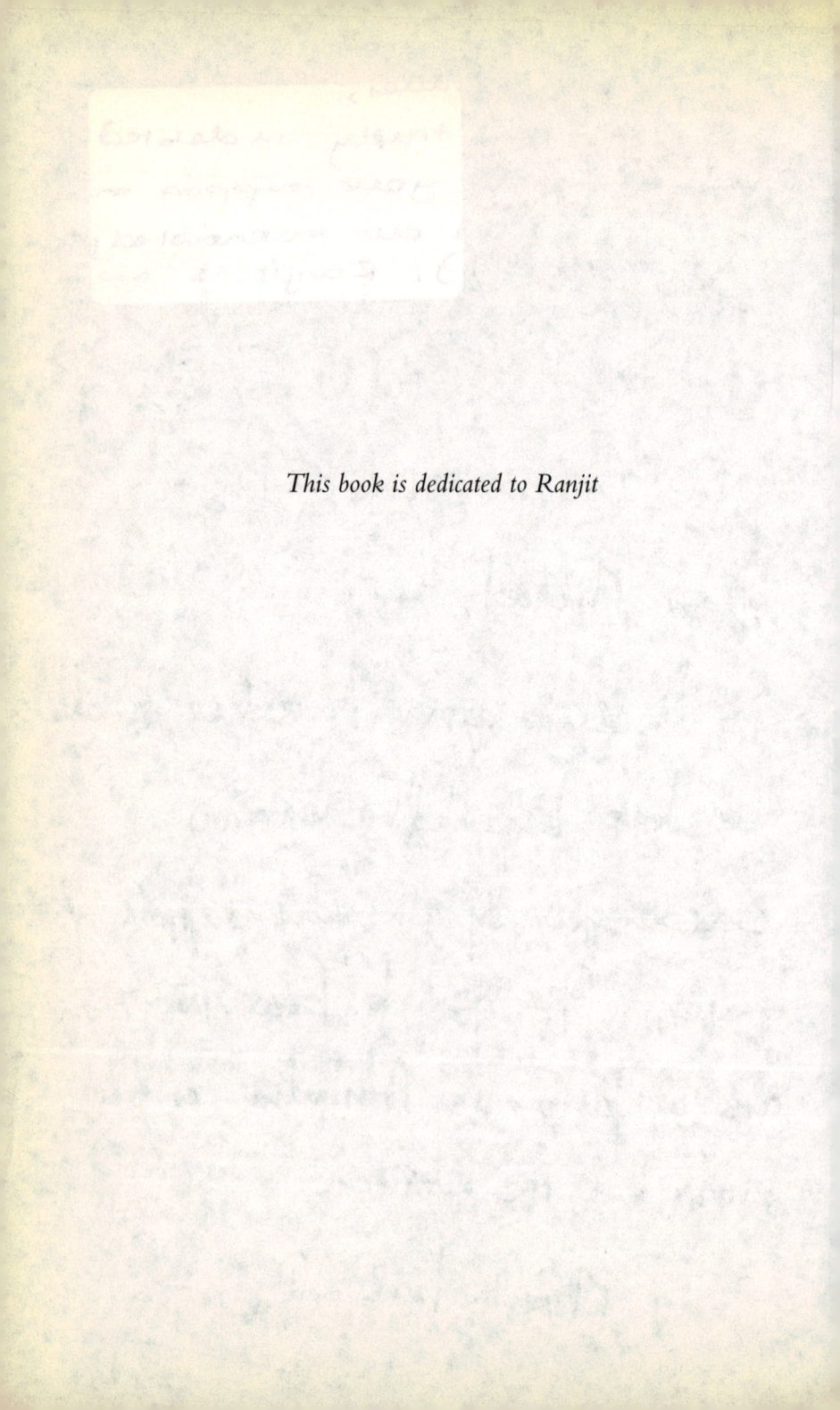

A STATE OF INJUSTICE

Robert N Moles

Lothian
BOOKS

Thomas C. Lothian Pty Ltd
132 Albert Road, South Melbourne, 3205
www.lothian.com.au

Copyright © Robert Moles 2004
First published 2004
Reprinted 2004

All rights reserved. No part of this publication may be reproduced, stored in a retrieval system or transmitted in any form by any means without the prior permission of the copyright owner. Enquiries should be made to the publisher.

National Library of Australia
Cataloguing-in-Publication data:

Moles, Robert N.
   A state of injustice.

   ISBN 0 7344 0597 9.

   1. Forensic pathology – South Australia – Case studies.
2. Forensic pathology – South Australia. 3. Death – South Australia – Causes – Case studies. 4. Death – South Australia – Causes. 5. Judicial error – South Australia – Cases. 6. Judicial error – South Australia. I. Title.

614.1099423

Cover design by Black Widow Graphic Design
Typeset in 11.5/15pt Bembo by Cannon Typesetting
Printed in Australia by Griffin Press

If guilt can be established, it should be established to the extent to which the system is capable. If innocent people are to be exculpated, then no questions should remain about the thoroughness of the investigation which might throw a doubt upon their innocence.

MR WAYNE CHIVELL,
THE CORONER FOR SOUTH AUSTRALIA

Finding of Inquest into the deaths of Storm Don Ernie Deane,
William Anthony Barnard, Joshua Clive Nottle
25 August 1995.

FOREWORD

This is a book about bad science and a flawed criminal justice system. Its setting is South Australia, but the challenge it presents is directed to the criminal justice system throughout Australia. The challenge is how Australians as a community face up to the reality of serious miscarriages of justice. Of course, everyone can accept at a purely theoretical level that miscarriages of justice occur, quite simply because the operation of the criminal justice system is a human endeavour and mistakes occur in all human endeavours. The journey from this comfortably distant theory through the factual realities and towards some uncomfortable conclusions is the route along which this book invites us to pass within its pages.

Allegations of injustices committed by the justice system are inevitably contentious. Outright denial and barely concealed anger are the predictable reactions from some who perceive the raising of this issue publicly as an assault on the criminal justice system as a whole. However, the experience of other countries is that public debate on this issue and the implementation of necessary reforms serve to strengthen the justice system and build public confidence in it.

In taking up the issue of miscarriages of justice, this book examines some examples of medical expert evidence about the cause and circumstances of deaths. The medical science of death investigation, or forensic pathology, is always an important part of any suspicious death or murder investigation. Getting the science right is clearly of critical importance, since an error may result in a killer escaping justice or a person being wrongly convicted. Both have happened in South Australia if the facts set out in this book are accepted. In examining the problems with forensic medical science, Australians might reflect on the British experience. After all, many of the forensic pathologists practising in Australia today trained in Britain, and the Australian practice of forensic pathology is closely linked to British practice. In the past few years allegations of incompetent practice by British forensic pathologists have resulted in a major reform program in Britain. These reforms are designed to ensure that forensic pathologists receive adequate training, are properly qualified for the work they undertake, do not practice beyond their expertise, keep up to date with advances in the discipline, follow accepted guidelines and protocols, work within systems subject to audit and quality control, and are subject to effective disciplinary procedures. It is against this backdrop that the criticisms raised by this book should be viewed.

The allegations and facts set out in the book should be examined with the care which their seriousness demands. Having done so, the reader might reflect upon a simple question: If I were an innocent person accused of murder would I be confident of not being wrongly convicted? The question is not an abstract one, since any one of us may be accused of a crime. The criminal justice system is truly a matter of concern for everyone.

Derrick Pounder
Professor of Forensic Medicine
Dundee

CONTENTS

Foreword vii
Acknowledgments xi
Introduction xv

PART 1: GENERAL ISSUES

1 **The criminal justice system** 3
2 **Police and forensic science procedures** 25
3 **Autopsies** 40
4 **Medical matters** 56

PART 2: THE CASES

5 **Time and Tide** 79
   Frits Van Beelen 1972

6 **Time and time again** 98
   David Szach 1979
   Stefan Niewdach and Alan Ellis 1992

7 **Arsenic and old cases** 109
   Emily Perry 1981

8 **No clothes, no files, no suspicions** 119
   John Highfold 1983
   Kingsley Dixon 1987

9	**There being nothing suspicious ...**	125
	Terry Akritidis 1990	
	Peter Marshall 1992	
10	**Seeing things**	139
	The Baby Deaths 1994	
11	**The one positive indication of murder**	155
	Henry Keogh 1995 — Part 1	
12	**No bruise, no grip, no crime**	180
	Henry Keogh 1995 — Part 2	
13	**No match**	193
	Michael Penney 1996	
14	**Justice for some or for all?**	209
	Plea-bargaining	

PART 3: WHERE TO FROM HERE?

15	**This is not good enough**	221
	Responses to miscarriages of justice	
16	**We can't face the future if we can't face the truth**	238

Glossary	260
Endnotes	273
Index	288

ACKNOWLEDGMENTS

Throughout this book I have decided to use the inclusive 'we' as opposed to the solitary 'I' because of the way in which it speaks of the author as a person supported by a very dedicated team of people who have been essential to its creation.

Robert Sheehan has been the researcher who initiated the inquiries and brought the issues to the attention of others. We now call him 'The Ferret' because of his dogged determination — and the fact that he disappears down every burrow.

Dr Tony Thomas has worked extensively in his own time assisting us to get to grips with the technical issues involved in anatomical pathology. He has worked with us at great length on the sections dealing with autopsies and medical issues, as well as in discussions of the cases. He is a man of great compassion and understanding.

Dr Harry Harding has been a key forensic scientist in South Australia. He believes strongly that standards must be improved and that the public must be informed. Every page of this book has been subjected to his exacting scrutiny and his demands for improvement to them. He has reordered and rewritten many sections to enable me to see more clearly what it was that I really wanted to say.

Arlyn Tombleson is a chiropractor and an early campaigner on these issues, being involved as he was in the Chamberlain, Van Beelen and Perry cases. He has provided us with much mental and physical therapy, and we are grateful to him for it.

David Cook is a senior police officer in the United Kingdom. Despite his very heavy case load of murder investigations in the London area, he has still found time to enable us to benefit from his knowledge and experience. It was he who first alerted us to the experience of the Criminal Cases Review Commission in the United Kingdom. In this electronic age, he inspires us to think more positively about the benefits of international collaboration, and we thank him for his contribution to it.

David Fuller, my old school friend, has very sensibly been a 'scene-of-crimes' officer with the Norfolk Constabulary in the United Kingdom. He has kindly provided much advice and guidance to me in the writing of the sections dealing with police procedures.

Kevin Borick QC and Chris Patterson (solicitor) are the legal representatives of Henry Keogh. They have given substantial support to all of the work which this book represents, and have become outspoken advocates for a review of the criminal justice system in South Australia.

We have had the privilege to work with journalists of considerable note. Lin Buckfield (producer) and Sally Neighbour (reporter) with the ABC *4 Corners* program first brought these issues to the attention of a national audience in Australia in October 2001 with their story 'Expert Witness'. Graham Archer (producer) and Rohan Wenn (reporter) of the Channel 7 *Today Tonight* program in Adelaide have completed a number of programs to further inform their South Australian viewers. They have all worked with consummate skill and judgment in putting together programs of considerable public interest on these issues. Their fearless devotion to the public interest has given us great encouragement to proceed with our work.

Much encouragement has been provided to us by Michael Parker in London. Pam Seaborn, our literary agent, and Averill Chase as commissioning editor of Lothian Books have given great support to this endeavour. Julie Stanton (editor) has worked wonders with the text. Sharon Mullins from Lothian Books has pushed through the publishing stage with great skill. We are indeed grateful to you all.

Above all, I must pay tribute to my wife Bibi Sangha. As law lecturer and co-researcher, she has carefully scrutinised all of the materials from which we have worked, and she has played a crucial and indispensable role in the formulation of the material that is presented here. In addition, she has had to bear the emotional turmoil to which work of this nature inevitably gives rise. If it had not been for her intellectual and emotional support, this task would never have been accomplished.

Finally, I must acknowledge the debt that we have to all of the people and families whose lives are the subject of the following chapters. They are the people who have had to bear the unspeakable burden of injustice. They have paid the price which is inevitably exacted every time the justice system fails to achieve its noble goals. I hope that in some small measure, this book will help to restore to them the dignity that was their due.

INTRODUCTION

A properly working justice system is fundamental to a civilised society. It is part of the social contract upon which modern society is based. The principle of the social contract is that each one of us gives up our right to use force against others on the basis that the justice system will protect our rights, if and when they are transgressed. This means that the justice system has a monopoly on the use of force. None of us is entitled to 'take the law into our own hands'. Where our rights have been infringed, we must look to the officials of the system both to recognise our rights and enforce them on our behalf.

In our modern and complex society, proper investigations of alleged infringements of rights depend on each of the people involved acting with integrity and skill. In more serious cases this will include a wide range of people with very different skills. For example, where there is a suspicious death, a forensic pathologist has to examine a dead body to determine how and when the person died. A forensic scientist may have to undertake microscopical examination of materials to help with identification, or with an understanding of the sequence of events. The police have to interview people and take statements. The prosecutor may have to prepare the case for trial. Other lawyers may be engaged to act for anyone who may be charged.

The result of all of this activity might eventually be played out before magistrates and judges. It is their job to ensure that the rules of evidence and procedure are adhered to. However, the ultimate test will be applied by people without any specialist skills. In the common law system of justice that applies in Australia (and the United Kingdom, Canada, India and the

United States of America, for example), the ultimate arbiters of guilt and innocence in serious criminal cases are normally ordinary members of the public — the jury. It is a cardinal principle of the common law system that ultimately people are subject to the judgment of their peers — their equals.

That is why we have determined to write this book for the general reader rather than the specialist reader. There is a developing public perception that all is not well with the criminal justice system in South Australia. In the following pages we will explain at least some of the reasons why that may be so.

The broad theme of the book is to canvass the possibility that there have been miscarriages of justice in South Australia in the last few decades. We will suggest that these have come about because, for various reasons, the normal checks and balances within the criminal justice system have failed to operate properly.

To get our bearings right, it is important that we have some agreement or understanding of how things *should* be done. To achieve this we have worked in close consultation with specialists in the various areas of investigations and legal work.

This book is divided into three parts. In Part One we discuss some of the general legal, scientific and medical considerations that should be kept in mind when reading about the individual cases. To help clarify how the problems arose in the cases we look at, we start by providing some understanding of the criminal law process, police and forensic science procedures, autopsy and pathology procedures and various medical conditions relevant to those cases.[1]

In Part Two we look at some cases which give rise to considerations about possible miscarriages of justice. Some of these cases involve pathology. We have given the Keogh case extended treatment because it encapsulates the wide range of problems found in other cases, and because it also demonstrates problems with the existing appeal processes. The Penney case, which involves a fire in a car, provides some understanding of the problems that can occur in the investigative stage of a case. It also highlights some of the procedural aspects of trials, in particular the special requirements in cases that depend on circumstantial evidence. We then look at some plea-bargaining cases that demonstrate the 'negotiated' aspects of criminal charges.

In Part Three we compare the systems in other countries and present information on how miscarriages of justice in the United Kingdom are being handled, and what happens in the legal systems of European countries. This will provide some food for thought on what may be done to put matters right in South Australia.

If we have been able to isolate a common element to the problems that have been identified, it could be summed up in the expression 'the inappropriate use of science'. All the other issues that we raise are discussed in the context of the inability of the criminal justice system to identify and correct the problems which have arisen from the inappropriate use of science and scientific methods.

By explaining what has been done, or sometimes not done, by the forensic pathologists, forensic scientists, police, lawyers and judges in a number of criminal cases, we will be asking whether these cases have been conducted and processed properly. In some cases, we look at problems which resulted in investigations being dropped or prosecutions not proceeded with. In some other cases we question whether the verdict was 'safe and satisfactory', as the lawyers say. Our inquiries suggest that they may not have been. As a result, there may have been a number of miscarriages of justice. More formal inquiries, with the ability to call witnesses and have them examined under oath, must now be established to get to the truth in these cases.

The law states that if, at the end of the trial, there is reasonable doubt as to guilt, then the accused is entitled to be acquitted and to retain the presumption of innocence. It follows then that the jurors at the trials that we discuss in this book were agreed that they did not have reasonable doubt as to the guilt of the accused. We cannot know how a jury evaluated individual aspects of the evidence in a trial because jury deliberations take place in secret, but there is no reason to believe that their conclusions were not fair and proper on the basis of the information *which was available to them at the time*. However, we will argue that in many ways the issues may not have been properly presented.

With the checks and balances that are built into the criminal justice system, we would have expected any shortcomings in a case to have been identified by the prosecutors, defence lawyers or judges at the time of the trial or, if not then, in the appeals. If that has not happened, then it can only be because there is some systemic fault. Perhaps the prosecutor failed to examine *all* the possibilities before accepting the view proposed by the pathologist. It may have been that the defence lawyer had an insufficient knowledge of the science involved and so failed to cross-examine the expert witnesses properly. It could even have been that the judge allowed the expert witness to venture opinions which went beyond the claimed area of expertise.

Each person involved in the justice process has to ensure that, at the end of the day, justice is done; that is, that the accused receives a trial according to law. Each participant has their own particular responsibilities and while their roles and functions differ, each also has to work closely with the others who are part of the process. The relationships must be based on collaboration, but they must also engage in critical evaluation of each other's approach for the process to work effectively. In this network of professional relationships, 'doing the right thing' requires strength of character and a commitment to one's sense of professional principles. Where either of these things is weak, the system is likely to fail.

We accept that it is in the nature of human activity that people will make mistakes. However, social systems should be so designed that when mistakes are made they will be identified and corrected as soon as possible. Obviously the amount of attention directed to picking up and correcting mistakes will depend on the potential importance of possible errors. To incorrectly determine that a person has committed suicide, for example, when in fact they were murdered, is a serious error. To determine that someone has been murdered, when they died of natural causes, would be an equally serious error.

The issues involved in criminal justice matters affect every one of us, and it is important that ordinary people are empowered by being given information that enables them to arrive at their own conclusions. It is not appropriate that such issues are monopolised by experts, for much of what they do is done in *our* name. As such, we believe the experts have a responsibility to account to us all for what they do. This presupposes that they will tell us what they are doing. The courts are open to the public, but that does not necessarily make them accessible to most people. We need to develop ways in which the evidence of forensic scientists and pathologists, and the way in which such evidence is handled by the lawyers, can be made more readily available for community scrutiny and comment.

We would not want this review of cases to be misconstrued as a policy of being 'soft on crime'. Every rape, assault or murder has a devastating effect on a wide group of people. This includes the families, friends and neighbours of those involved on all sides. Every such incident lowers our sense of confidence and wellbeing in society at large. It is important that the perpetrators of such wickedness be dealt with appropriately.

However, it is also important that we do our very best to ensure that we have identified the real perpetrators. It is important to reassure ourselves that we have not just latched on to some convenient scapegoat.

After every dreadful crime there is a social expectation that someone (or some people) be brought to account. There is often relief when an arrest is made and the trial commences. Perhaps this relief is partly because the most important and basic legal presumption — that people are innocent unless and until they are proven to be guilty — has been overlooked. In criminal cases in Australia, the standard is proof of guilt 'beyond reasonable doubt'. This means that any doubts must be fully investigated in order to determine whether or not they are reasonable. A doubt cannot be regarded as unreasonable simply because someone has determined that it would be inconvenient to explore that possibility. Such an attitude would be based on prejudice, which simply means that the issue has been 'prejudged'. All reasonable lines of inquiry must be pursued, whether the tendency is to inculpate (prove guilt) or to exculpate (acquit) some particular individual. Grave consequences follow a finding of guilt, especially for the more serious crimes. When we as a society subject people to those consequences, we must be sure that we have taken all reasonable steps to ensure that we are as confident as we can be in the outcome.

The social act of sentencing a person to a long period of imprisonment, if attributed to the wrong person, can be as damaging to them and their family as was the original crime to the victim. To do such a thing is to damage the fundamental fabric of our society. Our confidence in the ability to get it right is weakened. We may even stop caring about whether we have got it right, so long as we have someone to blame. By losing our respect for others, we inevitably undermine our own sense of self-respect. Where errors have been made, people's sense of self-respect can be restored (to some extent) by acknowledging those errors. We may even feel emboldened to say 'sorry' or to take other steps to make amends.

Sadly, it seems, our ability to re-examine cases improves only after the passage of significant periods of time. There seems to be an unwillingness to look at cases of concern at the time they occur. Maybe there is always the tension between 'doing the right thing', and avoiding 'embarrassment' to officials who hold high office. Once a person has been convicted of a serious offence, and exhausted all avenues for appeal, it may be that as many as twenty or so judges and other senior officials of the justice system will have concurred in the result. To find subsequently that they may have fallen into error may not reflect well upon them. It would seem that we have allowed ourselves to be overawed by 'authority', and find it is easier to wait until those involved are no longer around before asking potentially embarrassing questions.

The danger to justice lies not, however, in the challenging of some of its findings, but in *not* challenging them. The experience in the United Kingdom has been that admitting and rectifying errors does not undermine the system. On the contrary, it should give every citizen confidence that the system is there for *them* and to protect them — and that it is honest enough and robust enough to withstand legitimate scrutiny and valid criticism. The test of a legal system is not whether it makes mistakes, for all such systems do. The real test is the willingness of the system to correct errors when they are brought to the attention of the officials.

While the legal system can destroy a person's integrity and standing in the community by way of a judicial decision, it cannot so easily restore that standing by later revoking that decision. Insisting from the outset that lawyers and scientists be trained regarding thoroughness and proper ethical standards will mean that due diligence will be applied without exception. Unless we insist upon the rights of all, we cannot be confident about the rights of any.

While there are always costs involved in doing a job properly, they will always be disproportionately outweighed by the financial and social costs of not doing it properly. In 1983, it took a Royal Commission in South Australia over 190 hearing days and some $3 million to overturn the conviction of Edward Splatt. It took a hearing of only eleven days to convict him in the first place. It clearly would have cost a good deal less to have utilised the best expert advice *before* he was put on trial.

It is our view that many of the serious problems which have arisen in recent years have come about because lawyers (be they counsel or judges) have had difficulty in grasping the complexity of the underlying scientific and technical information. If proper procedures have been departed from, it is the lawyers who should be able to identify the shortcomings and call attention to them. South Australian lawyer and President of the Australian Criminal Lawyers Association, Kevin Borick QC, in referring to some of the cases we discuss, stated in the ABC TV *4 Corners* 'Expert Witness' program on 22 October 2001:

> I think you have to lay the blame directly with the legal profession and with the judiciary. It was our responsibility to make sure that something like this didn't happen and I include myself in the same criticism. It *did* happen. And now we have to put it right.[2]

Not only do we have to put it right, we have to try to stop it happening again. To put right injustice, we cannot avoid asking awkward questions. To minimise the possibility of such injustices occurring in the future, those who hold positions of responsibility within the criminal justice system must be called to account. The only form of accountability worthy of the name is that which follows hard upon the heels of the act in question. Proper performance of tasks will only occur when people are assured that substandard performance will be found out — and that the people concerned will be required to account for what they have done.

Accountability must not only be assured, it must also be democratic. It must apply to *all* within the system irrespective of rank or seniority. The failure to question or to hold accountable people in senior positions leads to a decline of standards and behaviour of those beneath them. Through 'alliances of convenience', subordinates can be discouraged from asking proper questions or insisting that proper procedures are followed. They can be encouraged to turn a blind eye to shortcomings. Whether the pressures are social, financial or tyrannical, some people acquiesce. In doing so, they allow the system of checks and balances to be manipulated and, in this way, they undermine their own integrity and that of our system of justice.

The only way to restore the system to robust health is by developing a system of accountability, which should have been there all along, and letting the cards fall where they may.

It is important to develop confidence in our legal procedures and institutions. But that presupposes that the procedures in place are correct and uniformly and fairly applied. Our research shows that in some cases the procedures for peer review and the appeals process have been deficient. This book is an attempt to raise awareness of the need to re-establish a sense of proper procedures. By looking at what has gone wrong, we can learn more about how to prevent those errors occurring in the future.

PART 1

GENERAL ISSUES

CHAPTER ONE

THE CRIMINAL JUSTICE SYSTEM

We begin our look at possible miscarriages of justice by describing how the criminal justice system works in the investigation and prosecution of crime.

The case of Edward Splatt

Edward Splatt was charged with the murder of Mrs Simper, a 77-year-old Adelaide woman who had been badly beaten, sexually assaulted and strangled in her bedroom. The case was complex, dealing with paint, wood, birdseed and biscuit particles found in her room. It was a rare case in that the only evidence leading to the identification of the accused was the scientific evidence. No one had ever seen Splatt with the deceased or in her house.

Splatt was convicted of the murder in 1978. His appeals were unsuccessful. However, Stewart Cockburn, a journalist with the Adelaide *Advertiser*, became convinced of the unsatisfactory basis of the prosecution case. He ran a campaign in the paper for about two years before the government agreed to a Royal Commission. Splatt's conviction was subsequently overturned in 1984 and he was paid some $300,000 by way of compensation.

The commissioner was highly critical of the conduct of the trial, especially the operations of the expert witnesses. He put forward a number of principles concerning the way in which lawyers and expert witnesses should work.[1] Had they been adopted, they may have prevented many of the apparent miscarriages of justice that appear in this book.

Before we look at these recommendations we will first explain some of the more important aspects of how the justice system works.

Criminal offences

In any criminal offence there are two elements — the physical and the psychological.

For someone to be successfully prosecuted for committing a crime there must have been a completed physical act (called the *actus reus*). This act forms the basis of the criminal offence. For example, goods were taken without payment, or someone was shot, stabbed or poisoned. No one can be convicted of just having 'bad thoughts'. Sometimes a person may be charged with an attempted crime, but even here there must be physical proof the person did something to prepare for the crime.

Also, those physical acts must have been undertaken with knowledge, understanding or intention (called the *mens rea*). That is, the person committing the act knew or was aware that the act was unlawful and that they were doing it. If someone is mentally ill or delusional, or perhaps suffering from the effects of medication or a brain tumour, and commits a crime, they may not have understood or even been aware of what they were doing. If so, they will have a defence to the charge. This defence generally does not apply to acts committed while under the influence of alcohol or drugs. In such cases, the mental element tends to shift to the taking of the substances. If the person took them consciously and knowingly, then they will usually be held responsible for what they did while they were under their influence.

Therefore, the first task of any investigation is to determine whether or not a crime has been committed. The competing rights of the victim and the accused are often spoken about, but even this may prejudge things. There cannot really be talk of a *victim* of a crime at all until it has been determined that some offence has been committed.

THE PRESUMPTION OF INNOCENCE

A basic principle of Australian law is that everyone is presumed to be innocent unless and until any criminality can be proved beyond reasonable doubt. This is important because it means that people do not have to prove their innocence. The State, through the prosecutor, has to prove their guilt. If there is reasonable doubt as to the guilt of the accused it means that the prosecution cannot succeed. It is for this reason that many people undoubtedly do not get convicted for things that they have done. Rightly or wrongly, the view which the common law system takes is that whenever there is reasonable doubt, it would be unfair to convict a person. It is said that it is better to allow an otherwise guilty person to go free than to run the risk of convicting an innocent one.

AN ACQUITTAL

Once someone enters the criminal justice system as an accused, the end result is usually a verdict of either 'guilty' or 'not guilty' after some form of hearing. If the verdict is 'not guilty', the accused will be acquitted by the court and cannot be recharged with the same or a similar offence that arises from the same circumstances, even if fresh evidence later comes to light. However, an acquittal does not mean that the person has been proved innocent. It means that the person has not been proved guilty and therefore retains the *presumption* of innocence. Bear in mind, though, that by the time an unsuccessful prosecution has finished, an accused may well have lost their job, their marriage and their self-respect. They may have spent all their savings and more on their defence. People who are acquitted are often surprised to find out that none of this will be repaid or compensated for by the prosecutor's office. It can be seen then just how important the role of the prosecutor is in the administration of justice.

Prosecutions

There are important differences between civil and criminal cases. In a civil case the action is between individuals, companies or public entities. The remedy being sought is usually some form of court order or compensation. This area is usually referred to as private rights.

In a criminal case the action is between the State on the one hand and an individual or group on the other. The remedy being sought is usually called a 'punishment' for having infringed some law and the duty which it imposes. These duties apply automatically to all citizens. For this reason, it is important that they are clear and well understood. Equality before the law means that rich and poor alike are required not to steal or engage in criminal damage or injury to others.

THE PUBLIC PROSECUTOR

Each state and territory has a designated official to enforce the law on their behalf. They may be called public prosecutors or Crown prosecutors. In South Australia there is an office of the Director of Public Prosecutions with a Director of Public Prosecutions (DPP) as the head of it. Responsibility for prosecutorial decisions, however, rests with the Attorney-General by reason of the power conferred by the Act governing the office of the DPP. The Attorney-General in turn is accountable to Parliament and ultimately to the public.[2]

The Office of the DPP is a publicly funded department that is independent of the police and the government. Whereas the police usually prosecute minor offences in the Magistrates or Local Court, the Office of the DPP prosecutes the more serious offences, such as murder and serious assaults. However, it is always important to determine where the line of responsibility is to be drawn. In the more serious cases, the decision to prosecute and how prosecutions are to be pursued is a matter for the DPP's office, not the police. The *investigation* of suspected criminal activity is the responsibility of the police who will (or should) jealously guard their independence in that respect.

The victim's family may pressure the police to bring charges against an alleged perpetrator. The police, who may have had a good deal of contact with the family, may find it hard to tell them that the evidence is not sufficient to support charges being laid or pursued. Rather than upset or anger the family by telling them this, the police may feel that the matter should be put to the DPP's office to let them make that decision.

Similarly, the DPP may come under pressure, by the family or by publicity or public interest in the matter. This applies particularly where there have been public outrages such as bombings or shootings, or where young children have been killed or sexually assaulted. Public confidence often requires a result. Laying charges against someone often reassures the public that the system is working properly and that they are again safe at last.

It is the role of the prosecutor to present the case against the accused in court, and to call evidence in support of it. It is the prosecutor's duty to ensure that the prosecution is lawful, that there is a reasonable prospect of conviction, and that it is not vexatious or trivial. It is also their duty to ensure that the evidence, be it scientific or otherwise, meets the appropriate standards and is presented fully and fairly.

The pressure to get results might mean that the prosecutors lay charges when the investigation is still proceeding or the evidence is still not adequate. Once this happens, then tunnel vision can set in and the only goal appears to be firming up the evidence against the accused person. Other possibilities fall by the wayside and it is 'all hands to the pumps' to pursue the conviction 'successfully'.

Our study of legal systems shows that this phenomenon has been the cause of a number of miscarriages of justice. The cases show that even judges and juries can be caught up in the zeal to convict someone for the wickedness that has happened. Obvious examples are the Lindy Chamberlain case (the 'dingo' case) in Australia, or the terrorist cases of the Guildford Four and the Birmingham Six in the United Kingdom. It is often forgotten that the importance is not just punishment, but punishment of the *right* people. It is important to remember that if the wrong person is convicted, then it is likely that the real villain is safe to walk the streets. One imagines that they may well go on to commit further offences.

DEFENCE COUNSEL

'Defence counsel' is the term used for the lawyer who is representing the accused person in court. It is their role to test the evidence brought by the prosecution. They might do this by calling witnesses (expert or non-expert or both) to present evidence, or they may do it only by cross-examination of the prosecution witnesses to explore any doubt, error, prejudice or dishonesty of the witness. For expert witnesses, this cross-examination may be about the extent of their training, knowledge and expertise in the tests conducted, the interpretation of such tests as were done, or why other or further tests were not done. The examination might probe the integrity of the exhibits and the chain-of-custody of the items that have become exhibits in the case.

To cross-examine experts effectively, counsel needs to have at least some knowledge of the subject, which is normally achieved best by consultation with relevant experts, who may or may not give evidence later on behalf of the accused. Counsel is obliged to put their client's case to the best of their ability, and a well organized, sound and probing cross-examination is essential to the proper functioning of our justice system.

In addition to representing their client, however, a lawyer is an officer of the court. This means that in addition to their duty to the accused they also have an overriding duty to the court to ensure that it is not misled.

PLEA-BARGAINING

Plea-bargaining is an important part of the criminal justice system and is widely used to minimise delays in the handling of cases in the courts. Normally, where it is alleged that a person has committed a crime, the prosecution and defence counsel will exchange views about the most appropriate charges. It is the responsibility of the prosecution to lay charges or to continue with prosecutions only where they have 'reasonable prospects of success'. In these discussions, the defence lawyers will, no doubt, argue that the evidence is weak and that lesser charges — or perhaps none at all — might be more appropriate.

It is accepted that most prosecution services have a very substantial workload, and that it is in the interests of all concerned to obtain negotiated outcomes without the need for a trial, provided that the rights of the accused are not jeopardised nor the expectations of the community diminished. In 1994 a national set of guidelines was introduced to deal with the plea-bargaining process.

How plea-bargaining works is that sometimes the accused will accept that the evidence or the circumstances are not in doubt, and their lawyers will then try to persuade the prosecution to go for the lowest reasonable charges in return for a guilty plea. At the same time, the prosecution will be making it clear that a guilty plea at an early stage could be taken into account by the judge in determining the sentence.

In the case of doubtful circumstances, the prosecution will have to form a view as to whether it is better to deal with the matter at that time or await the outcome of further investigations. On pleading guilty, the accused person will be bound to accept whatever sentence the judge imposes. Judges can refuse to accept a guilty plea if they take the view that the evidence does not match the charge. As we will see later, a number of people in South Australia who were initially charged with murder were subsequently convicted for dangerous driving or manslaughter as a result of plea-bargains.

COMMITTAL PROCEEDINGS

Once the prosecution decides to go to trial, they face the first public check in the prosecution process, which is the preliminary or committal hearing. This hearing is held to review the evidence against the accused and to satisfy a magistrate that there is a sufficient case to go for trial. This is similar to the Grand Jury part of the proceedings in the United States. There only needs to be a prima facie case at this stage. 'Prima facie' means 'on the face of it' or 'at the first examination of it', which means that there must appear to be sufficient evidence to provide a reasonable prospect of securing a conviction. It will not be known at this stage whether any of the evidence will be ruled inadmissible at the trial, whether further evidence will come to light in the meantime, or whether some of the evidence will be eliminated by cross-examination during the trial. Sometimes committal proceedings are handled in written form and involve an exchange of the relevant statements and reports (called a 'hand-up' committal). Alternatively, witnesses can be required to attend for oral examination as in a trial. The oral form of committal proceedings takes longer and either side can request it. It gives the lawyers a chance to test the witnesses in the absence of a jury. They can get the measure of a witness and assess whether they are likely to be convincing before a jury. The main focus for the magistrate is to say whether the evidence presented *at that time* would be sufficient to secure a conviction if it proves to be both admissible and convincing.

The jury trial and the adversarial system

The Australian legal system is an adversarial system. This means that each side puts its version of events to a jury by presenting witnesses and taking them through their evidence by asking questions. The witness's testimony is then 'tested' by the other side through cross-examination. It is the role of the jury, after hearing the evidence, to determine what the facts are. The judge acts like an umpire to ensure that the two sides play by the rules.

In contrast, the European legal system is an inquisitorial system. They have an investigating magistrate and the judges and magistrates take a far more active part in the investigations and the proceedings in court. The judges are entitled to engage actively in asking questions and in seeking the truth of what happened. Some argue that this system works better — we will discuss this later.

THE JURY TRIAL
If a magistrate commits someone for trial for a serious offence, it will be heard in a higher court. In South Australia this will

be either the District Court or the Supreme Court, depending upon the seriousness of the offence. Some financial assistance, or legal aid, is normally provided to those unable to afford legal representation, especially on more serious charges. Indeed it is now the law that if a person is unable to pay for their legal representation on serious criminal charges, and the State will not pay for their defence, then the prosecution cannot proceed (the Dietrich principle).[3]

Normally, serious criminal offences are heard in front of a jury. One of the early tasks in a trial therefore is to empanel the jury which will be selected from names on the electoral role. Some people are excluded automatically because of their occupation — police officers, lawyers and politicians are obvious examples. Jury selection in Australia is not the sophisticated operation it has become in the United States. Usually either side may ask a few preliminary questions to determine if there is any obvious bias or inability of a proposed juror to approach the matter with an open mind. Anyone related to the accused or any of the witnesses is excluded as usually are those with more extreme social or political views. The experience is that most ordinary people appreciate the seriousness and importance of the task. The legal system takes the view that people are ultimately to be tried by their peers, being ordinary people just like them. It has resisted the idea of specialist juries. In earlier times, ordinary people were expected to be property holders, or those with some obvious investment in the community. Nowadays, one simply has to be old enough to vote.

Many trials are complex and involve sophisticated science, accounting or other specialist knowledge. Jurors, however, cannot ask the witnesses questions, nor may they talk to the judge or to counsel about why the case is being handled as it is. They can ask the judge for clarification of any legal matters that they have to consider.

The prosecution and defence counsel try to persuade the jury to their point of view; the judge sums up the case and may put suggestions to the jury. Counsel and judges cannot go beyond that.

The important task for the jury is to determine a guilty or not guilty verdict in the matter before them. (The term 'verdict' is derived from the French words *ver* and *dit* and means literally 'a speaking of the truth'.) If they need to know any law, the judge will direct them in relation to that and they must take the law as the judge explains it to them. It is said that the facts are for the jury to determine and no one else can tell them what the facts are. However, at the end of the case, there is really no way of knowing what facts the jury actually accepted. All that is known is their verdict. From that the public can attempt to infer what facts the jury accepted but they can never really know.

WITNESSES

The normal role of a witness is to give evidence in court about what has been experienced directly (what they saw, heard or felt). They are not allowed to give evidence about what they have been told by others (hearsay), nor about their deductions as to what their experiences might mean. The jury has to assess whether the witnesses are truthful and correct.

Psychological studies have shown that eye-witness testimony is notoriously unreliable. Without any conscious awareness of doing so, witnesses edit their version of events to fill in any gaps and sometimes to fit in with their expectations of human behaviour. If you were close to an event when it happened, you may be reluctant to state that you do not know or cannot remember the size or shape of the vehicle involved, or of the offender. The police might subtly suggest some alternatives and within a few minutes there may be clear agreement on matters which moments before were in doubt.

EXPERT WITNESSES

The role of the expert witness is different to that of the ordinary witness. Experts must have credentials upon which their expertise is based. Qualifications, courses of study, being well read and well regarded in the area of their expertise are what one would expect to find.

Like ordinary witnesses, expert witnesses give evidence about what they have seen, as in the case of a pathologist who gives evidence on the observations at an autopsy. However, the expert witness is the only type of witness who is allowed to give an *opinion*. This means that they are allowed to speak about what inferences may be drawn from the facts as they are or may be established. This is done to assist the jury in their interpretation of the evidence. The expert can say that if there are red stains in a tissue section, then that can be understood to mean that there was bruising on the victim. The jury is free to accept or reject the expert opinion and, not infrequently, experts will be called to contradict each other on key points. The expert is therefore able to suggest an *interpretation* of the facts which an ordinary witness is normally not allowed to do. A forensic pathologist, therefore, would be both a witness and an expert, and it is important to distinguish what a pathologist (as witness) *saw*, and what a pathologist (as expert) might *infer*.

In some of the cases in this book, this important distinction seems to have been blurred. There are instances where the facts are based on assertions made by the expert witness without the slides or photographs that would corroborate or substantiate those facts being put into evidence. It is also important that when the expert is stating an opinion about what the given facts mean, the reasoning that led the expert from the facts to the conclusion should also be clearly stated. Again, in some of the cases which we discuss, this does not appear to have been done. The conclusion appears to have been based on little more than a bald assertion — to be accepted or not.

The standing and demeanour of an expert witness can have a significant effect upon the jury. Also, an expert witness should be able to explain their evidence in a manner and with wording that the jury can understand, yet still be scientifically correct.

ADMISSIBILITY AND RELEVANCE OF EVIDENCE
One of the most important tasks for the judge in the adversarial system is to determine the admissibility or inadmissibility of evidence. For example, to be admissible, the judge must be persuaded that the evidence is both relevant and probative. This means that if accepted, it would tend to prove the facts in relation to the charge — for example, that the person was at the scene at the time of the incident. However, the judge must also accept that the evidence is not unfairly prejudicial. If the evidence showed, for example, that the accused held extreme or unpopular views, then if not essential to the charges before the court, the judge might say that it was inadmissible because it would prejudice the jury against the accused. The rules of admissibility of evidence are some of the most complex and technical in all of the criminal law. In South Australia, the practitioner's 'bible' is *Criminal Law South Australia* by Robert M Lunn. It consists of about 5000 pages in loose-leaf volumes and is updated six times a year.

THE *VOIR DIRE*
Sometimes the lawyers for each side want to have lengthy arguments about the admissibility or otherwise of certain evidence, or whether a particular witness is an expert or not. They know that their prospects of success and failure in a case will depend on the judge's rulings on these issues. When they

get to the point where that evidence is about to be put before the court, the opposing lawyer will tell the judge that there is a matter to be discussed 'in the absence of the jury'. The jury will then be sent out of the courtroom while the judge hears the arguments from each side. If the matter is the acceptability of a witness, the witness may be examined and cross-examined by the respective counsel. When the matter is resolved, the jury is brought back into the court and the trial then continues — with or without that evidence, depending upon how the judge ruled on it. The jury is never informed what the issue was or what the judge's ruling was. This type of hearing, with the jury absent, is often called 'a trial within a trial' or *voir dire*, which is from the French words 'to see' and 'to say'.

TRIAL PROCEDURES
At the start of the trial, the prosecution and defence lawyers make opening statements, outlining the case and the evidence they intend to put before the court. This is to give the jury an overview of what is to come. They must keep to things that they will subsequently put forward in evidence. The prosecution then brings its witnesses to give evidence-in-chief. This means the prosecution, via questioning, takes the witness through the written statements they made and signed before the trial. These statements have been made available to the other side. After this, the defence will bring forward their witnesses who will give their evidence-in-chief for the defence, and then be cross-examined by the prosecutor.

Generally, counsel is not allowed to ask a leading question. This is a question in which the appropriate answer is contained within the question itself. For example, it would not be appropriate to ask, 'Did you arrive there at 9 pm?' because the question suggests what the answer should be. The question has to be 'What time did you arrive there?'

After a witness has given their evidence-in-chief, counsel for the other side will then cross-examine. This is the most skilful and unpredictable part of all legal proceedings. The legal advisers for each side will have a fair idea of what their own witnesses will be saying, because they questioned the witnesses while drawing up their statements. However, this is the first time that counsel is able to directly address the witnesses for the other side. Skilful cross-examiners must be extremely knowledgeable about the subject matter and able to think on their feet. A cross-examiner's task is to cast doubt in a jury's mind about the testimony. While the experience may be unpleasant, nerve-racking, even intimidating, the truthful witness will have little to fear, as they have simply to say what they know. Those who are untruthful will have much more to be nervous about when facing the skilled advocate.

It is improper for a lawyer to 'coach' a witness, that is, to tell a witness what to say. However, it may be appropriate to make suggestions about how to say it. Telling a witness what to wear and to remain in control and speak clearly is entirely proper. To suggest, in any way, that the witness either be economical with the truth, or prevaricate with it, is quite improper.

A difficult situation arises when an accused confesses to their lawyer that they committed the acts in question. Defence counsel can still subject the prosecution witnesses to cross-examination. However, in the presentation of the defence case, defence counsel is not allowed to try to defend the client by saying that the accused did not do the acts in question. The lawyers have an overriding duty not to mislead the court, and this applies even where their client would want them to do so. The prosecution must still prove all elements of their case beyond reasonable doubt.

In many jurisdictions it may be possible for an accused person (the defendant) to opt to have a trial before a judge alone. This option might be taken if the evidence is particularly ghastly — offences against children, for example, where the accused may feel that the photographic evidence of injuries to the child might prejudice a jury.

In a trial, the defendant can call witnesses on their behalf if they wish. If they do so, defence counsel will lead the witness by questioning to bring out their evidence-in-chief. They will then be cross-examined by the prosecutor. With regard to the defendant giving evidence personally, there are three possible courses of action. Firstly, they can give sworn evidence and be cross-examined by the prosecutor. Secondly, they have the right to make an unsworn statement to the court, and this is not subject to cross-examination. Thirdly, they can choose to remain silent, and the jury is not allowed to draw any adverse conclusions from this.

THE JUDGE'S SUMMING UP
After all the evidence is given, the prosecution and the defence lawyers have an opportunity to sum up their cases to the jury. Following these, the judge gives a summing up. This is a very important part of the trial. The jury might be trying to discern what the judge's views are. The skilful judge will always be careful not to fall into that trap, as the jury must make up its own mind.

> The facts are for you to determine, ladies and gentlemen of the jury and for you alone. However, you are bound to accept my instructions upon the legal principles which you are to apply in your deliberations. You will now retire to consider your verdict.

Appeals
If the accused is found guilty then the question of an appeal will arise. The prosecution might appeal on sentence if they

consider it to be woefully inadequate, but most appeals are made by the defence lawyer after a conviction. To appeal successfully, the lawyer must argue that the legal principles governing the evidence and procedures were not properly applied. A person can't appeal just because they are unhappy about the verdict. Possible reasons for an appeal might be that admissible evidence was excluded, or that inadmissible evidence was allowed in. The appeal might claim that the judge acted unfairly in the closing remarks to the jury, or that the judge incorrectly advised the jury of the relevant legal principles. Appeal courts are always mindful that the jury was able to make their own assessment of the witnesses and arrived at their conclusion beyond reasonable doubt.

In South Australia, the first level of appeal in serious cases is made to the Court of Criminal Appeal, which is usually made up of three judges. Having three judges gives the court greater authority, and prevents the possibility of an even split in the judgment. Appeal courts are state based and sometimes appeal court judges are those who at other times will conduct Supreme Court trials. In the United Kingdom, however, judges serving on the Court of Appeal usually do not conduct trials. The cases in this book bring into question the effectiveness of the Australian appellate procedures in this regard, a matter that we will come back to in the final chapter.

If the first level of appeal fails, an appeal can be made to the High Court of Australia. This is the equivalent of the House of Lords in the United Kingdom or the Supreme Court in the United States. At this level there are usually five judges to hear the appeal, but there could be seven if the matter is particularly important. It is recognised that the courts at this level have a significant role to play in developing legal policy, and that they must interpret the law to give clear guidance to the courts below them. These judges work full time in hearing cases at this level and they seldom sit in courts below, although it may be technically possible for them to do so.

At each level of appeal one has to obtain 'leave to appeal', which means to get permission for the appeal to proceed. To get this permission, the lawyers will set out the issues that give rise to the appeal, and the points of law which they involve. At the first level, the permission may be granted by the trial judge whose decision is being appealed, or by the appeal court. Permission to appeal to the High Court can only be granted by the High Court. This means that the High Court has exclusive control over the cases that it hears.

If the verdict is overturned on appeal but without an acquittal, then it will be for the prosecution and not for the appeal court judges to determine if there should be a retrial. This will depend on whether or not the prosecutors feel that the case would have reasonable prospects of success if tried again.

After appeals to all levels of the courts have been exhausted, one normally has to live with the final outcome. However, there are two additional opportunities for a further review.

The first is a petition to the governor of the state involved to exercise the prerogative power of mercy. This can be on compassionate grounds, such as when the governor is asked to recommend the immediate release of a person suffering from a terminal illness, without any suggestion that the conviction was faulty. It may also be done where there has been a perceived miscarriage of justice. A prerogative power is really the last remnant of the power of the 'sovereign' to do as it pleases without the normal constraints of rules or law. However, it is now the custom or convention for the governor to take the advice of the governor's ministers — being the ministers of the government in power. This avoids any possible conflict between the sovereign on the one hand and the government on the other. The appropriate minister to advise the governor on these matters is the attorney-general, who will in turn consult with other members of the government and other legal officials. The attorney-general (as the most senior law officer) should make the decision on legal and not political grounds. The other alternative available under the petition procedure is for the governor, on the advice of the attorney-general, to refer the matter back to the Court of Criminal Appeal and to have it reheard as if it were an appeal.

The final procedure is to set up a Royal Commission. A Royal Commission usually means that a judge or a retired judge is asked by the government to conduct an inquiry. The scope of the Commission will be set out in the formal document establishing it. A Commission can be used to look at any matter, not just convictions. It may be given the power to overturn a conviction, or to recommend to the governor the overturning of a conviction. A problem with Royal Commissions, or other commissions of inquiry for that matter, is that governments are extremely reluctant to set them up because of the cost involved. They are often therefore only achieved as a result of public agitation through the media. The case of Edward Splatt, described at the beginning of this chapter, is one such example. It illustrates not only how hard it is to get a thorough review of some aspects of the criminal justice process, but also how such reviews (when they do occur) can lead to many important and positive outcomes.

Recommendations from the Splatt case

The Splatt case is important because it was an authoritative source by which proper procedures could be identified. Judge Shannon, the commissioner, was critical of the procedures which had led to the conviction.[4] In his report he adopted the recommendations about how things should be done for the future made by the scientific experts that had been called in from the United Kingdom. He said that some of the scientists involved in the original case appeared to have had a dual role. This meant that when analysing what they said and what they did, it was difficult to determine whether they were acting in an investigative role (like the police) or as an objective observer (like a scientist).

Judge Shannon pointed out that this sort of confusion could only happen in a system which was 'an incorrect one with serious defects'. He said that some of the original evidence which had been given by the expert witnesses involved completely non-scientific statements that were more like police investigatory suggestions.

He also emphasised that a system which did not distinguish between scientific observations and deductions by police in their investigatory capacity, was 'a defective and therefore a non-acceptable forensic system' and said that 'in each instance the dual roles are, in my opinion, incompatible'.

THE PROPER ROLE OF EXPERT WITNESSES

The commissioner said that every scientific operation or observation must be documented on the case notes and documented in such a manner that they would still be comprehensible perhaps even years later. He said that all major observations must be checked by an independent observer who must indicate, by initialling the notes, that the proper checks had been made. In our view, these basic requirements should apply to forensic scientists and forensic pathologists alike. The commissioner also said that it was not acceptable for the scientific expert witnesses to say that it was no fault of theirs if the court was left with the wrong impression of their evidence because they were not asked the right questions by the lawyers; *they* had a responsibility to ensure that their evidence was not misused in that way.

THE PROPER ROLE OF LAWYERS

The commissioner also expressed his view on the proper role of lawyers. He said that during the conduct of a trial there is a serious obligation on the lawyers conducting the trial. He said that the critical responsibility is that they should ask such detailed and probing questions of the scientists as are most likely to elicit the proper information.

Some of the cases that we discuss in this book illustrate the results of the legal system of South Australia failing to adopt those sound principles across the range of forensic investigations.

Miscarriages of justice

People frequently ask how there could possibly be miscarriages of justice if a person can be tried, found guilty and then have some two levels of appeal after that. The simple answer is that there are many issues which, if not corrected at the trial, cannot be picked up on the appeal. The appeal courts will not see any witnesses; they work only from the transcripts of the trial and the arguments which counsel make in relation to them. They generally are concerned with errors on the part of the judge or jury, and whether all the legal requirements have been satisfied. Appeal courts are not there to reinvestigate the case. They cannot determine that a witness has been untruthful or mistaken. They will not know about any missing links that were not presented at the trial. Concerns like these escape detection in the course of the ordinary appeal process. The Keogh case, which we examine in detail in this book, is a classic example of this sort of dilemma.

So while the appellate system has a job to do, it has become increasingly apparent that it is not up to the task of revealing all the inadequacies which might take place during the modern trial process. This is particularly so where the testimony of expert witnesses has been crucial in bringing a conviction, as seen in the high profile cases mentioned earlier of Lindy Chamberlain, the Birmingham Six and Guildford Four, and in the Porter case in the United States. Porter had spent some seventeen years in prison in Illinois and had come within two days of being executed when his conviction for murder was overturned. It was a class project by journalism students which led to his case being re-examined.

To tackle the inadequacies in the process, a mechanism is required that will allow the role of judges, prosecutors, defence counsel, investigators and the witnesses of a trial to be more fully investigated. In the United Kingdom there is a Criminal Cases Review Commission (CCRC) which does just that. It investigates cases of alleged miscarriages of justice and refers them back to the Court of Appeal for reconsideration if required. Miscarriages of justice are not as uncommon as one might like to think — in the first year or two some 4000 applications were made to the CCRC. The value and necessity of such a Commission can be seen from the fact that of the first 94 cases so referred, 64 were determined to be miscarriages of justice. In some, information had subsequently emerged about the unreliability of witnesses. In others, it seemed that the police had either been untruthful or dishonest. Some of the cases were up to 50 years old and in four of them, those convicted had been hanged. We will discuss the role and function of the CCRC in more detail later when we explore how miscarriages of justice in South Australia might be dealt with.

CHAPTER TWO

POLICE AND FORENSIC SCIENCE PROCEDURES

Police duties include a wide range of activities such as education, crime prevention, directing traffic and managing their own resources. However, their principal duty is to investigate crime or possible crimes. In criminal investigations, the duty of the police (just like that of the prosecutors) is to serve the interests of justice and not just to obtain convictions.

In their investigation of crime it is necessary for the police to work with a wide range of technical and specialist people. Among the most important of those are the forensic scientists and pathologists. The word 'forensic' is derived from the Latin word *forens*, meaning a 'tribunal'. It means 'in connection with the courts'; it does not of itself mean 'scientific'. Forensic *scientists* are those who use their science training for the investigation of crime; for example, biologists and chemists who examine blood, fluid or powder residues from a crime scene. Their expertise helps the police determine what might have happened and who may have been involved. The forensic *pathologist* is a medical doctor who has specialised in the study of pathology and works in the court environment. This often involves the examination of a dead person to collect appropriate samples or evidence. Forensic pathologists generally do not work with living victims, such as those of sexual or other assault, fires or road accidents. This is normally the province of a police medical officer.

The arrangements for the delivery of forensic science services vary between the states. In Adelaide, forensic scientists and pathologists are based at the Forensic Science Centre. Sometimes the Coroner's office will be located with the forensic services (as it used to be in Adelaide) or near to it. The police forensic unit may also be nearby. In South Australia, if a person has died in circumstances where the cause of death is either unclear or where unlawful behaviour is suspected, the body is usually taken to the mortuary at the Forensic Science Centre. Under the instructions of the Coroner, a forensic pathologist will then examine the body (conduct an autopsy) and take samples for further examination. At the same time, police technical services officers will be working on the crime scene collecting other samples for examination by the scientists. The police forensic science section might also employ scientists to do some of this work. This chapter sets out the way in which the police are expected to approach the examination of a crime scene and the principles which they should have in mind when doing so.

Provision of forensic services

While forensic science centres may be organisationally independent of the police, the fact is that the bulk of their work comes from the police, who pay for the scientific services provided to them. This is important because the basic principles of science are neutrality and objectivity. In contrast, the basic principle of human and social organisation might be said to be 'the one who pays the piper calls the tune'. A recurring concern within this area of work is whether the police are getting objective advice from the scientists — or advice that supports their need to secure convictions. A dilemma for defence lawyers is whether they can trust forensic scientists to provide them with objective and impartial advice when the scientists are so close to the police — or when they might be working with the police on the same prosecution case.

There is no particular reason why forensic science organisations have to be government departments or even substantially dependent on government funding. In some countries there has been a move away from such arrangements. In the United Kingdom and the United States, a number of commercially based and independent forensic science laboratories have been established, and it has been recommended that the government system in the United Kingdom be privatised.[1] When the police or defence lawyers in those countries have forensic work they are able to send it to any of the independent laboratories. Choice will be based on cost, turnaround time and quality of service. Such laboratories can provide services to anyone who requires them and for any reason. They might do testing for the prosecution, the defence, private individuals or commercial organisations. The people who require such facilities have a range to choose from, and the laboratories become accustomed to servicing a wide range of needs from a diverse group of clients.

Whatever the local laboratory arrangements, it is clear that the need is for good experts such as pathologists, biologists, physicists and chemists who can assist with the criminal investigation process.

Forensic specialities

The police use many types of specialists and scientific disciplines to investigate cases. The more commonly used are the following:

Anatomy is helpful in understanding the cause of death or of injuries when dealing with skeletal remains; for example, to discover if the bones found in the back garden are human remains or a long dead pet. While not very accurate as yet, facial reconstructions from skulls are increasingly resorted to in investigations.

Botany and geology are used to determine where bodies, clothes or tools have been. Leaf, twig and soil samples left on clothes, tools or vehicles can be precise indicators of localities where events have occurred.

Chemistry is important for much of the standard work of the forensic scientist or pathologist. A detailed knowledge of chemistry is needed for the examination of powder residues from gunshot wounds, the aftermath of explosions and the identification of accelerants used to start fires in arson cases. Chemical tests help to identify materials and whether they are likely to have a common origin. Chemistry is also essential in the examination of documents and inks used in printing or writing. Histology, the procedure of preparing tissue samples for examination using the microscope (for example from an organ such as the heart or lung) relies on chemical staining processes to detect the features being analysed. Likewise, toxicology uses chemistry in the detection of drugs and poisons. Chemistry is also used to detect fingerprints, bloodstains, semen, urine and paint marks in almost every type of material and surface.

Entomology is useful where there has been insect infestation of a dead body — especially by blowflies — as this can help establish a time of death. This is particularly the case where death has occurred in the open and the body has not been found until after about 48 hours, when the other methods of timing death are less helpful.

Molecular biology helps to identify semen, saliva and other bodily fluid deposits or stains that are significant in sexual assault cases, as well as blood, which is often fundamental in bodily harm and homicide cases. The detection, analysis and storing of fluid and tissue samples, and their use for DNA typing purposes, involves complex chemistry. DNA analysis has become very important to the investigation of crime and to the reconsideration of convictions.

Odontology is used for identification. Tooth enamel is the most resilient material in the body and the teeth may be the only way to identify remains that are skeletal, charred or decomposed. Bite marks can be very useful. On occasion, a thief has regretted leaving an apple core or half-eaten chocolate bar at the scene of a crime. Bite marks have also been used to identify assailants in cases of sexual assault and child abuse.

Physics provides an understanding of how things come into contact with each other. From ballistics to blood, from vehicles to knives, physics can help determine speeds and angles, which in turn may indicate the order in which things happened. This enables the police to check the stories and explanations that people have provided. Ballistics is the part of physics dealing with guns and ammunition. Fluid dynamics is the physical basis of bloodstain pattern analysis, which can reveal a good deal of information about the scene, including the way in which a weapon was used. Variable wavelength light sources are used to check for glass, fluid and powder residues, including traces of blood, semen, drugs and other materials. They are important in colour comparisons of fibres, paint chips and inks. The physical matching of fingerprints, foot marks, tyre marks, tool marks, bullets and guns, all involve complex pattern-matching techniques — and an understanding of the physical dynamics that cause impressions in different materials and surfaces.

The principle of transference

Investigators gather physical evidence to establish if a crime has been committed, who may have been involved and how it may have been undertaken.

From his study of dusts in France in the early 1900s, Dr Edmond Locard developed what is now a fundamental tenet of forensic science — that when a person commits a crime they will leave at the scene something that was not there before, and carry away with them something that was not on them previously. This is now known as Locard's principle of interchange (or transference) and is the basis of scientific crime detection (and the 'clue' in detective stories!). It is often summarised as 'every contact leaves a trace'.[2] Thus, when a person has been murdered, the killer will leave vital clues at the scene of the crime — and also take away some material with them (on their shoes or clothing, for example) which will connect them with that scene. They may leave fingerprints, footprints, hairs or fibres, tool marks or car tyre marks at the scene. They may take with them mud, scratches, traces of blood or fibres from the victim or traces of broken glass or wood particles from a broken window.

Relevant evidence may be found on anyone knowingly or unknowingly associated with the incident. A fundamental operation, therefore, in any criminal investigation is to quarantine the scene immediately to avoid contamination and to preserve as much information as possible. The scene should be kept cordoned off until everything has been fully examined and recorded.

Contamination of crime scenes

Contamination means that the scene has been altered or interfered with after the criminal event, which makes reconstruction of the scene difficult. This may be accidental, as in the case of someone stumbling over the victim in the dark, or it may be intentional, as is the case with the criminal who wipes the fingerprints from the gun before placing it in the victim's hand.

Contamination can also result from transference. The principle of transference applies as much to investigating officers as it does to criminals. It is the investigating officers who are the most likely people to accidentally transfer material into the scene and also between the scene and the suspect's location. Officers who have attended at the crime scene should not be involved in interviewing suspects without taking considerable care to avoid transferring material to suspects and thus contaminating any evidence they collect from them.

Police forensic procedures

Any organisation has to have rules which identify the people who have the power to act for it. The police call their rules *General Orders*. Every police force will have rules relevant to the control and examination of crime scenes. In South Australia the police 'Crime Scene and Forensic Procedures Manual' is part of the 'General Duties Manual', which in turn is part of the *General Orders*.

A police forensic procedures manual contains the *minimum* operating standards crime scene examiners must follow when investigating physical evidence. Such a manual spells out the command and responsibility issues such as who is in charge of each situation and who does what. It covers matters such as securing the scene, the role and responsibilities of the crime scene investigators, preparations and procedures for the examination of crime scenes and the preservation of evidence, communications (codes and procedures) and case management. It deals with practical topics such as photography, equipment and supplies required (such as adhesive tapes, fingerprint powders, plastic bags, gloves, overalls, cameras and film).

In this book we elaborate only on those aspects that are pertinent to the cases which we discuss.

THE CRIME SCENE EXAMINER

Crime scene examiners are usually part of the technical services branch of the police service. They are specially trained and are responsible for providing high quality physical evidence services to, or beyond, the standard specified in the guidelines. Where an examiner considers the task is beyond their knowledge or experience, they must seek assistance from a more experienced examiner or supervisor. Other police officers take statements and generally seek any relevant information to help determine what has happened.

QUARANTINE THE SCENE

The police procedures state that for any unexplained death, the scene is to be cordoned off immediately. This means that crime scene tape is placed around the scene, leaving only one point of access. A guard is stationed at that point to control access and must have clear instructions about who is allowed in. A list is kept of all those entering and leaving the scene, including times of entry and exit, and such details as the protective clothing being worn. A crime scene examiner enters the scene via a route which permits access without disturbing any evidence.

Crime scene examiners must assume sufficient control of the scene to ensure that they can undertake their duties without interference. The police in charge of the investigation should be informed when the scene can be released to them and they can be shown through it.

The scene examiners wear gloves, overalls, shoe covers, face-masks and head coverings. This is to protect not only the scene from the examiners, but to protect the examiners from the scene. They do not know if anyone there has been suffering from an infectious disease or whether there may be chemical agents or poisons present. Fluids at the scene might be bath water or bodily fluids. Everything has to be treated with the greatest suspicion.

It is important to think about what counts as the 'scene'. Other locations and vehicles may also need to be secured. Where this is the case, a scene coordinator should be appointed to ensure that there is no cross-contamination. For example, a person attending at the scene should not be sent to interview suspects, or to attend at other locations.

CRIME SCENE EXAMINATION

The procedures require the police to investigate the circumstances surrounding a sudden, violent, unnatural death, or other death when it is not possible to obtain a death certificate from a medical practitioner. The investigation should provide accurate and detailed information on the manner and cause of death and the identity of the deceased. Deaths can be classified as natural (that is, died of natural causes such as a heart attack or old age) or unnatural. Unnatural deaths are further subdivided into accidental, suicidal or homicidal. The cause of death is usually provided by a pathologist.

An unexplained death is where a person is found dead but there are no immediate means of determining how death occurred. The next step is to decide if the death is suspicious or non-suspicious. The mere fact that a death is as yet unexplained does not necessarily mean that it is suspicious. However, police are trained to treat every unexplained death as suspicious (a homicide) until an explanation is forthcoming which either confirms or removes the suspicion. Indeed, the South Australian Police Forensic Procedures Manual states specifically: 'Initially (regardless of the probable category) crime scene investigators must *treat every death as a homicide* to ensure that no vital evidence is lost.'[3] [Emphasis in original]

It is essential to treat a suspicious death more carefully than a non-suspicious one. Normally, the doubts cannot be resolved until the results of the autopsy are known.

In unexplained deaths, the deceased is the most important part of the scene and safeguards must be in place to ensure that no unauthorised access to the body is permitted.

THE CHAIN-OF-EVIDENCE

In criminal investigations, all relevant evidence collected must be clearly linked to the source from which it arises. The explanation from a piece of evidence to its source must be complete and unbroken. This is called the chain-of-evidence and it is of critical importance if criminal charges are to be laid. All items should have an item number, description of item, location, time and date of collection, identity of person collecting (initialled), general location (room, address) and, if being handed the item by another, that person's identity. Proper records should be kept of the transfer of all evidence each time it passes from one person or place to another, as well as of all processing that is done to it. This is especially important in relation to body tissue samples taken at the autopsy since these are subjected to a number of processes as part of the examination procedures.

A complete and unbroken chain-of-evidence will eliminate any queries regarding potential contamination of the item. Details and batch numbers of specific chemicals used could be important to any later verification of processes.

TEMPERATURES

It is fundamental to record the body temperature at an unexplained death. This is usually done by a pathologist. To estimate the time-of-death it is necessary to know also the ambient temperature, that is, the air temperature, both within any room where the deceased is found and outside. Likewise, the temperature is needed of water in baths, pools, rivers or the sea in which a body is found.

Without disturbing the body unduly, detailed examination and recording of features is undertaken. After death, physical changes can occur quickly and the pathologist performing the autopsy later needs to be provided with detailed information of any markings, colouring, swelling or other features seen on the body when first found, as these could change before the autopsy begins.

PRESERVATION OF EVIDENCE
Physical evidence refers to anything which is of a physical nature that can be seen by the naked eye. It can include vehicles or buildings, fibres or obvious footprints and fingerprints.

Latent evidence is evidence that is invisible until it is enhanced in some way, such as fingerprints that cannot be seen until treated with powder or light. It may also refer to microscopic evidence such as traces of dust or fibres.

Destruction of evidence means that evidence has been lost, removed or transformed in some way so as to make it unavailable or unusable. Clearly the first priority of police arriving at a scene is to ensure that evidence does not get destroyed. Criminals may deliberately try to destroy the physical evidence or cause the evidence to be contaminated or misinterpreted; for example, by wiping away fingerprints, or burning the car that was stolen or used in a robbery.

Evidence can be destroyed accidentally, particularly if there has been a lack of planning in the approach to the scene. For example, if a body is found in a car, it might be the most natural thing in the world to open the car door to check that the person is in fact dead or to identify the body. However, the existence of any flies within the car might help an examiner to determine how long it has been since the car door was last open. Merely opening the door might result in the loss of such valuable evidence.

Contamination of evidence, just as for contamination of crime scenes, occurs where evidence has been exposed to contingencies that make its interpretation unreliable. If physical evidence is to be used to prove the presence of a person at a particular place, and that person has either visited or been brought to the scene, then the reliability of the evidence may be put in doubt. For example, if a police officer had been involved in a murder or robbery, but was later present at the premises as part of the investigating team, then any physical evidence linking that officer with the scene is contaminated by the later lawful presence at the scene. This is why any crime scene must be cordoned off until all the physical evidence has been obtained.

From the start of any investigation the approach must be that everyone is a suspect. One cannot assume that any of the people who turn up to the crime scene are beyond suspicion. This applies as much to the investigating officers as it does to the family and friends of a deceased person.

SEARCH STRATEGIES

It is important to think through possible search strategies from the outset. The principles of inclusivity and non-reversibility must be understood and remembered. Once information or material has been contaminated or destroyed it cannot be recovered. Therefore the initial information gathering should be as inclusive as possible. The basic rule is 'never trust anything to memory'. Diligent observation and recording are mandatory. Crime scenes are often charged with emotion, but all involved must remain calm and in control at all times. The examiner in charge of the crime scene should not relinquish control until confident that all relevant information has been retrieved and secured.

PHOTOGRAPHS AND VIDEO

Photographs are taken to record the scene and also for use later to help reconstruct the scene and the sequence of events. Police services provide for specialist photography and processing. Video recording of the scene should always be considered as it enables larger and more complex scenes to be understood in terms of scale and the relation of items to each other. Lateral thinking is important in determining what counts as the 'scene'. It could, for example, include cars or people in the area. It is not unknown for perpetrators to remain in the vicinity of a crime to watch the product of their work unfold. Sound and movement can obviously be of value. Also, video can also allow the officers outside the cordon to appreciate what has happened so that they can take appropriate action.

Where there is a suspicious death, the body is the most important component of the crime scene. Crime scene examiners should photograph the body at the scene and at the subsequent autopsy using colour film and electronic flash. Photographs should include general, mid-range and detailed photographs of the body, photographs of the body in the body bag, and any other photographs requested by the pathologist. 'When it comes to crime-scene photos, more is always better, and great is always best.'[4]

When objects or items are moved at the scene, it is important to retain precise details about where they were in relationship to other items. Photography, video or a grid reference might be appropriate depending on the circumstances. A photograph of an object in a cupboard might be relevant, but a photograph of a gun or knife on the ground outside or on a beach may not be sufficient to identify its precise location. A proper system of measurements should be devised, so that afterwards people will be able to reconstruct the relationships between items.

Before items are removed or examined, any possible trace evidence on the item itself or in its immediate vicinity must be preserved. This may involve fingerprints or dust on the item, or dust-free areas revealed when the item is moved. This can indicate if the item has been recently used, removed or placed in that location.

In certain circumstances, it may not be possible to move evidence without damaging it. Footprints, tyre marks and tool marks in friable soil, or on non-removable items or materials, will not be able to be moved. In this case, photographs and plaster or flexible casts can be used to retain the distinctive features of such evidence.

CASE MANAGEMENT

A log of events or running sheet must be established by the first officer arriving at the location. It should record the names, arrival and departure times of everyone entering and leaving the scene and any other relevant information. The police and the Coroner's office keep running sheets as a record of what is happening in relation to each of their cases. Each case will have a case number and once this is established, a continuous note is then kept in relation to the handling of the case. Each time a request for information is made it will be entered into the running sheet. When the matter has been attended to, that will also be entered into the sheet. It is then easy to identify at any stage which requests are still outstanding.

As soon as possible, it must be established who has been at the scene prior to the arrival of the police and whether they have moved or touched any items. This will indicate if any evidence has been lost or contaminated, or whether there is a chance that it may be misinterpreted.

Case management meetings are an important part of the organisation between the various people involved in the investigation. They should include the primary (operational) investigative team, crime scene examiners, technical services experts and forensic experts. The initial meeting should be held as soon as practicable and follow-up meetings held regularly afterwards. It is important to have a meeting of everyone involved before any arrest, trial or other conclusion of the matter. It is important also to debrief and to assess performances at the end of the inquiry. Accurate notes of meetings should be made and kept in the case file.

STRATEGIC THINKING

Communication strategies should be properly stated. It might, for example, be improper for the scientific officers to be in direct communication with the investigative officers. It might be improper for them to attend at the scene, or at an interview with a suspect. There should be procedures for peer review of autopsy and laboratory observations. Control samples, which are samples that do not come from the scene but from a known and independent source, should be used to test and demonstrate the accuracy of the system.

The biggest cause of contamination, however, will be because investigators have arrived at an explanation of what happened too soon. Once one can *explain* what has happened, there is an inevitable tendency to see only what fits that story, and not to see other (inconsistent) elements.

An assumption is the death of a good investigation.

CHAPTER THREE

AUTOPSIES

A death in sudden or unexplained circumstances comes within the jurisdiction of the Coroner. It is usual practice for a police officer attached to the Coroner's Office to attend such incidents. This officer liaises with the other police at the scene to determine if a forensic pathologist should be called in before the body is moved or removed. The Coroner's police officer arranges for the removal of the body to the mortuary for an autopsy. Under the Coroner's Act, the Coroner has to determine, if possible, the cause of death and if any further steps need to be taken. After the autopsy is done, the Coroner has to decide if there is a need for an inquest, which is a formal and usually public coroner's hearing into a death.

The autopsy
The procedure of examining a dead body to determine the cause of death is called an autopsy. The word comes from Greek words meaning 'to see for oneself'. The procedure is sometimes called a 'post-mortem examination', or even (colloquially) just a 'post-mortem' or 'PM'.

A forensic autopsy in the case of a suspicious death differs from a hospital autopsy. Whereas a hospital autopsy is primarily an internal examination of a body for disease, the forensic pathologist doesn't look only for disease but also for signs of trauma, injury or foreign objects such as bullets, as well as clues to a suspect, to try to determine how and when the death occurred. This information may exclude a suspect by showing that the death was really a terrible accident, for example. Equally, it may show that a suspect's account of how the death occurred is not true.[1] Thus a timely and competent autopsy is fundamental to the proper investigation of any suspicious death. Basic knowledge of the procedures involved and what they can show is therefore helpful to an understanding of some of the cases in this book and for this reason we now discuss how an autopsy is done.

The pathologist must be objective and operate in accordance with proper scientific standards. The obligation is to elicit as much information as possible to enable an assessment of the cause of death, and to record the observations in such a way as would enable another pathologist to provide an independent and properly informed opinion.

In unexplained deaths where there is access to a relevant medical history and there was medical supervision prior to the event, the pathologist will have some idea of what to look for and expect. With suspicious deaths, the examination is far more extensive and many more tissue samples are taken. The first thing to establish is whether the death resulted from an accident, homicide or natural causes. As someone may later be charged with murder, for example, based on the autopsy results, the evidence from the pathologist must be able to prove the cause of death *beyond reasonable doubt*, if at all possible. Therefore the pathologist must be open to all explanations for the death, including those consistent with innocence, and these must be excluded before a finding of guilt can be achieved. For example, where a person has been assaulted and is now dead, it might be natural to think that the assault caused the death.

However, that is only one possibility — one that needs to be confirmed beyond reasonable doubt. Another possibility is that the assault was merely incidental or coincidental to the death. The person could have died from a heart defect. The assault may have had nothing to do with the death. The pathologist has to examine (and exclude) any other reasonable alternative, as well as provide positive information which connects the observable injuries with the outcome. A proper chain-of-causation has to be established, so that each of the events leading to the death can be placed in their proper order. It is essential to establish, for example, whether the deceased died before or after being stabbed, or before or after the car they were driving crashed.

The pathologist must read all the background information about the person. If acting under coroner's instructions, any further information can be obtained via the Coroner's Office, as it has the power to demand information be provided. In such a case, a Report of Death to the Coroner form will have been completed. The Coroner has to issue proper instructions for the autopsy to proceed. The appropriately completed forms and permissions should be kept on the file.

PREPARATION FOR THE AUTOPSY
The pathologist wears the normal surgical theatre dress — boots, surgical gown with plastic apron, gloves and goggles. The mortuary technician has the various pieces of equipment ready. These include an array of knives for cutting, forceps for moving, a ladle for dealing with fluids and a saw for cutting bone. The saw used is an oscillating saw specially designed to cut hard surfaces such as bone. It will not cut soft tissue, such as the pathologist's fingers.

A crime scene examiner should be present at the autopsy of all suspicious or unexplained deaths. The officer takes notes of the procedures and colour photographs or a video recording of the sequence of the autopsy.

The pathologist keeps personal notes of observations and procedures, which are written up afterwards. A pathologist may be conducting a number of examinations shortly after each other and it would be easy to be unsure of specific observations, even a little time later. Some pathologists dictate notes into a tape recorder, others write them as they go. Examination suites nowadays are likely to be fitted with closed circuit television to enable video recording of examinations. This also allows easy observation by colleagues or trainees.

The notes, tapes, photographs and samples must be clearly identified and kept secure. There should be a clear audit trail in relation to each item which identifies who has accessed it and when.

The external examination of the body

The body is undressed and any jewellery removed (where appropriate) and documented.

The pathologist conducts a full external examination of the body. If written notes are being used, then a body chart (a pre-printed outline sketch of a person) is used to provide details of locations where injuries are found.

There must be full documentation of all details including birthmarks, skin blemishes, tattoos, scars, colour of hair and eyes, false teeth, missing teeth, lacerations, bruises, fractures and injection sites. It must be confirmed that the body is the same as that from the scene of the death and recorded in the register book or computer records. It is important to turn the body over and examine the back, and to look for possible trace contact material. This evidence might include fibres, semen or soil stains and scrapings from under the fingernails, all of which must be recorded and collected.

At this point X-rays may be taken to identify or confirm fractures (especially in children), detect bullets in shooting cases, or to check against dental records for identification purposes in the case of an unknown person or a badly mutilated or decomposed body. Fingerprints may also be taken.

The internal examination of the body

As far as possible the pathologist ensures that marks from the autopsy do not show above the shroud or shirt in which the body will be later dressed, as friends and family will want to make their farewells after the examination.

OPENING THE BODY CAVITY

Frequently the mortuary technician makes the initial cuts, although the pathologist attends to any areas where there may be complications. What we say about the standard procedures will always have this caution in mind. If, for example, the person had been strangled or shot, then any procedures would have to ensure that evidence of those injuries is preserved.

The pathologist makes various cuts with a scalpel across and along the body to open it up. The skin and soft tissues are peeled back and the ribs and breastplate removed so that the organs can be accessed for examination. The neck and bottom part of the jaw are cut such that the tongue, throat and mouth can be examined in detail.

ORGANS RELEASED

The connections to the organs are severed so that the organs can be removed in one block. The blood vessels that supply the legs are disconnected. About 50 ml of blood is taken from these vessels to test for various drugs (including alcohol) and poisons. Some may be kept for DNA testing to resolve any identification issues. A sample of urine can be obtained by making a small cut in the upper surface of the bladder.

The next step is to remove the organs, which are removed as a block. Once this is done only the body shell remains. The blood and other fluids will be ladled or sponged out by the technician and the pathologist will look inside to check the linings and coverings for fractures, bruises or other signs of injury or disease.

INDIVIDUAL ORGANS SEPARATED
The individual organs are cut away from the block and examined, commencing from the back. The major blood vessels, the inferior vena cava and the aorta, are identified and opened along their length to expose their interior and then removed. The vessels branching from those are also examined. The pathologist is looking for signs of an aneurism (a rupture to the blood vessels), blood clots or other blockage, or injury or disease. The renal arteries which lead to the kidneys are checked and the kidneys removed. Sometimes the organs may not be removed but just cut along their length to examine their interior. This is less thorough than removing each organ separately and weighing and examining it. The ureters, which conduct urine from the kidney to the bladder, are then examined, as well as the adrenal glands.

The thoracic and abdominal blocks are then separated. The oesophagus is released for removal with the stomach as part of the abdominal block. The diaphragm is released from the abdominal block and removed with the thoracic block.

ABDOMINAL, PELVIC AND UPPER THORACIC BLOCKS
From the abdominal block, the oesophagus and stomach are opened and a sample of the contents of each is taken. The

various abdominal organs are inspected in situ. The pelvic block is removed from the abdominal block and the pelvic organs, such as the prostate in men and the ovaries in women, are examined. The heart, which is in the thoracic block, is removed by cutting the vessels which lead to it. That block is then turned over, and the airways examined, including the larynx, trachea, bronchi and lungs. The vessels of the heart are opened, as is the part of the aorta leading from it. All the remaining organs are dissected out: the lungs, heart and thyroid from the upper block; and the liver, spleen and pancreas from the lower block. Each organ is weighed and then examined in detail.

The further examination technique depends very much on what is required. One approach is to cut down the bronchi and airways of the lungs. However, as any technique for examination will (at the same time) destroy the organs or vessels, the pathologist will be very much guided by whether there is a need to demonstrate some process, or to obtain samples for further testing.

With the heart there are many different techniques. One is to work through the chambers and open up each of them in the order in which the blood flows through them. However, this might lead to them being unrecognisable afterwards.

Photographs are an important part of recording both the sequence of events and the findings, especially in traumatic deaths, whether the death arises from assault or car, workplace or recreational accidents. In criminal matters, a full sequence of photographs must be taken, usually by the crime scene examiner.

Ancillary investigations

All autopsies should be complete and the examination not restricted to areas of presumed or obvious pathology. An autopsy is not considered complete unless it is accompanied by the appropriate ancillary microscopic (histology) and chemical (toxicology) investigations.[2]

HISTOLOGY

Histology is the examination of body tissues using a microscope. This detailed examination is an essential aspect of an autopsy. In a suspected criminal case, the pathologist should take as many tissue samples for histology as possible. It is better to take too many samples rather than not enough in such cases, as it is impossible to know what questions will eventually turn out to be important.

Tissue samples should be taken from organs such as the heart and lungs at least. The minimum required for each lung is four samples — two from the upper (left and right) lobes and two from the lower (left and right) lobes. In addition, it is essential to take samples of any abnormality. With the heart, tissue samples should be taken from the different areas of the blood flow within the heart, and of portions of the coronary arteries that supply blood to the heart itself. The arteries are opened and examined for blockage. A heart attack caused by a blocked artery does not necessarily show up as damage to the heart itself. The failure to appreciate this can lead to an impaired diagnosis of ischaemic heart disease or the failure to diagnose a heart attack (myocardial infarction). *Ischaemia* means an inadequate supply of blood to a part of the body. A *myocardial infarction* is where the muscle of the heart is irreversibly damaged due to a loss of blood supply. It may not always be possible to find evidence of infarction as it takes about six hours for the effect of this to show up within the heart. Thus, if the person dies within one hour of the heart pain, for example, then heart tissue samples taken at an autopsy would not reveal anything even when examined using a microscope. However, by opening up the coronary artery, the pathologist can see any thrombus (clot) within it. Sound practice is to take samples from the coronary arteries for histological examination.

When pathologists see evidence of a heart attack, they have to relate these observations to what has occurred. Did the heart attack cause the accident, or was the accident the cause of the heart attack? The people who were present at the incident may not be able to relate accurately whether the person was alive or dead when they were stabbed. This may be due to their incomplete knowledge of the circumstances or to the fact that they may have been affected by drink or drugs.

The procedure for taking histological specimens is to cut representative blocks of tissue from areas of abnormality and also from normal tissue (as controls) for comparison. These blocks are placed in formalin, which fixes (hardens) the tissue. The next day, the hardened tissue can be sectioned. To do this, pieces about 2 cm × 1.5 cm in size and about 2–3 mm thick, are cut from the original blocks, trimmed to fit in a cassette and impregnated with molten wax. Additional procedures ensure that the tissue is properly positioned within the wax block and that the block itself can then be positioned so that it can be placed on a microtome — a machine which will take off very fine slices (sections). In effect, the wax is holding the hardened tissue in position so that wafer-thin slices can be machined off it. The sections are adhered to microscope slides and stained with various dyes that will react with the tissues to produce different colours so that they can be properly identified using a microscope. The piece of tissue finally examined by the pathologist is quite small and its selection from the larger piece of tissue should be done by the pathologist and not by the technician. Under the National Association of Testing Authorities (NATA) accreditation (which is the Australian standard for laboratory accreditation) the pathologist is not allowed to get the technician to cut up the tissue specimens. Where it is just a matter of the tissue being transferred, say from the microtome to the slide, then the technician may do that, but if *selection* is involved, then it is the pathologist who must make that selection. This is demanding on the pathologist's time, as they have to return to the laboratory 24 hours after the block tissue sample has been taken from the body to do the next stage. However, good laboratories should insist that the pathologists do the trimming and selection of tissue samples and organise schedules accordingly.

Samples for histology of lung, heart, spleen, liver, brain, kidneys and any abnormality should be routine. If a death is suspicious, then it is essential to take many more than that. If a body is found at home and is of a young and apparently fit person, and an autopsy as described above had not revealed any apparent cause of death, then it would be essential to take further action.

TOXICOLOGY

Usually decisions about toxicology are taken at the end of the examination. If the autopsy and histology have been of little help in revealing the cause of death, a full toxicology screening should be done. Initially this involves screening the blood and (perhaps) urine as well. Samples of liver tissue and stomach contents, and sometimes bile, might be taken. The pathologist screens the urine and blood for drugs such as cannabis and amphetamines as well as alcohol — this is where any known social history of drug taking can be of great help. It is very important to know what drugs or medications were found at the scene and for screening to be undertaken for them. Samples from containers taken from the scene would need to be analysed as well, as it would be unsafe to assume that the contents of containers corresponded with the description on the labels. If a volatile solvent, such as chloroform or petrol is thought to be involved, lung tissue will reveal if vapours from such a solvent have been inhaled.

It is important that the pathologist is given as much help as possible in what to look for. Lawyers and police should appreciate that the social and medical history is important and that any relevant information should be provided as quickly as possible to the pathologist so that appropriate tests can be conducted quickly and some of the possible causes of death eliminated.

SPECIALIST EXAMINATION
The most obvious organs for more detailed examination are the brain, heart and liver. The first thing to consider is if the brain should be sent to an expert neuropathologist. The whole brain needs to be sent as it is better for the specialist to section it because the tissue is so soft.

The brain
To examine the brain, the top of the skull is removed and nerve connections are examined and cut. The connection to the spinal cord is also examined and cut. Removing the brain is a delicate job, and must be done carefully. The brain is then examined externally for haemorrhage or swelling.

Death caused by a haemorrhage, such as a subarachnoid haemorrhage can be seen on visual inspection. This is bleeding outside the brain itself but beneath the membrane which covers the outer edge of the brain (the arachnoid membrane). An internal brain haemorrhage is likely to be seen either by the blood spilling out through the tissues of the brain or where an area of the brain looks swollen. If such a haemorrhage is observed at this stage, the pathologist may decide that this is sufficient evidence to diagnose the cause of death and will not send the brain to the specialist.

If the brain is being sectioned at autopsy, the pathologist takes a long knife and slices through the centre of the brain to minimise damage. At this stage there will be some leakage of red cells, which would (to the untrained eye) look like bleeding. However, a pathologist should be able to distinguish such leakage from bleeding that had occurred during life.

It is often said that loss of consciousness has no pathology. So, if someone has lost consciousness before death there may be no physical evidence of this in the examination of the brain at autopsy. If a dead person has (external) bruising to the head, it may be difficult to determine whether they hit their head and became unconscious or became unconscious and then hit their head. There may be no physical signs within the brain of the initial loss of consciousness. Epilepsy is perhaps the most common occurrence of such an event, but it is by no means the only possible cause.

The heart

At a normal autopsy, somewhere between four to twenty tissues samples may be taken of the heart. When a specialist cardiac pathologist examines the heart, some 300 to 400 samples may be examined. This enables the specialist to pick up on faults or damage within the heart which would not otherwise be apparent.

What a specialist can bring to an examination highlights the need for peer review in forensic pathology, and the need for all pathologists to be in constant contact with other specialists in their field so that they can check each other's cases and keep each other informed. Where a pathologist is working essentially on their own, without frequent exchanges of files, slides and ideas with colleagues, there is a potential problem.

Lack of knowledge or missed opportunities for updates go unnoticed. Any quality management procedure should require regular, routine and systematic peer reviews to be undertaken. Blind checking by pathologists from another laboratory of notes, files, reports, analyses and procedures used, is one way of doing this. It is an integral part of risk management.

General issues

BRUISING

A pathologist must be able to substantiate the fact that a mark is a bruise as opposed to any other form of skin discolouration or blemish. Bruising results when blood vessels are damaged sufficiently to allow blood to escape through the walls of the vessel into the surrounding tissues beneath an intact skin, leading to discolouration which can be seen through the skin.[3] Not all bruising is visible to the naked eye. Blood has to escape in sufficient quantities for it to be visible through the tissues and skin. Many factors, for example skin colouring and the existence of tattoos or other marks, influence the extent to which a bruise can be seen on visual examination. Peeling back the skin over suspected areas of bruising can confirm bruising, as can taking tissue samples for microscopical analysis.

Normal procedure is to photograph the visible mark or suspected area, peel back the skin and photograph the tissue, then take a tissue sample and photograph the area again. Thus a complete record is kept of each stage of the procedure. Microscopical examination can then confirm the existence of red blood cells within tissue where blood is not normally found.

The body reacts to ruptured blood vessels by utilising fibrin to stem the flow of blood and sending neutrophils (a type of white blood cell that acts as a scavenger) to mop up the escaped blood. If neutrophils are seen in tissue samples taken from the site of the bruise when examined using a microscope, bruising is confirmed.

It can take up to 24 hours, and sometimes longer, for this neutrophil reaction to take place. In one person it may happen within two hours, and for another person it may still not have happened after 24 hours. Therefore telling the age of bruises based on this process is a vexed question. All the pathologist can do microscopically is to determine whether or not the reaction has occurred, but not when the injury that caused the bruise occurred.

The pathologist should try to determine if any bleeding is along the septal planes (that is, *between* the tissue surfaces), or whether it is diffused *within* the tissue. This is because it is not uncommon to go back to the body after 24 hours and see bruising which was not apparent upon the first examination. Bruising sometimes appears more obvious a day later. However, if the pathologist doesn't notice bruising at the first examination, but does notice it at a subsequent examination, then careful consideration must be given to the fact that it could be bruising (or bleeding) which has been caused by the process of the autopsy itself (artifactual bruising).

Because the autopsy process involves cutting through tissues, it invariably causes bleeding. If proper care is not taken, such bleeding might subsequently be thought to have occurred during life. For example, when the scalp is peeled back from the skull, the process causes blood to escape from the many tiny blood vessels across the scalp. It is likely that this blood will collect along the line where the scalp is still joined to the skull. Gradually, blood will seep between the skin and the tissues. If the scalp is then peeled back further after a period of, say, 24 hours, a pathologist would expect to find some pooled blood in the tissues where the skin was further taken back. Any bleeding or bruising found in such areas must be distinguished from bleeding or bruising which had occurred during life.

VIRTOPSY

The term virtopsy was created from the words 'virtual' and 'autopsy' to describe a virtual autopsy — an autopsy performed without dissecting the body. It uses computerised imaging and radiology technology to create two dimensional and three dimensional reconstructions of the body from which an objective and reproducible assessment can be made. This procedure is not yet in general use, but studies show it to be practical and reliable and it could become an established technique. Its advantages include its non-invasiveness, its potential for teleconsultation between colleagues, and its ability to use the data for teaching and in court reports and demonstrations.[4]

DOCUMENTATION PROTOCOLS

For a sudden or unexplained death investigation, a properly documented medical history is essential. In Australia, a person can seek medical assistance from a number of practitioners, none of whom may know about the others. The only way a pathologist can be confident of obtaining relatively complete information on someone brought in for autopsy is to check through the Medicare system. Medicare maintains records of payments and treatment providers and the Coroner has the power to request such information.

In suspected criminal cases, the pathologist must avoid any unauthorised contact with the family or friends of the deceased, just as a judge would do during a trial. While it can sometimes be helpful for the pathologist to discuss matters relating to the deceased with the family or friends, it is necessary to get the permission of the Coroner before doing so.

The autopsy report

At the completion of the autopsy a formal report is prepared. A typical report begins with information concerning the identification of the body, followed by a description which includes age, sex, race, height and weight.[5] Clothing is described and then the findings from the external examination are described — items such as hair and eye colour, scars, tattoos and any other identifying features. Injuries are described in detail.

The information from the internal examination describes the various systems of the body — respiratory, cardiovascular, alimentary, renal, endocrine, haemopoietic, central nervous and skeletal — and follows the pattern of the dissection. A record is made of the results and meaning of samples that have undergone histological testing and of material taken for toxicological testing.

The report concludes with comment on what was directly or indirectly responsible for the death — the 'cause of death'. The language used for this should be as simple as possible as it needs to be understood by non-medical people such as lawyers and possibly jurors. In some cases it is appropriate to comment on the 'manner of death'. For example, commenting that the injuries found are likely to have been self-inflicted.

In a court hearing, an expert witness is often pressured to be more accurate than the science sometimes allows. It is always inappropriate for an expert witness to express views that go beyond their own scientific capabilities. The pathologist's findings must be based on what they have actually observed, and their interpretations on accepted scientific principles. Speculating on the circumstances surrounding the death should be absent or kept to a minimum[6] — it is not the job of the pathologist to speculate as to how something may have happened, only to be able to prove that it has.

CHAPTER FOUR

MEDICAL MATTERS

The medical issues involved in the cases discussed in this book can be complex. So that a better understanding and assessment of these cases can be made, this chapter explains some general medical principles and also describes some of the procedures in detail.

The circulatory system

The blood, together with the heart and its system of blood vessels, the arteries and veins, is the transportation system of the body. It brings nutrients absorbed through the stomach, and oxygen absorbed through the lungs, to all the tissues and cells of the body. It transports the waste products away, with the kidneys acting as the waste filtration system. The blood is pumped out of the heart through the arteries and eventually into small, thin-walled capillaries. It then returns to the heart by way of the veins.

The average adult human body has about 5 litres of blood. About half the blood volume is made up of a straw-coloured liquid called plasma. The remaining half of the blood is made up of blood cells which are of two main types — red cells and white cells.

The red cells are in the vast majority. They contain haemoglobin, an iron-containing substance that gives blood its red colour, which binds oxygen to transport it around the body.

The white cells include cells such as neutrophils which scavenge for bacteria and dead tissue. For example, where blood escapes from a blood vessel which has been damaged (as in bruising), it is the neutrophils which come along to pick up the blood which has escaped into the surrounding tissues. The white cells also include the B cells which produce antibodies in the presence of foreign substances such as bacteria and viruses. It is the white cells that contain the DNA used for typing for identification.

Blood samples tell the pathologist much about the condition of the person before and after death. The presence of alcohol, drugs or poisons can be seen from toxicological analysis of the samples. Blood spattering provides information about the location and movements of a person during an attack. The way in which the blood settles in the body (lividity) tells about the timing and circumstances of death.

It is important to appreciate that bleeding does not require a person to be alive, nor does it require the heart to be beating. It simply requires there to be fluid blood in the vessels. If those vessels are torn or damaged, then the fluid blood within them will escape, and this is what is called bleeding.

BLEEDING TO DEATH

The aorta is the main artery leading from the heart. It comes from the top of the heart, like a large hose, then arches over, rather like an inverted U-bend (like this ∩) and goes down through the centre of the body. The bend is called the aortic arch and it is anchored quite firmly to the surrounding tissues and bones. Although the membrane surrounding the heart (the pericardium) is also firmly anchored, the heart itself is not so firmly anchored, and it hangs off the end of the aorta. If someone receives a violent blow to the chest, especially with a slightly downward momentum, the heart can be pushed downwards within the chest. With the heart moving down and the aorta firmly anchored, the aorta will tear near the top of the arch.

This type of injury is commonly found in car accidents where the driver's chest hits the steering wheel. Such an injury could also be caused by someone stamping on the chest of another person lying on the ground. This topic is usually covered in the forensic pathology books under sections headed 'Blunt trauma injuries of the trunk' or 'Blunt force injuries of the chest'.

If the aorta is ruptured in this way, the heart will pump blood into the tissues or the body cavities until it stops beating. Death would occur rapidly. However, this does not mean that there could be no external bleeding. This would depend on the nature of any cuts or damage to the tissues. Even when the heart stops beating, bleeding will result from any wounds which cut across blood vessels, organs, tissues or cavities which still contain fluid blood. If an autopsy is done before the blood has become fixed, there will be bleeding each time the pathologist makes a cut into the tissues. Indeed, as discussed in the chapter on autopsies, it is an important issue for the pathologist to distinguish post-mortem bleeding (artifactual bleeding caused by the process of the autopsy) from bleeding that has occurred before death.

It is not hard to see that it is possible for a pathologist to accidentally create signs of 'murder' while in the process of looking for them.

Drowning

While the idea that someone has drowned is familiar to everyone, the term itself can give rise to confusion. This is because 'drowning' explains the *circumstances* in which death occurs; it does not, however, explain the particular biological *mechanism* which has caused the death. Drowning may mean that water has filled the airways and the lungs, causing the person to suffocate. Or it might mean that the person has fallen into water, and the shock has killed them before water has entered the lungs. Someone might die because the sudden immersion in water caused them to have a heart attack. If the heart muscle stops working, or the coronary artery narrows, then the blood supply to the brain, and the oxygen which it contains, ceases. This is like a mechanical failure and can cause loss of consciousness and death if the supply is not restored within a few minutes. After just a few minutes, brain damage is likely to result even if the person were to be revived. Sudden immersion can also cause the brain to stop working in another way which is more like an electrical failure. Shock or fear can affect the nervous system directly and produce vagal inhibition. This is where the nervous system stops sending the electrical signals that keep the heart and lungs working. In each of these circumstances (mechanical or electrical failure) the originating cause of the death is different, but it would be quite accurate to say in each of them that the person had drowned.

To know the cause or mechanism of death, as opposed to the circumstances giving rise to it, it is necessary to understand the body's functioning systems and to determine the order in which they closed down.

BREATHING AND OXYGEN ABSORPTION
Human beings need to absorb oxygen continually to keep their system ticking over. They breathe in through the nose and mouth, filling the lungs with air to supply the blood and other tissues and cells with oxygen. To breathe, the diaphragm and chest muscles cause the lungs to expand and take in air. The air travels along the bronchial tubes to the alveoli, which

are rather like the little branches on broccoli. The alveoli contain irregular chambers which make for a large surface area. The very thin membranes of the alveoli allow the oxygen from the air to be absorbed by the blood. The oxygen is taken into the red blood cells where it binds to the haemoglobin and is circulated throughout the body. Likewise, the carbon dioxide that is produced by the body is sent back via a similar process to be discharged into the lungs, and then expelled from the body when we breathe out.

When this process is interrupted for any period of time, death occurs. Some cells of the body are especially sensitive to a reduction or loss of oxygen, particularly the cells of the brain and the heart. Loss of oxygen to the brain can cause permanent loss of function. Loss of oxygen to the heart can affect the heart muscles and produce an irregular heartbeat (arrhythmia).

ASPHYXIATION

In a drowning caused by asphyxiation (suffocation), the water fills the airways and obstructs the intake of air, thereby halting the oxygen absorption cycle and causing death. The crucial factor here is the blockage that prevents the intake of oxygen. What actually causes the blockage is not so important. Therefore, there will be similarities in asphyxiation cases where a pillow is placed over someone's face, where a person has been buried alive, or where a person is immersed in any fluid or fine grains or powders. If someone falls into a silo containing grain or flour and sinks because their bodyweight takes them under the surface, they would drown just as surely as if they had fallen into water.

When a person submerged in water loses consciousness, the air in their lungs and stomach is replaced with water. As the water enters the confined spaces of the lungs, it forces the air out of them and back up through the throat and mouth.

This is what is happening when we see bubbles appearing after a person has been submerged for a short time.

Drowning is sometimes classified as wet or dry drowning, although some pathologists do not like to use these expressions. Wet drowning means that the water has been taken into the system while the person was alive, and the water in the lungs and stomach has been carried into the bloodstream. Dry drowning is where the water has not reached the lungs while alive. This may happen when a spasm of the larynx, for example, blocks the passage of air (and hence water) into the lungs while the person is alive.

WATER ABSORPTION

If the lungs of a dead person appear to be 'waterlogged', a number of possibilities need to be considered.

Of immediate importance to an investigation is to determine whether the person has aspired (taken in) water as part of the process of drowning, the water seeped into the body after death has taken place, or whether the fluid in the lungs is, in fact, oedema. Oedema occurs when the clear fluid (plasma) of the blood separates from the blood under certain conditions and which cannot, for various reasons, be returned to the veins and arteries. The excess fluid becomes dispersed in the tissues, causing swelling or weals like blisters. Oedema can affect all organs, causing swelling in the lungs and brain as well as the skin, where it looks like a weal, a blister or generalised swelling. After death, the whole body may become swollen by this leaked vascular fluid, especially the face and neck. The walls of the lungs are very thin and where additional fluid builds up in the tissues, it will pass through the thin lung membranes and drain into the lung. When oedema of the lungs occurs from heart failure, the lungs can have the same weight and appearance as if they were waterlogged from drowning.

Where drowning is thought to be a factor in a death, it is particularly important to retain the integrity of the organs at autopsy. All organs should be removed and weighed, especially the lungs. There are standard weights for people of different sizes and types. If the organs are heavy, tests should be conducted to determine if the cause is through water or oedema, and to exclude all other possibilities.

HAEMOLYSIS

If fresh water enters the lungs while someone is alive and the heart is still pumping, the intake of water into the blood vessels can be rapid. When this happens, the total number of red cells in the blood remains the same but the volume of liquid becomes much greater, which reduces the blood's oxygen carrying capacity. The dilution of the blood changes its chemical balance, causing the red blood cells to swell and burst. This is called haemolysis. When the red cells burst, the haemoglobin is released and becomes ineffective. This further diminishes the capacity of the blood to carry oxygen at a time when the heart requires more oxygen, not less, because of the much greater demand put on it to circulate the extra fluid taken into the blood. The net result is likely to be heart failure.

The released haemoglobin can stain the linings of some of the blood vessels, particularly the aortic artery, which is the largest vessel extending from the top of the heart. However, caution must be exercised before making a diagnosis of heart failure due to drowning based on such staining. This is because some medications and other medical conditions can also cause haemolysis and produce this staining, and may well be a cause of death. Samples must be taken of the fluid the person is said to have drowned in, so as to assist in determining the likelihood of haemolysis. Salt (sea) water, for example, may have a different effect to fresh water. Domestic bath water may include bath salts (which include sodium chloride), oils and soaps which, if ingested, could also affect the chemical balance of the blood.

In a suspected drowning where signs of oedema are present, it would be important to check for any physical obstruction of the airways, because if this was found it might mean that the person had choked to death and not drowned. Such obstructions could be caused by swallowing something which has blocked the airway or could be inhaled vomited material, or could be an allergic reaction that narrowed the airways. Removing and examining the airways and lungs should be done carefully and, if vomited material and/or some other blockage is present in the airways, then it is important to determine whether the physical blockage or the water blockage occurred first. Photographs are essential during and after the removal of the organs.

FROTHING

Frothing of the mouth is caused by fluid mixing with the mucous fluids and is a common sign of drowning. It is not always present in drowning deaths and it can also occur in natural deaths. The frothing may be white or pink. The latter is from the leakage of the red blood cells into the space surrounding the lung. Normally the alveoli are open, however salt water destroys the surface tension of the lining of the lungs, causing the alveoli to collapse and the surface fluid of the alveoli to become part of the fluid in the lungs. Rather like soap, this substance causes frothing within that fluid. Damage to the alveoli may be difficult to identify as it may not always be possible to see the frothing microscopically. This is because the process of preparing the tissue sections on the microscope slides dehydrates the sample. This same consideration can apply where there may be foreign matter (such as smoke particles or dirt) in the water within the space around the lungs. The slide preparation process is like washing, and material in the tissue sample such as vomit, smoke or dirt may be removed during that process and not show up on subsequent examination of the slides.

THE DIATOM TEST

Diatoms are microscopic, unicellular algae found in all sources of fresh and salt water. They have a silica body that is hard, acid-resistant and can be seen using a microscope. Different species of diatoms have different shapes and structures and these are used to determine the species. The species (or combination of species) help identify the geographical location of the water source in a drowning death.

To detect diatoms, a section of body tissue is treated with strong acid. Because diatoms are acid resistant, they will remain after the tissue is broken down and can be put onto slides and viewed with a microscope. The number and shapes of diatoms found can be compared with diatoms from a sample of water taken at the scene. This sample should be taken as close as possible to the time at which the drowning is said to have occurred.

Diatoms can enter the bloodstream of a drowning person if the lungs fill with so much water that the alveoli break. This allows the water (and any diatoms contained in it) into the bloodstream. The presence of diatoms in lung tissue alone cannot discriminate between drowning and immersion in the water after death. Diatoms can also be present in the air and enter the lungs by being inhaled. Thus, to show conclusively that water has been taken into the system while the person was alive and while the heart was still beating, rather than just passively draining into the lungs after the person died some other way, it is necessary to test organs other than the lungs for the presence of diatoms. This means that tests should be conducted on organs such as the kidneys and the bone marrow. Finding diatoms in enclosed tissue such as bone marrow indicates that the drowning caused the death. The test, however, is often of limited usefulness because of the low numbers of diatoms in some waters and the very small number of diatoms recovered from the body. It is critical that control samples be processed to check for contamination which could be caused, for example, from diatoms in the reagents and the water used in the laboratory.[1] To be meaningful, the species of diatoms found in the body tissue must also be found at the site of the drowning. If there were no site sample, a diatom test on the tissues alone would not be likely to provide any useful information.[2]

DEATH BY DROWNING

How long does it take for a drowning person to die? Experience shows that it varies from immediately to much longer and may well depend on the definition of death. For someone to be pronounced dead, it usually will be reported that the eyes are fixed and the pupils dilated, and that there is no respiration or pulse. When blood is not circulating, brain damage occurs fairly quickly through lack of oxygen. If this situation continues for any period of time, the brain is irreparably damaged. The heart can continue to pump after breathing has ceased, but the blood will not be conveying oxygen. When the lungs fill with water there is (in effect) complete asphyxiation. Although the heart can beat, if the airway can't be cleared, death is inevitable. If the airway is blocked, attempts can be made to remove the blockage by either sucking it out or dislodging it. If this can't be done, the airway can be pierced below the blockage to get air into the lungs. A hollow tube (tracheotomy tube) or needle is inserted through an incision below the blockage. In emergencies it has been done by inserting the plastic tube of a ballpoint pen.

Electrocardiograms record the electrical activity associated with the heartbeat. Where there is no beat, the heart is said to be asystolic or straightline (as it shows on a monitor). Where there is an irregular beat, the heart is said to be suffering from arrhythmia, and in extreme cases it will be in a state of fibrillation. Fibrillation is where the heart muscle is twitching but not moving enough to pump blood. It may be possible to get the heart muscle beating properly again by using a defibrillator to apply an electrical shock across the chest. It is often thought that the defibrillator is used when the heart has stopped beating. It is in fact only possible to get the heart beating again where it is fibrillating. Another way of doing this is to use manual cardiopulmonary resuscitation (CPR) to keep the heart and airflow going.

DIAGNOSIS OF DROWNING

In some instances the autopsy findings on a person who has died by drowning may be no different to those found in other forms of death by asphyxiation. When death has been rapid, and the deceased immersed only for a short time, there may be few, if any, external signs of drowning.[3] When positive evidence of drowning (say from an eye-witness) is lacking, a 'diagnosis by exclusion' is all that can be made. This means that when all other reasonable causes have been excluded, and macroscopic, microscopic and toxicologic examinations have revealed nothing, then the pathologist might attribute the death to something which reasonably could be inferred without there being specific physical signs of it.

Allergies

An allergy is an inappropriate or excessive immune response to antigens.[4] An antigen is a substance that stimulates the production of antibodies when it enters the body. It is the role of the antibodies to bind to the antigens to remove them from the system, hopefully before they cause any harm. Antigens which trigger allergic reactions are called allergens. Common allergens include pollen (particularly ryegrass pollen in the Adelaide area), house dust-mites, penicillin, insect stings, yeasts and moulds, and foods such as shellfish and eggs.

ALLERGENS AND HYPERSENSITIVITY

People who suffer from an allergy are said to be hypersensitive to the particular allergen. Hypersensitivity begins with the process of sensitisation, which is the initial exposure to an allergen that leads to the production of antibodies, specifically, large antibodies called IgE (immunoglobulin E). The IgE antibodies are made in the B cells, a type of white blood cell. People who make a lot of IgE antibodies tend to have allergic reactions more than those who do not. The tendency to produce IgE antibodies in response to specific allergens may be genetically determined.

MAST CELLS AND HISTAMINE

There is a time lag between initial contact with an allergen and the production of antibodies. Because of this, it might be that the first exposure to the allergen does not produce any observable symptoms of the reaction that is beginning to take place. The IgE antibodies produced from this first contact become attached to the cell membranes of what are called mast cells, millions of which are in the tissues lining the surfaces of the body in the skin, ears, lips, eyes, nose, mouth, lungs and intestines. Once the IgE antibodies are bound to the mast cells the system is prepared for the next exposure to the same allergen. When the next exposure happens, the antibodies already bound to the mast cells will bind the allergen immediately, which stimulates the mast cells to release histamine and other chemicals that they contain into the surrounding tissues. These chemicals attract scavenger cells to the area which then release their own chemicals, extending and exaggerating the responses initiated by the mast cells. This is called an allergic reaction.

A rapid and massive inflammation of the affected tissues may result. The severity of the reaction depends on the individual's sensitivity and the bodily location involved. If allergen exposure occurs in the skin, the responses may be restricted to that area. It often appears as localised redness and/or swelling and involves itching or hives (urticaria). An allergic reaction in the nose causes a runny nose (rhinitis) and sneezing. When this is combined with irritation of the eyes (conjunctivitis) it is called hay fever.

ANAPHYLACTIC SHOCK

If, however, an allergen enters the bloodstream, as with a bee-sting for instance, it can rapidly come into contact with the mast cells throughout the entire body and the response could be a systemic (whole body) reaction. This is known as anaphylactic shock. It can be swift and lethal. In anaphylactic shock the mast cells throughout the body release histamine into the blood vessels. As a result, the linings of the blood vessels become more porous, and plasma (the clear fluid part of the blood) leaks out into the surrounding tissues. This quickly produces swelling and oedema in the outer layer of the skin. Raised welts, blisters or hives may appear on the surface of the skin, especially on the face where the tissue is soft. The histamine causes the blood vessels to expand to allow the white cell reaction to speed up. The white cells are important to the healing process.

However, if this process gets out of control, the oversupply of histamine can cause real problems. Extensive and rapid expansion of the blood vessels occurs. The heart tries to keep the blood pressure up but as the space in the 'pipes' through which the blood flows may double in size, it has to pump faster and harder in an attempt to keep the vessels full with blood. This produces a sudden fall in blood pressure that can lead to circulatory collapse (heart attack).

The histamine may also cause the smooth muscles along the respiratory passageways to contract or spasm. As these muscles tighten up, they narrow the air passages and make breathing extremely difficult. The combination of breathing difficulties, increase of heart rate and loss of circulatory pressure can cause either or both systems to stop.

Certain drugs and diagnostic reagents can also directly trigger mast cell histamine release.[5]

Anaphylaxis may occur rapidly or slowly. Many of the symptoms of anaphylaxis can be prevented by the prompt administration of antihistamines. People with a susceptibility to this can carry a puffer or inhaler which will deliver an antihistamine dose directly to the airways. As its name implies, the antihistamine blocks the effect of the histamine that has been released into the system. The treatment of anaphylactic shock in a hospital setting involves antihistamine, corticosteroid and epinephrine injections.[6] It may also require adrenaline and intravenous fluids, plus artificial ventilation. Intubation (passing a tube into the trachea) may also be necessary to deal with the problem of airway swelling.

Systemic anaphylaxis is characterised by an appearance of a generalised flush, weakness, anxiety, dizziness, palpitations, tingling of the fingers or toes or of the tongue, hives (urticaria), swelling of the lips, tongue, neck and face (angio-oedema), nausea and vomiting, and uterine and gastro-intestinal cramps. Vomiting occurs in 10 to 15 per cent of people with anaphylaxis. The entire range of symptoms can develop within seconds or within minutes of contact with or administration of the drug or particular allergen to which the individual is sensitive.[7]

If not treated, the reaction may progress to respiratory distress, over-contraction of the muscles (hyper-peristalsis), irregular heartbeat (arrhythmia), cardiovascular collapse (heart attack), seizures, coma and death. Death can occur within 30 minutes.[8]

Most anaphylactic reactions are due to insect stings, food allergies or pharmaceuticals.[9] Penicillin and even aspirin can produce these problems.[10] In a drug-induced allergy, the reaction is most likely to occur at the start of a new course of treatment, or with a previously used drug which may not have caused allergic symptoms at earlier times. However, anaphylactic hypersensitivity can exist for many years in the absence of any known exposure to the drug.

In South Australia in one year recently, there were two rapid deaths from anaphylactic shock caused by bee-stings. In highly sensitive people, just having the substance on the skin or in the air may produce a similar response. There are examples of sensitised people developing the reaction by merely being in a restaurant where the allergen has been included in a sizzling dish which has been carried past their table. Anaphylactic reaction to the presence of peanuts is not uncommon.

DIAGNOSIS OF SUDDEN ANAPHYLACTIC DEATH
Forensic pathologists have long recognized anaphylaxis as a cause of sudden death.[11] However, diagnosis at autopsy is complicated by the relatively non-specific and inconstant pathologic findings seen in these cases.[12] If the death is the result of asphyxia the findings would be similar to those seen in other types of asphyxia, including drowning, but often there

are no specific visual autopsy findings that indicate an allergic death.[13] This reflects the rapidity and mode of death, which is often the result of shock rather than asphyxia. Where this shock is established within minutes of the start of the reaction, there may be no time for other features to occur. It is possible, however, to confirm the diagnosis of anaphylactic shock by testing for elevated levels of tryptase in the blood serum.[14] Tryptase is an enzyme which is released from the mast cells at the same time as the histamine. In contrast to histamine, however, it is relatively stable in serum and can therefore be measured in autopsy samples, including after storage at −20°C.[15] A study in the United Kingdom has shown that the absence of specific findings at autopsy does not exclude a finding of anaphylaxis and thus the possibility of anaphylaxis should be considered in *all* cases of sudden unexpected death.[16]

Epilepsy

Epilepsy is a discharge of electricity within the brain that causes the body to convulse. It often leaves no visible signs within the brain to be found at autopsy. It may be possible to infer an epileptic seizure from cuts or bruises on the body, especially from a cut to the tongue, which is why it is prudent to look for evidence of trauma (bite marks) to the tongue.

Where an epileptic fit occurs in a person in a potentially dangerous situation, such as when driving a car, in a bath or while swimming, it may result in death. While the traumatic cause of death (the injuries resulting from the car crash) will be evident at autopsy, there will be no evidence of the epileptic fit that caused the driver to crash.

DIAGNOSIS OF EPILEPSY
As with drowning, the diagnosis of epilepsy is a diagnosis by exclusion.

In chronic cases of epilepsy where there have been repeated attacks, it may be possible to take samples of tissue from the correct areas of the brain and show damage to the neurones, but in the case of a first attack this can't be done. Where a dead person is known to be epileptic, it might be possible to attribute the death to epilepsy without seeing specific physical signs of it.

Time of death

There are several methods for estimating the time of death, all of which are subject to variables that affect their accuracy.

BODY COOLING

The cooling of a body after death is known as algor mortis. The temperature of the body when found and the rate at which it is cooling can be used to estimate a time of death.[17] The temperature, which is measured in the rectum or alternatively in the liver via an abdominal stab, is taken as soon as possible after death, with further recordings being taken at regular intervals afterwards. This information can then be used in calculations[18] or, better, applied to a nomogram, which is a mathematical diagram that relates temperatures with times and body weights to help determine a time of death.[19] To calculate as accurately as possible, it is necessary to know the ambient (air) temperature in the room where the deceased is found, and also the temperature outside the room and outside the building, to help calculate the rate at which the temperatures have changed. Likewise, the temperature of water in baths, pools, rivers or the sea in which a body is found needs to be recorded.

A number of variables affect the accuracy of a time of death calculated by body cooling. Some, such as the size of the person and the amount of clothing they were wearing at the time of death, can be measured and factored in. Others, such as the person's temperature at the time of death and any changes in the ambient conditions since their death, are unknown and have to be assumed.[20]

Environmental factors, such as the humidity, whether the area is open or closed, and how windy, wet or otherwise it is, should be noted. The value of temperatures and other information recorded at the scene is that they are always available for later review and evaluation by an expert.[21]

LIVIDITY

If a body lies undisturbed for some time after death, the blood, without the heart to pump it around the system, settles at the lowest parts of the body producing areas of discolouration under the skin. These areas, which can be seen through the skin, turn red and then purplish as the blood pools and changes colour. This is called lividity (also livor mortis or hypostasis). Those parts of the body which are in contact with the ground will show white patches (blanching) because the pressure of the body on the ground stops the blood from settling in those areas. This means that if a body is discovered some time after death, the pattern of discolouration and blanching can help the pathologist to understand fairly accurately the way in which the body was lying after death.

The blood eventually becomes fixed in position, so the pattern of colouring and blanching will remain, even if the body is moved subsequently. If the pattern of discolouration and blanching is not consistent with the way in which the body is lying on the ground (or other surface) when discovered, then it can be inferred that it has been moved some time after death. This is why colour photographs of the body at the scene and at the autopsy are so important.

Lividity is usually apparent about one hour after death, but may be noticeable as soon as half an hour, depending on the conditions.[22] If a person were to die in a warm bath, then the process may be speeded up, because the blood vessels would be dilated (expanded) and so hasten the draining effect of the blood. It appears earlier in asphyxial (suffocation) deaths. It is usually complete within 8 to12 hours.[23]

RIGOR MORTIS

Rigor mortis is the stiffening of the muscles after death.[24] The muscles of the body need a continuous supply of the chemical adenosine triphosphate (ATP) to enable them to contract. The production of ATP stops at death, but it is still used by the muscles. When the ATP is used up, the other chemicals present in the muscles combine and set to produce the stiffening known as rigor mortis.[25] A number of factors affect the rate at which rigor develops. Strong exercise or increased temperatures prior to death will speed up the use of any ATP that is still in the muscles after death, and thus speed up the process of rigor after death. Cold or freezing will delay the onset of the rigor, as well as prolonging its presence. Rigor gradually disappears as the body begins to decompose. Usually rigor appears within 2 to 4 hours of death, fully develops in 6 to 12 hours, and is gone after about 36 hours.

INSECT INFESTATION

After the first 24 to 48 hours of death, the processes of rigor, temperature and lividity become less useful in determining a time of death as decomposition progresses. This is where the study of insects becomes most helpful. By understanding the life-cycle of insects attracted to a decomposing body, a specialist may be able to determine a time of death. The blowfly is the most common of these insects, especially where a body has been in the open. Eggs or live maggots may be laid on the body, and then develop as maggots which leave the body and, when a metre or so away, burrow into the ground to pupate. It is important to examine the ground in the vicinity of the body to see if this has occurred. Any investigation of insect infestation requires the advice of a specialist forensic entomologist.

STOMACH CONTENTS

An examination of the gastric contents can sometimes be used to give an estimate of the time interval between eating and death. If the time the deceased last ate is known or can be found out from witnesses, for example, then this estimate of the time interval can be used in combination with other factors found at autopsy to indicate an approximate time of death.

'Normal' stomach emptying times range from less than an hour to 6 hours.[26] There are a number of factors affecting these times, and in a death investigation many of these are imponderables. No precise estimate is therefore ever practicable, and evidence of time of death derived in this way must be treated with great reserve.

There are some obvious factors that need to be taken in to account in making such estimates. They include the size and type of meal — the larger the meal, the longer the emptying time — and the types of food (liquid or solid) and the specific food involved. Others factors are not so obvious and some certainly not easily determined. They include the energy value of the food, the age of the deceased, the 'normal' emptying time of the stomach of the deceased (which usually isn't known or knowable), and their physical, mental and emotional states in the interval between eating and death and at the time of death (also often not known or knowable). Delayed emptying of the stomach is well recognized in shock, trauma and unconsciousness. Fear and anxiety also may cause great delay.[27]

Estimates of time of death can be expected to cover a range of some hours.[28] The degree of imprecision is considered by some specialists to be unacceptable and that as such it is liable to mislead the investigator and the court.[29] The stomach is a poor 'forensic clock'.[30]

PART 2

THE CASES

CHAPTER FIVE

TIME AND TIDE

FRITS VAN BEELEN 1972

Part One describes some aspects of the way in which police officers, lawyers, judges, scientists and pathologists should go about their work and how the criminal justice system should operate. This then gives us an appreciation of how factors such as faulty expert evidence, for example, or the failure of defence counsel to properly conduct the defence, or the failure by the judge to properly instruct the jury, or the failure of the prosecutor and the courts to act on new evidence about the reliability of a witness, could lead to miscarriages of justice.

It might be thought that if any of these things happened they would be picked up during the process of the trials and appeals of the cases. But they may not have been. By looking at a number of cases, this section will show that problems like these could have been going undetected in South Australia for years and miscarriages of justice may well have resulted.

We look first at a number of cases involving pathology evidence. These cases reveal that there were problems with the investigations. They also serve to demonstrate the pivotal role of the forensic pathologist in the delivery of justice. A common factor in these cases is that they involve the work and evidence of Dr Colin Manock, who was in charge of forensic pathology in South Australia for nearly 30 years. He claims to have completed some 9000 autopsies during his career, so it is obviously beyond our capabilities to examine more than a small number of his cases.

The issues involved in these cases have given rise to such widespread concern that they have become the subject of parliamentary questions[1] and television programs.[2] We do not suggest that Dr Manock alone is responsible for what has happened in the cases he was involved in. Because jury deliberations take place in secret, the extent to which his or any other evidence might have influenced an investigation or a trial, and the effect of this on the outcome in the courts, cannot be known. However, we will be suggesting that, from our examination of the cases, there may have been serious deficiencies with the way in which the verdicts and conclusions were arrived at.

We will start by providing some background information about Dr Manock. We will then take a look at some cases, starting with the case of Frits Van Beelen.

Dr Manock

Dr Colin Henry Manock came from England to South Australia in 1968. Documents explaining Dr Manock's background were lodged with the court in South Australia during an action he took against his employer in the 1970s. As a result they have become part of the public record and the following information is taken from them.

In March 1968, Dr Manock applied for the position as the head of forensic pathology in South Australia. His covering letter, addressed from Morley, near Leeds in Yorkshire, stated that he wished to apply for the post of director of forensic pathology in the Institute of Medical and Veterinary Science (IMVS).

He enclosed a list of postgraduate positions he had held and of his experience of medico-legal work. This list showed that he graduated from the Leeds Medical School with the degrees MB, ChB (Bachelor of Medicine, Bachelor of Surgery) in 1962. Following that, he had several six-monthly placements: medical officer to a clinical toxicologist and to a cardiologist at St James Hospital, Leeds; senior house officer to a group of neurosurgeons at Leeds General Infirmary; and senior house officer to a consultant obstetrician at Leeds Maternity Hospital.

In February 1964 he was appointed an assistant lecturer in the Department of Forensic Medicine, Leeds University, and appointed to the permanent staff of the university as a lecturer in October 1966.

Concerning the details of his experience, he stated that he had been in the department for four years and had carried out 1200 coroner's autopsies, 'of which 30 were murder cases for which I was personally responsible'. It also included 150 suicides and 90 accidental deaths. He said that he had also attended the autopsies of a further 30 murder cases.

He noted his special interests as firearms and firearm injuries and stated that he was granted a firearm dealer's certificate in 1966.

He listed the papers he had given to the British Association of Forensic Medicine as 'Peripheral carbon monoxide due to shotgun injury' and 'The use of papain for extracting bullets from bone'.

Dr Manock was appointed Director of Forensic Pathology at the IMVS in December 1968. This was some years before the new Forensic Science Centre was built. He was instrumental in starting the South Australian Branch of The Forensic

Science Society of the United Kingdom. Dr Manock retired from his position of Senior Director of Forensic Pathology at the Forensic Science Centre in 1995, just before he gave evidence at the Keogh trial.

A few years after his appointment, Dr Manock applied to be registered as a Fellow of the Royal College of Pathologists of Australasia (RCPA). His application showed that he had provisional medical registration in England and Wales from July 1962, full registration from July 1963, and British Commonwealth registration from 1970. He was granted a provisional certificate by the South Australian Medical Board from 2 December 1968. He obtained registration in the Northern Territory from February 1970 and a South Australian practising certificate from September 1970.

To gain admission to the college, Dr Manock was given only an oral examination and, as stated in an interview given by Dr David Weedon of the Royal College of Pathologists to Sally Neighbour on the ABC *4 Corners* program, he was exempted from the normal requirements:

SALLY NEIGHBOUR: Dr Manock was admitted to the College of Pathologists in 1971. It gave him the qualification he'd lacked, at least on paper. He was exempted from the normal five years of training and two written exams.
DR DAVID WEEDON: Well, it was the practice in those days for members who held very senior positions in Australia, and who had British qualifications, to be given a viva examination — that is, an oral examination only.
SALLY NEIGHBOUR: But Dr Manock didn't even have British qualifications.
DR DAVID WEEDON: So I believe.
SALLY NEIGHBOUR: So why would he have been given this oral-only examination?

DR DAVID WEEDON: Because of the seniority of the position he held. It would probably have been about 20 minutes, and he would've been asked questions related to forensic pathology.[3]

Dr Manock was admitted to fellowship by the council of the RCPA on 7 September 1971. No date of 'completion of training' is stated on the records, but there is a note to say that 'Dr Manock had completed up to five years'. The effect of granting Dr Manock his FRCPA was to give him an important qualification. It indicated that he was a person of high standing within the profession of pathology. Yet he had undertaken no formal postgraduate training in pathology and had never sat a formal written examination in the subject since his graduation as a doctor.

In the 1970s, an attempt was made by the IMVS to appoint a Senior Director of Forensic Pathology. Dr Manock took action in the courts, arguing that this was tantamount to a constructive dismissal of him as *he* had been appointed as the head of the department.[4] The IMVS responded by saying that his title as Director was more of a courtesy title, and was not meant to convey that he was the department head. Dr Bonnin, the Director of the institute, pointed out during the court proceedings that the IMVS was in an awkward situation; they had a person (Dr Manock) in a specialist's job, but without the necessary specialist qualifications.

Dr Bonnin said: 'We had to make other arrangements for the work, particularly the histopathology which he was unable to do certifying the cause of death because of his lack in histopathology …'[5]

The court upheld Dr Manock's claim, and his position as the head of the department of forensic pathology was confirmed.[6]

Some time later Dr Manock was again back in court. He said that as he could be called out at any time, he was 'on call'

24 hours per day, seven days a week, and hence was entitled to an allowance for this. The matter was settled.[7]

The Van Beelen case

This case is significant because it was the first criminal case in South Australia to rely entirely on scientific circumstantial evidence and, at the time, it was the longest criminal trial in the state's history.[8] The time of death was pivotal, and the case is notable from the pathology point of view because the precise determination Dr Manock made of the time of death was, and still is, controversial.

DEBORAH LEACH MURDERED

On Thursday, 15 July 1971 at about 3.30 pm, 15-year-old Deborah Leach left Taperoo High School in Adelaide with a girlfriend. They walked home together as far as Deborah's home, which was about 300 metres from the school. Deborah went into her house, dropped off her school bag and a cake she had baked at school that day, and changed into a pair of tartan slacks and a brown jumper. At about 4 pm, a witness saw Deborah and her dog running across the paddock opposite her home and down towards the beach. At 4.40 pm, Deborah's mother came home from work and found the cake on the kitchen table. She looked out through the front window and saw the dog playing alone on the seagrass covering the beach. Deborah's mother crossed the road and retrieved the dog. She called out Deborah's name several times but got no reply. By 6 pm she was beginning to worry and rang her husband at work. He came home and, together with a neighbour and Deborah's dog, they went to look for Deborah. It was dark by this time and they had to use torches. The seagrass was piled up all over the beach, in places up to about 2 metres. During the search they found tyre marks and boot prints (of the type

Deborah had been wearing) but there was no sign of the teenager. They went home and called the police several times. By midnight the police had launched a full-scale search.

There was intermittent rain throughout the night. At 4 am a police officer found some of Deborah's belongings lying close together on the edge of a bank of seagrass. They were her right boot, her small transistor radio and a dog leash. At 4.20 am, one of the senior detectives found Deborah's partially clothed body buried in the seaweed about 3 metres from where her belongings were found.

Dr Manock arrived at the scene soon after. He examined the body but did not take the body temperature. He later conducted the autopsy and concluded that Deborah had died by drowning in seawater. There were no signs of bruising to the body. Dr Manock concluded that she had been murdered. He also determined that she had been sexually assaulted after her death (rather than before her death) as there was a small triangular tear in her vagina but no bleeding or bruising associated with it. In his evidence-in-chief, he was asked about the bruising and tearing by the prosecution:

PROSECUTOR: You told the jury that in relation to the laceration that there was, I think I quote you, 'No evidence of bruising'.
DR MANOCK: That is correct.
PROSECUTOR: Was there any evidence of bleeding externally or internally near the site of the laceration.
DR MANOCK: No, there was not.
PROSECUTOR: Is there any significance in the absence of bruising and the absence of bleeding, both externally and internally.
DR MANOCK: The significance is that had the injury been caused during life then bleeding would have been apparent. I therefore come to the conclusion that this was a post-mortem injury.[9]

FRITS VAN BEELEN

Frits Van Beelen was an unemployed carpenter who often went to the beach for a walk or to do some jogging. He had two previous convictions, one for indecent exposure and the other for attempted rape. He did not come forward in response to the police requests, but was traced through his car registration number which had been noticed by other visitors to the beach that day. Two weeks after the discovery of Deborah's body, police interviewed Van Beelen. He said that on the day of Deborah's disappearance he had driven to the beach at about 4 pm and walked along the beach for about half an hour. He could not recall having seen anyone else on the beach at that time. He said he left the beach and drove into the centre of Adelaide to pick up his wife from work at 5 pm. It was estimated that it would have taken him about 30 minutes to get into the centre of town from the beach. Almost three months after Deborah's death, Van Beelen was arrested for her murder and subsequently brought to trial in July 1972.

Much of the evidence against Van Beelen during the trial was scientific. The clothing he was said to have been wearing on the day of Deborah's death had been vacuumed in the police forensic laboratory for possible traces of evidence — microscopic fragments of paint, fibres, hairs or anything else. In all, 27 different areas of expert scientific evidence were presented by the prosecution. All areas were contested by the defence. At the end of a trial which lasted three and a half months, the jury found Van Beelen guilty of murder. He was sentenced to death. His appeal against the conviction was upheld by the Court of Criminal Appeal on several grounds, one of which was that the trial judge had misdirected the jury in the way they were to regard the scientific evidence. The head note in the law report of this case reads as follows:

> In a criminal trial, the judge is required to direct the jury that they cannot convict unless they are satisfied of the guilt of the accused beyond reasonable doubt, and it is usual, *in a case of circumstantial evidence*, for the judge to tell the jury also that *they cannot convict if there is any rational hypothesis or reasonable probability consistent with the innocence of the accused*. [Emphasis added]

This is a point that we will make a number of times. The appeal judges also said:

> ... if we had been members of the jury ... we think we might have been tempted to abandon in despair the task of trying to make sense of the scientific evidence and to concentrate on the other evidence ...[10]

A new trial took place one year and nine months after Deborah's death.

At the second trial the prosecution again relied largely on scientific evidence, but the original 27 categories were now reduced to four. For example, the evidence of Dr Manock and a police expert witness concerning human and dog hairs, which had been the subject of much dispute in the first trial, was not presented at this trial. The defence had been able to show that both Dr Manock and the detective sergeant had mistaken an effect that had been caused in the mounting of the hairs on slides for microscopical examination for 'pigment' and 'fluorescence' and had mistakenly used this as a basis for comparison. The jury themselves picked up that the experts gave the diameter of the hairs as ten times too big. It was further revealed in cross-examination that the police expert, who had been giving this sort of evidence for years, wrongly believed that hair grew from the tip end.

The prosecution, however, presented three types of evidence derived from the application of the Locard transference principle. These were: minute paint particles, details of which were heard only in the *voir dire* and which the judge subsequently ruled were not admissible as evidence as they proved nothing one way or the other; red and black fibres found on the upper part of Deborah's singlet that were said to have come from Van Beelen's red and black jumper; and fragments of shell and sand embedded in Van Beelen's jumper, although this was objected to and subsequently ruled out.

The defence was again critical of the quality of the scientific work and its interpretation.[11] Indeed, during the second trial, Dr Bevan, a professor of chemistry at the School of Physical Sciences at Flinders University, was moved to remark during his evidence that he saw 'no reason why, if the legal processes were going to use science, it should not use proper science'.[12]

The prosecution argued that the red fibres and black fibres found on Deborah's singlet were the same as those from Van Beelen's red and black jumper taken by the police from his home. Initially Van Beelen said he was unsure whether he had been wearing his red and black jumper or his blue one. He then said he remembered that he had been thinking of going for job interviews that day and so he wore his best jumper — his blue one.

The defence argued that the fibres were not uncommon, had not been tested adequately and could even have come from the tartan slacks Deborah had been wearing that day. The most that can be said about fibres of this sort is that they are *similar to* other fibres. The value of fibres as evidence is based on an estimation of how commonly they are found in the community.

THE PATHOLOGY EVIDENCE

Pathology evidence was the fourth category introduced by the prosecution. When Deborah's body was found, twelve hours after she was last seen alive, rigor mortis was present, as was lividity. The skin did not blanch under pressure, showing that the lividity had become fixed. This meant that she had probably been dead for at least six hours. The prosecution claimed that this evidence was consistent with death occurring between 3.30 and 4.30 pm the previous day. However, Dr Derek Pocock, a forensic pathologist who gave evidence for the defence, explained that the evidence about rigor was also consistent with death having occurred up until around 11 pm that night.[13]

Time of death

Throughout the trial, the timing of the death was a crucial factor. Deborah had last been seen alive at 4 pm and Van Beelen had an alibi from just after 4.30 pm. If he was to be found guilty of murder, then it was essential to the prosecution's case to establish that Deborah was dead by 4.30 pm. An accepted way for a pathologist to calculate a time of death is by taking body temperatures, but Dr Manock did not take the body temperature when he arrived at the scene. He said at the trial that in view of the seaweed and cold wind, this was not a reliable indicator in this case. Other pathologists say that this explanation does not excuse or properly explain his failure to record the temperatures.

The most contentious of the evidence was the way Dr Manock fixed the time of Deborah's death as between 3.30 pm and 4.30 pm. He did this by relying on an analysis of Deborah's stomach contents. Dr Manock gave evidence to say that it was 'virtually certain' that Deborah was dead by 4.30 pm, and most probably around 4.15 pm. His calculation was based on the rate at which a stomach is emptied of its contents. According to Deborah's school friends, she had apparently eaten a pie or pasty, some chips and a carton of milk around midday. Dr Manock then 'calculated' how long the stomach would take to process the food and to pass it through the system. He asserted that by examining the contents of the girl's stomach, he could be certain that her death had occurred by 4.30 pm, *and no later*.

As Kevin Borick, who had been Van Beelen's counsel at the trial, later said in an interview with Sally Neighbour for *4 Corners*:

> KEVIN BORICK: He [Dr Manock] was dogmatic about the time of death and we believe he was wrong about that.
> SALLY NEIGHBOUR: The time of death was crucial. The dead girl had last been seen alive heading to the beach at 4 pm. Van Beelen had an alibi from 4:30. To get a conviction, the Crown had to show she'd died within that half-hour.[14]

In a scientific article subsequently published by Dr Derrick Pounder, now Professor of Forensic Pathology at Dundee University, the method used by Dr Manock in the Van Beelen case was reviewed and evaluated. Professor Pounder concluded that the most that could be said about this approach to the timing of death was that it could narrow the possibilities down to 'a range of some hours'. He stated that any suggestion that this method could be exact to 'within a half an hour as given in … the Van Beelen case in Australia would seem to be scientifically unsound'.[15] This is important, because Dr Manock's testimony in this case was said to be both expert and scientific. Dr Manock was not called upon to detail the basis of his expertise in this respect. In 1984, under cross-examination in another case, however, Dr Manock was questioned on Professor

Pounder's statement about the Van Beelen case. 'I did see that comment, yes,' he replied. Defence counsel went on:

> COUNSEL: And would you agree that estimates of time of death on the basis of stomach contents are very unreliable.
> DR MANOCK: I do agree with that.[16]

Unfortunately, this concession by Dr Manock was of no assistance to Van Beelen. There are many important factors in making an estimate of time of death from stomach contents. Dr Manock had no way of knowing Deborah's standard rate of digesting food. He had no test results to see how her rate of digestion of different food types progressed. He had no test results to compare how her rate of digestion varied with differing physical and psychological states. He had no knowledge of how long she was in each of those states. Even if Dr Manock's assertions about Deborah being killed about four hours or so after her last meal were to be accepted, there is no way to be sure that the meal she had at midday was in fact her last meal.

NO BLEEDING

Dr Manock's evidence that the lack of bleeding in the tear in Deborah's vagina meant that the injury occurred after death was one factor used to rule out another person who had actually confessed to the murder, as we will see in a moment. The surprising thing is that the same evidence should also have ruled out Van Beelen. On the facts, Deborah went to the beach around 4 pm, and Van Beelen left the beach around 4.30 pm at the latest. Therefore, if he had been the perpetrator, and if he had killed Deborah and then had sexual intercourse with her body, there could only have been an interval of a few minutes between her death and the intercourse, at the very most. This is insufficient time to prevent bleeding in the manner Dr Manock described. Dr Manock's statement that bleeding does not occur after death is imprecise. Bleeding occurs as a matter of course at autopsies that are conducted expeditiously after a death. Bleeding will occur while the blood remains fluid in the part of the body tissues which are torn, cut or damaged.

The only way bleeding will not occur in such a circumstance is when the interval between death and damage to the tissues is sufficiently extended that there is no longer fluid blood in the vessels. This can be for one of two reasons: either it has drained from those vessels, as it may do with the process of lividity; or, it has become fixed and is no longer fluid. This fixing process takes at least one or two hours, depending on temperature and the position of the body. It doesn't occur either instantaneously or within a few minutes. As a result, Dr Manock's observations about the damage to the tissues and the lack of bleeding, properly interpreted, should have been sufficient to clear Van Beelen of suspicion.

Diatom testing
Dr Manock's diatom testing in this case also requires re-examination. In suspected drownings the tissues can be tested to see if the diatoms in them are similar to those in the water in which the person was found. In a number of cases where drowning has been involved, including this one, Dr Manock has said that he tested only the lung tissue for the presence of diatoms. Testing lung tissue is inadequate to confirm drowning; it is more appropriate to examine the kidneys and bone marrow for the presence of diatoms.[17]

THE RADIO MYSTERY
One of the most intriguing elements of the whole case, and one which was never explained, was the fact that when

Deborah was found her radio was nearby. It appeared to have been left switched 'on' to full volume, and that the batteries had run down. The outside of the radio was damp but the inside was dry, and when the batteries were replaced the radio immediately worked. This was curious because Deborah's body and the radio were found below the high water mark. In fact, shortly after her body was found, the tide was coming in and the body had to be moved to prevent it from being covered with water. The previous tide had come in at about 8 pm the night before. This would have meant that if her body had been there at the time, it, and one assumes the radio, shoe and dog leash, would have been under water during the course of the night. If that was not the case, then Deborah's body (and/or radio) had been placed on the beach after that last high tide — long after Van Beelen had been near the beach that day.

The interesting point about this is that if there is one piece of objective or scientific evidence that is not consistent with a guilty verdict, then the accused must be acquitted. In many cases it is difficult to determine if any piece of objective evidence is actually inconsistent with a guilty verdict. In this case the inconsistencies should have been clear. Because the radio was dry inside, it must have been placed at that location on the beach after the last high tide. If so, it couldn't have been Van Beelen who put it there. Therefore, by implication, it is unlikely that he committed the murder and assault. However, the judges in the appeal said that the evidence about the tides was before the jury, and it was for them to accept or reject it as they thought fit. This seems to suggest that the jury could ignore the irrefutable evidence about the high tide. It seems a little strange to suggest that the jury could arrive at a result that is inconsistent with the known laws of physics.

We take the view that the case, because of its inherent defects, should not have been put to the jury at all. The evidence about the tides, properly explained, or the evidence given by Dr Manock about the absence of bleeding, properly explained, should have established reasonable doubt that Van Beelen caused the damage to the tissue which Dr Manock reported.

CONVICTIONS UPHELD

Although there were two trials and numerous appeals, including an appeal to the Privy Council in London, Van Beelen's conviction for the murder was upheld. He had been sentenced to death, but it was the practice at that time to commute a death sentence to life imprisonment.

However, the case refused to go away. In 1974, the Adelaide *Advertiser* reported that a juror at the second trial claimed that the stress of circumstances and pressure in the jury room influenced the juror's vote. 'It was a moment of weakness which I have lived to regret,' the juror said. After much thought and receiving counselling, the juror felt compelled to 'speak out about it'.[18] The same issue of the paper carried the first of two substantial articles discussing the case. The paper said that they were written 'in the public interest'. The articles elicited a response in the form of a Letter to the Editor from Sir Roderic Chamberlain, a former Crown prosecutor and Supreme Court judge. Sir Roderic wrote that 'the unanimous findings of two separate juries, confirmed by the State Full Court' made it 'difficult to see how the public interest is served by publication of material that can only throw doubt on the justice of the conviction'. He went on to say that the public interest might have been better served by a tribute to the skill of the police homicide and scientific bureau officers and their expert advisers.[19] A number of university scientists, who had been involved with the defence, responded with a Letter to the Editor pointing out that the bulk of the prosecution's scientific evidence was either withdrawn or rejected, and it was this which should be 'a matter of public concern'. They said that the length and cost of the case was largely caused by the necessity to expose and correct the many 'scientific mistakes and misconceptions' which were made and held.[20]

Other suspects

There were two other curious facts about this case. At the time of the murder, police, through the media, had appealed for anyone who had been on the beach that day to come forward. They were particularly interested in talking to a man with a limp that had been seen in the area at the time. He did come forward and he confessed to Deborah's murder. He then retracted that confession. However, the police dismissed his confession because, among other factors, he had at one time been institutionalised for mental problems, and because he said that he had raped Deborah *before* he killed her. Dr Manock had said that Deborah had been raped *after* she had been killed. The defence lawyers were not told of this man's claims. If they had known about this in good time, they could have conducted their own investigations of the matter, and perhaps they would have formed a different conclusion. What was unusual were the remarkably accurate details that this man gave about Deborah's dog, her clothes and the drowning in his statement to the police, which was only three days after her death. These matters had not been covered in such detail in the newspaper reports. He later said that he only knew the details because he had heard some police officers talking about them in the pub. Those officers were never identified, nor was their presence in any pub ever confirmed.

The other interesting matter surfaced in 1988, when a woman who had been living near to the beach at the time of Deborah's death told the authorities that she suspected that her former husband might have killed Deborah.[21] He had apparently been sexually interested in young children for some time, and was known to frequent the toilets in the area of the beach.

The wife thought that it seemed possible that he had the opportunity to commit the crime, and to return to the scene later to move Deborah's body, and she thought that this should be investigated.

It was, however, many years after Van Beelen had been convicted that the woman had come forward and by that time she had been divorced from her husband for some years. The police were no longer sure of his whereabouts, it being thought that he had moved interstate.

The Legal Services Commission sought the advice of Mr Mullighan QC (now a Supreme Court judge). He concluded that, on the basis of the information available to him at the time, there was insufficient evidence to pursue the overturning of the conviction of Van Beelen. It was considered that while the wife may have thought that her husband's behaviour at the time looked suspicious, there may well have been perfectly innocent explanations for it. It also had to be considered that the wife had delayed for so long before bringing the matter to the attention of the authorities.

Mr Mullighan concluded by saying: '… the new evidence is not capable of establishing the innocence of Mr Van Beelen or of removing the certainty of his guilt (as determined by the jury) …'

But people are never required to prove their innocence. The most that they should be required to do is to establish reasonable doubt as to their guilt.

It becomes clear in the course of the report by Mr Mullighan QC that the evidence of Dr Manock was at that time still regarded as an important part of the prosecution case.

Yet as has been shown, Dr Manock failed to take temperatures of Deborah's body when he first arrived at the scene, and his timing of Deborah's death has been described as 'scientifically unsound'.

Conclusion

Throughout the years since his arrest, Van Beelen has continually asserted his innocence. Because he would not show contrition for the offence for which he was convicted, the Parole Board would not release him on parole until he had served over seventeen years. It was at that time quite common for those sentenced to life imprisonment to be released after eight or nine years. Van Beelen was a model prisoner. He continued to be a keen jogger and was from time to time allowed day-release from prison to compete in races. He frequently competed alongside judges and senior lawyers. He now lives in Adelaide and has been gainfully employed since his release from prison. He still says that he didn't do it.

CHAPTER SIX

TIME AND TIME AGAIN

DAVID SZACH 1979
STEFAN NIEWDACH AND
ALAN ELLIS 1992

The timing of death is important in any murder case because it helps to narrow down the range of people who could be regarded as suspects. In the Van Beelen case the estimated timing was so tight that, even though it has been called 'scientifically unsound', it eliminated all but Van Beelen from suspicion. But Van Beelen is not the only case in which serious questions have been raised concerning the evidence given with regard to the timing of a death. One such case is that of David Szach who was convicted of the murder of the Adelaide lawyer Derrance Stevenson.[1] Stevenson's body was found with a gunshot wound to the head, in a freezer at his own home.

Another case in which the evidence on timing of death was important concerned the death of Gerald Warren.[2] In estimating the time of death, the pathologist, Dr Manock, took into consideration factors of blow flies and bird droppings that were not really relevant. In this case there were also problems caused by Dr Manock's failure to identify correctly the weapon used and the manner of death.

Szach charged with murder

David Szach, 19, was in a relationship with the 44-year-old Derrance Stevenson. According to the autopsy report, Stevenson is said to have died at some time between 4 and 5 June 1979. It appears that Szach had driven from Adelaide to Coober Pedy (about 850 kilometres north of Adelaide) on the night it was thought that Stevenson had died. Szach had originally bought a bus ticket for the journey. However, he was reimbursed for the ticket shortly before he left Adelaide, and travelled overnight to Coober Pedy in Stevenson's rather 'flash' car. Police regarded this as suspicious at the time as Stevenson was said to have been possessive about his car.

Szach was questioned by the police in Coober Pedy, and later there was some confusion about the precise timing and content of these interviews. The defence argued at the trial that the police deliberately didn't tell Szach before the interviews that he was regarded as a suspect in the murder in the hope that he might inadvertently reveal something of value to them. It is a breach of police procedures to interview a suspect without properly informing them of their real purpose. It would, for example, be unfair to Szach if he thought that he was being interviewed on a charge of car stealing, while the police were actually trying to obtain information against him on a charge of murder. The police said that the interviews had taken place before they had received phone calls from the police in Adelaide telling them of the murder.

Szach was charged with murder and tried in the Supreme Court in Adelaide, in November and December 1979.

TIMING OF DEATH
Stevenson's body was found in his freezer. The pathologist, Dr Manock, calculated the time of death by utilising a formula which had been developed from experiments where bodies

had been frozen in the prone position (that is, lying flat). When Stevenson's body was found, however, it was bent round in the foetal position with his back uppermost and his arms and feet downwards.

Dr Manock said that he used the formula to calculate the time the body took to cool, adjusting the formula by 40 per cent because Stevenson's body was doubled over rather than prone. In those circumstances, he said, there would be a reduced surface area of the body exposed and it would therefore take longer to cool down. This is correct. The difficulty arises in how much the formula is to be modified. A modification of about 40 per cent can hardly be classified as an 'adjustment'. In his autopsy report, Dr Manock stated:

> A body will cool 85% of the temperature differential within 28 hours. However, where the effective surface area is reduced, the time is lengthened and in the above circumstances it is my opinion that the lengthening of cooling time would be about 40%.

Dr Manock did not provide any scientific basis for such an adjustment. This is an example of a fact being accepted into evidence on the basis of an assertion without any properly established evidence or studies to support it.

The ultimate effect of this evidence was to make Szach a plausible suspect because he was in the vicinity at the calculated time of death. It also meant that another 'person of interest' to the police had an alibi.

PATHOLOGY EVIDENCE REVIEWED

Some years after the trial, Dr Byron Collins, a consultant forensic pathologist, reviewed the pathology evidence. In his report he said:

Dr Manock's formula was initially proposed by Fiddes and Patten with their work being published in the *Journal of Forensic Medicine*, 1958. On the review of the paper, it becomes transparently obvious that it was not applicable to the circumstances of Derrance Stevenson's death.[3]

A basic principle of scientific work is that the procedures are capable of being replicated. This means that they can be spelled out in such a way that another scientist could go through the same procedure and arrive at the same answer. In his report, Dr Collins outlined the reasons for his view that it was not appropriate for Dr Manock to use the formula to calculate time of death in this case. He pointed out that the authors of the research report, which was based on experiments on bodies frozen in the prone position, stressed that their findings were not to be used or applied in circumstances which varied significantly from those of the experiments.

Dr Collins noted in his report that fundamental to the reliability of any formula is the accuracy of its individual factors. He went on to say that none of the variable factors that Dr Manock used in his calculations were matters that could be properly substantiated.

For example, Dr Manock substituted a liver temperature for a rectal temperature. He did not explain why he thought that one could just be substituted for the other.

The running temperature of the freezer was unknown at the time the body was placed in it. In normal mode it would have been $-20°C$, but in superchill mode it would have been $-28°C$, a significant difference.

The core body temperature at the time of death was assumed by Dr Manock to be $37°C$, but he provided no evidence to support this assumption. In normal circumstances, bodies begin to cool down after death and Dr Manock had no way of determining the time between the shooting and when the body was placed in the freezer. Without knowing the room temperature and the length of time between death and refrigeration, Dr Manock would have had little idea of the body temperature at the time it was placed in the freezer.

SZACH CONVICTED
Szach was convicted of murder and sentenced to life imprisonment. He appealed, and this was heard in March and April 1980, but was unsuccessful. In 1991, Michael David QC inquired into the matter on behalf of the Legal Services Commission to determine if it should fund a further appeal. He advised against it.

Throughout his time in prison Szach refused to apply for parole because he claimed that he was in jail because of the shortcomings of the legal system. He claimed throughout that he did not commit the crime and that he would not apply for parole as that would amount to an admission of guilt. Eventually the law in South Australia was changed to enable the Chair of the Parole Board to apply for a non-parole period on behalf of a prisoner. Szach was released in 1993.

Gerald Warren killed
Gerald Warren, an aboriginal youth, was having a drink on a road outside Port Augusta, South Australia, when he threw his empty beer bottle at a passing utility vehicle. Little did he suspect at the time that such a thoughtless act would lead to his death. The two men in the vehicle took offence at his action and determined to make this apparent to him. They bought some beers, came back and enticed Warren into the vehicle to join them for a drink. They drove a short way out of town with him and battered him to death.

His body was found on a dirt track on 28 December 1984. Dr Manock, who happened to be in Port Augusta that day, arrived at the scene at 10.45 pm. He noticed that the injuries Warren had on the back of a hand and his face had fine parallel lines within them. In his autopsy report dated 14 May 1985, Dr Manock said he thought that these injuries had been made by Warren's corduroy trousers pressing against his face and hands. After examining the rest of the injuries, Dr Manock said, 'It is my opinion that the deceased received his injuries as a result of leaving a moving vehicle'. As a result, it was not clear if the death resulted from an accident or from criminal activity.

In 1991 two men, Stefan Niewdach and Alan Ellis, were separately apprehended for various offences and they confessed to killing Warren. They explained that they had beaten Warren with a brass rod with a threaded end. Then they had driven the vehicle backwards and forwards over his body. At their trial, Dr Manock was asked to explain the discrepancy between their story and his own explanations in his autopsy report.

Dr Manock said that if Warren had been beaten with a threaded rod, or if he had had corduroy pressed against his skin, he would be left with similar injuries. He then went on to say that if Warren had fallen out of a car, or if the car had been driven over the top of him, the resulting injuries would also have been similar. The following extracts of the prosecutor's questions to Dr Manock are taken from the trial transcript:

> PROSECUTOR: That damage [to Warren] could possibly have been caused by the body being run over by a motor car, could it?
> DR MANOCK: Yes.
> PROSECUTOR: Or it could have been caused by the body leaving a motor vehicle?
> DR MANOCK: Yes. The forces involved in either scenario are very similar.

In a later exchange, Dr Manock responded to defence counsel in cross-examination as follows:

> COUNSEL: The possible cause that you gave for those marks [on the back of Warren's hand and face] was the fabric of corduroy, wasn't it?
> DR MANOCK: Yes.

Warren happened to be wearing corduroy trousers. Dr Manock said that Warren had tumbled from the vehicle and 'the tumbling was required to bring corduroy in contact with hands, face.' This was how the corduroy could have been 'impressed' against the back of his hand, or indeed his face. Defence counsel continued:

> COUNSEL: I take it that's still, in your view, a possible cause of those marks.
> DR MANOCK: It would certainly produce a patterned mark.
> COUNSEL: So, while you agree with my learned friend that those marks may have been caused, as she asked you to hypothesise, by the thread of a piece of iron, and you agreed that's consistent with that.
> DR MANOCK: Yes.
> COUNSEL: But also consistent, you would still say I think, with the pressure from the corduroy of the pants.
> DR MANOCK: Yes.
> COUNSEL: You'd have no reason to resile from that view.
> DR MANOCK: Correct.

When used to inflict blunt injuries, threaded metal rods leave a characteristic pattern of abrasion on the skin, with or without a central laceration (tearing of the skin).[4] Recognising this characteristic injury may categorise the weapon and lead to its discovery. The suggestion that a blow to the face with the threaded end of a metal rod would leave the same mark as corduroy being impressed against the skin isn't correct. Likewise, the proposition that the 'same forces' are involved if someone 'leaves' a moving vehicle, as having a vehicle driven backwards and forwards over them is also incorrect — the injuries would have been different. Being thrown out would have caused impact injuries and probably a lot of grazing; being run over would have caused crushing injuries.

Evidence of being beaten by a metal rod would strongly suggest that Warren had been seriously assaulted by another. Evidence that his corduroy trousers had been 'impressed against his skin' suggests he could have done that himself. The important point is that the two interpretations open up the possibility of it being either an accident or a crime. The same can be said about the deceased either falling out of the vehicle or having the vehicle driven over the top of him.

It can be seen that the arguments for injuries from corduroy and for leaving a vehicle are not consistent with the rest of the evidence as it is now known. It is important to bear in mind the way in which *circumstantial evidence* like this is to be used. If there is a rational explanation consistent with the accused's innocence (and the evidence is circumstantial) then the court should not convict the accused. This does not mean that the two alternatives can be weighed and the court (or the jury) can decide what is thought to be most likely. So long as the two possibilities exist, then the court should not convict the accused. This was the principle stated by the South Australian Court of Criminal Appeal following the Van Beelen trial, as we saw in the previous chapter.

OTHER PROBLEMS

An examination of the trial transcript in this case reveals a series of unscientific or unsubstantiated statements by Dr Manock.

Explanations about bruising

Dr Manock said that 'there was nothing to indicate there had been repeated blows to the body'. This is difficult to understand. It is now known that the injuries on Warren's hand and face were the result of blows from the metal rod, and that his body had been driven over by a vehicle at least twice, with four wheels going over his body. The injuries from the rod and the vehicle could not have been caused simultaneously.

Explanations about the placing of the body

At the trial Dr Manock said that he took the view that the body had been placed where it was found, rather than tumbled or rolled there. He also said that he had not put that in his report because he had no firm evidence to say the body had been moved. However, there was in fact no evidence for it at all.

Dr Manock said that 'his opinion' that the body had been placed there was based on the observation that the grass around the deceased's leg was still standing and not flattened. He agreed, however, that the leg could have gone over the grass, rather than through it. He thought that if the leg had 'brushed through' the grass it would have flattened it more, because he had observed that the grass was quite brittle. Given, though, that he had just admitted that the leg could have 'gone over' the grass instead, his observations about the grass not being flattened were not significant or relevant and do not constitute evidence for or against anything at all.

Missed information

Dr Manock agreed that in a photograph of the deceased at the scene 'it looked as though' there was a wet area on the body, but he could not say what it was or how it might have got there. His evidence was that the body had been on the track on a particularly hot day and that, based on his time of death, it had been there at least from 'noon to 4 pm'. If indeed there was a 'wet area' on the body, it could have been an important clue, as it does not fit that situation. At the very least he should have examined it, recorded it in his report and taken samples of it for testing.

Blowfly activity
In his autopsy report, Dr Manock said that he timed the death on the fact that the body was not fly-blown. At the trial, in cross-examination by the defence counsel, he said:

> COUNSEL: How is it then that you are able to say it was unlikely that death had occurred after 4.00 p.m. on that day?
> DR MANOCK: The main reason that I came to that conclusion was that the body was not fly blown extensively and I felt blow flies would be active in the early evening. I have since learned on very hot days blowflies are not active at all if temperatures are very high and will not cause fly strikes.

He said he also thought at the time that the activities of scavengers, such as crows, may have discouraged the flies. Blowflies and their activity are an important method of determining the time of a death that has occurred in the open. However, blowfly activity only becomes valuable some 48 hours after death, which was not the situation here. Within the first 48 hours, rigor mortis and lividity are usually more precise indicators.

Dr Manock had also considered the amount of bird droppings in making his estimate. On further questioning he agreed that his observations in this respect were just his 'layman's observations'. However, he was supposed to be giving evidence as an *expert* witness.

Incorrect time of death
In his report, Dr Manock said that Warren's death had occurred between noon and 4 pm on the day he was found. It was

revealed, at the trial, however, that the death had actually occurred around midnight of the previous day. When pressed about which bits of his reasoning still supported his conclusion, Dr Manock said, 'I don't think I was restricting the timing. That I chose to simply put a relationship for the putrefaction change until that was related to the total picture.'

It is not clear what Dr Manock may have meant by that. He seems to be saying that 'noon to 4 pm' was consistent with 'not restricting the timing'. When he was asked why he hadn't 'widened the ambit' he said, 'I didn't put any range of possibility to any great extent'. When Dr Manock had explained that the process of putrefaction would produce gas within the body, he was asked by defence counsel for more details.

> COUNSEL: Was there any gas production within the organs?
> DR MANOCK: Not of any great significance, no.
> COUNSEL: Was there any at all?
> DR MANOCK: No.

It appears that there was no putrefaction change to be related 'to the total picture'. It also appears that the expression 'not of any great significance' was the same to Dr Manock as 'none'.

In his autopsy report, Dr Manock fixed the time of Warren's death with some degree of confidence. Between noon and 4 pm he claimed. Obviously this would be significant if the police were considering making criminal charges. If the death had occurred around midnight of the previous day, as was subsequently found, then the perpetrators could be somewhere else between noon and 4 pm the following day. They would then have a 'cast-iron' alibi in connection with the alleged murder of Warren. It would not be hard to imagine that if anyone else had chanced to be around at the scene between noon and 4 pm that day, then they might have ended up being accused of the murder.

CHAPTER SEVEN

ARSENIC AND OLD CASES

EMILY PERRY 1981

This case is an interesting example of the problems caused by speculation and inferences. There were no problems with the autopsy — there wasn't one because there was no deceased. The person, who according to the prosecution was supposed to be the victim, was still alive, but was never examined by a forensic pathologist.

Attempted murder of Ken Perry

Mrs Emily Perry was charged with two counts of attempting to murder Ken Perry, her third husband. The prosecution alleged that between July and November 1978, and again between February and October 1979, she administered poison to him with the intention of killing him. Mrs Perry was convicted on both counts and sentenced to 15 years' imprisonment with hard labour. There was no evidence directly implicating her, and no suggestion that she had poisoned her husband unintentionally. So as to establish a 'course of conduct', the prosecution relied on inferences that she had also been responsible for the deaths of three other people with whom she had had a close relationship.

Her appeal to the Court of Criminal Appeal in South Australia was dismissed. She then appealed to the High Court on the basis that the judge had wrongly admitted evidence which, according to the prosecution, showed that her second husband, her brother and a de facto partner had died of poisoning.

The High Court accepted that at various times Mr Perry had become ill from poisoning by lead and arsenic, probably in the form of lead arsenate. It was clear that Mrs Perry had the opportunity to administer the poison to him. She also stood to benefit financially from his death under various insurance policies. The defence claimed that Mr Perry had accidentally ingested the poison and that Mrs Perry had no involvement in that. Mr Perry liked to renovate old pianolas and organs and these often had rat or insect poison in them. The defence claimed that the poison contained arsenic and the instruments also contained dust from crumbling lead pipes. The pathologist on the case, Dr Manock, did not examine Mr Perry's workshop.

As part of their case, the prosecution alleged that in an 18-year period Mrs Perry knew three people who were said to have died in suspicious circumstances. She was never charged in relation to these deaths at the time when they occurred. Nevertheless, with the benefit of hindsight, the prosecution included those three deaths as part of the narrative of her wrong-doing, and evidence in relation to them was given at her trial although they were not part of the charges before the court. As it turned out, the High Court was critical of the inclusion of this other evidence.[1] The appeal was successful and a new trial was ordered. The prosecution then conceded that there was no adequate basis upon which they could proceed to trial again. The three deaths that were raised in Mrs Perry's trial were as follows.[2]

ALBERT HAAG

Albert Otto Haag, Mrs Perry's second husband, was a police officer. It was said at her trial that Haag had died on 13 March 1961 of acute arsenical poisoning. He had been ill in December 1960 and again in January 1961. Mrs Perry was said to have stood to benefit from insurance policies on his life. The defence said that he might have eaten some corn that had been sprayed with weed killer which may have contained arsenic. Otherwise, he might have committed suicide. The prosecution said that Mrs Perry had some knowledge of poisons, that she had bought the weed killer which Haag had used for spraying, and that she had the opportunity to administer it to him. There was some evidence of domestic problems, and that Mrs Perry had made false statements about her knowledge of the insurance policies and the state of her relationship. An inquest had been held but no charges had been laid against her.

FRANCIS MONTGOMERIE

Francis William Montgomerie was Mrs Perry's brother. He died on 9 April 1962, about one year after Albert Haag. It was said at her trial that he too had died from acute arsenical poisoning. He had been an alcoholic and given to moodiness and depression, and he had been admitted to a psychiatric hospital on at least two occasions. He had been living with a woman who had left him just two days before he died, after he had attempted to strangle her. The day after the woman left, Mrs Perry took her mother to Montgomerie's house so that she might look after him. Mrs Perry said that he was incoherent, as he usually was after drinking heavily. She left her mother there and picked her up again at the end of the day. The next day, 9 April, Mrs Perry telephoned Montgomerie and, receiving no response, she went to his house where she found him dead. It appears that the lining of his stomach was badly burned from ant poison that he had apparently swallowed. Mrs Perry might well have been the last person to see him alive, and the first to find him dead.

Some bottles were found on a bedside table, including a bottle containing a small quantity of wine and some arsenic. The autopsy showed the presence of arsenic in the body. There was evidence that one of Mrs Perry's sisters had bought some weed killer a few days before, but the evidence did not establish what type it was. However, it seems that it had been placed by Mrs Perry on a shelf at her mother's house. It was said that this showed that she had access to the poison. The defence argued that the facts pointed to suicide. The prosecution argued that if it had been suicide, then one would have expected to find the container which had had the arsenic in it before it was put into the wine bottle. None was found. However, there was evidence that some old bottles at Montgomerie's house had been cleared up and thrown out by Mrs Perry and her sister on the morning of his death. It was also said that she gave her name as Emily Hulse, Hulse being the name of her first husband. Many of the facts that the prosecution put forward were contested. Montgomerie had no insurance policies and Mrs Perry did not stand to gain from his death. The prosecution argued that the motive was to rid the family of a tiresome burden.

JIM DUNCAN

Mrs Perry had a de facto relationship with John Alfred Jameson, also known as Jim Duncan, who died on 21 March 1970 from an overdose of barbiturates. Duncan began to live with Mrs Perry from the end of 1967. She had arranged insurance policies on his life during 1968 and she received payment under them after his death. He had swallowed about twenty barbiturate tablets. It was unlikely that she could have forced him to take them. The prosecution suggested that she may have persuaded him to take them, but there was no evidence of this. Medical evidence showed that Duncan was in poor health long before being acquainted with her.

Duncan was also a heavy drinker and it was possible that he had committed suicide. However, the prosecution put forward evidence that Duncan had suffered from arsenical poisoning over a considerable period before his death. He had had operations for haemorrhoids in 1944 and 1957. By the beginning of 1968 he was seeking medical treatment for anal trouble and had another operation for haemorrhoids during that year. Around the end of 1968, he was complaining of some loss of bowel control and pains in his lower abdomen. By the end of 1969 and in 1970 he was complaining of diarrhoea, incontinence, vomiting, pain and other symptoms, including enlarged breasts. None of the many doctors who examined him diagnosed heavy metal poisoning, and no test was made before his death or at the autopsy for the presence of arsenic. Dr Manock had performed the autopsy. He said at Mrs Perry's trial that the symptoms described to him were consistent with, but not specific for, lead arsenate. However, he said that he had seen no signs of heavy metal poisoning when he conducted the autopsy of Duncan.

Another doctor who had been involved in the case thought that such a diagnosis was unlikely, with some signs that were not consistent with heavy metal poisoning. The prosecution accepted that if Duncan's case was viewed in isolation it would be insufficient to find that he died of heavy metal poisoning.

The case against Mrs Perry
In summary, the case against Mrs Perry involved the allegation that she had attempted to murder her husband, Ken Perry, with arsenic. The associated allegations, which were introduced to

show a course of conduct, were to the effect that she had murdered two previous partners and her brother in a similar manner.

A doctor who had been treating Mr Perry at the hospital sent the case notes to Dr Manock seeking his opinion. Dr Manock said that the symptoms were consistent with poisoning, and suggested that investigations should be made into the possibility of malicious administration. In his letter to the doctor, Dr Manock said that 'the information contained in the case notes seems to have excluded the common accidental sources'. He reached his conclusions even though he had not examined Mr Perry, nor had he been to his place of work. Mr Perry has stated that the first time he saw Dr Manock was when Dr Manock was in court giving evidence. He said that Dr Manock had formed his opinions from reading the other doctors' reports in the various cases, and had made no attempt to examine him or conduct any tests.[3]

The High Court appeal

The appeal to the High Court took place in 1982.[4] The prosecution conceded that if each of the alleged poisonings was considered in isolation, the evidence would not justify a finding that Mrs Perry had poisoned any one of them. The prosecution said that it was the cumulative effect of the evidence relating to all four of them which justified the verdict of guilty. That is, the prosecution was claiming that the only rational explanation for the deaths of Haag and Montgomerie, the sickness of Duncan and the poisoning of Ken Perry was that Mrs Perry had deliberately poisoned all of them with arsenic.

Justice Lionel Murphy (in referring generally to 'the modern forensic scientist') said that the prosecution's evidence fell far short of the proper standard. He said that if the expert assistance available to the prosecution in this case was typical, then the interests of justice demanded an improvement in both the investigation and the interpretation of data — and their presentation to the court by witnesses who are *substantially* and not merely *nominally* experts in any subject which calls for expertise.

Justice Aickin, who was on the court, died before the judgment was delivered. All four remaining judges agreed that the verdict could not stand. Justice Murphy was the most critical of the four judges who delivered the judgments. Chief Justice Gibbs said that his principal reason for overturning the verdict was that the evidence in relation to Duncan and Montgomerie was inadmissible. Justice Brennan pointed out that in relation to Duncan 'a pathological test gave a result which may have been inconsistent with arsenical poisoning'.

In referring more directly to Dr Manock's evidence, Justice Murphy said that Mr Perry had had a history of motor bike accidents, including severe injury to his facial structure and nasal passages which led to symptoms such as rhinitis (running nose). He said that the prosecution's expert witness had attributed this condition to arsenical or lead poisoning by Mrs Perry. The only problem with this theory was that the condition had existed years before Mr Perry had met her. The condition had, in fact, been the subject of a published medical article on facial reconstruction.[5]

Justice Murphy then went on to say as part of his general criticism of the case:

> The evidence, particularly in relation to Duncan, but also of the other alleged poisonings including that of Mr Perry, revealed an appalling departure from acceptable standards of forensic science

in the investigation of this case and in the evidence presented on behalf of the prosecution.[6]

He said that in his opinion, 'The evidence was not fit to be taken into consideration'. He pointed out that, in his summing up, the trial judge had said that no one had even thought of lead or arsenic as even a possibility until the case against Mrs Perry began.

The cases of Haag, Montgomerie and Duncan had been introduced by the prosecution as evidence of 'similar facts'. The Chief Justice of the High Court (Gibbs, CJ) said that in the way in which the prosecution case was presented, it was necessary to *assume* Mrs Perry guilty of the offences she was charged with in order to render admissible the evidence regarding the death of Duncan. He said that such a line of reasoning was obviously objectionable.[7]

The prosecution had raised the issue of the 'Brides in the Bath' case (*R v. Smith*). This was a nineteenth-century English case where a Mr Smith had sequentially married a number of young women, each of whom he drowned in a bath. In referring to this part of the prosecution case, Justice Murphy said that the case against Mrs Perry was not 'in the same universe of discourse' as *R v. Smith* or other similar-fact cases. The judge went on to explain that because the evidence was circumstantial, it was admissible only if there was no rational explanation of the victim's sickness consistent with the accused's innocence.[8] This is a point which prosecutors and judges appear to have ignored in some of the cases detailed in this book, and which we have already pointed out in the judgment in the Van Beelen case.

Fortunately, in Mrs Perry's case, there was additional forensic evidence. As Justice Murphy remarked, there was important evidence in the form of a pathological test as well as that of an expert pathologist, which overwhelmingly discredited the notion of arsenical poisoning in the case of Duncan. But, Justice Murphy went on to ask, what would have happened here if the evidence of the pathological test had not been available?[9]

Justice Wilson referred to the fact that Dr Manock had conducted the autopsy of Duncan and did not detect any sign of arsenical poisoning at that time. Cremation of the body meant that there couldn't be any further examination.[10] This underscores concerns about using forensic evidence in trials where the body has been prematurely cremated, thus precluding the defence from properly examining the prosecution evidence.

Justice Murphy said that one of the greatest dangers of cases like the Perry case was that the presumption of innocence tends to be brushed aside. In the criminal justice system every person is taken to be innocent unless the contrary is legally proved. No one should be found guilty on appearances, suspicions, conjecture or anything but evidence establishing guilt beyond reasonable doubt. Moreover, the judge said that in Mrs Perry's case there was a great temptation in weighing the evidence, and more particularly in deciding admissibility, to ignore the presumption of innocence and to replace it with a presumption of guilt.[11]

Justice Brennan said that if one attempted to prove a certain fact by a chain of reasoning which assumes the truth of that fact, then that would of course be a fallacy 'repugnant alike to logic and to the practical processes of criminal courts'.[12]

Justice Wilson also pointed out that the evidence of Dr Manock was equivocal and, therefore, that fact alone should disallow its admissibility because it was a circumstantial case.

He said that when all the other evidence is taken into account, the conclusion that Duncan suffered from arsenical poisoning was unsupported by cogent evidence. There could have been other causes for the symptoms displayed. Without there being persuasive evidence of the presence of arsenic, he said, the evidence possessed a speculative character and it should not have been admitted.[13]

IN SUMMARY

One of the judges said that the details of all three previous cases should have been excluded. Another judge said that two of them should have been excluded, and two judges said that one of them should have been excluded. However, they were all agreed that the conviction could not stand.

CHAPTER EIGHT

NO CLOTHES, NO FILES, NO SUSPICIONS

JOHN HIGHFOLD 1983
KINGSLEY DIXON 1987

The Highfold and Dixon cases are similar — both cases involved the death of a prisoner and in each case their clothing went missing and could not be examined. Both cases were the subject of a coroner's inquest and subsequently were among the first cases dealt with by the Royal Commission into Aboriginal Deaths in Custody held between 1987 and 1989.

John Highfold

John Highfold, 30, was an Aboriginal man who was found dead in his cell at Adelaide Gaol on 4 January 1983.[1] He was known to be epileptic and was being treated for it by medication. The pathologist, Dr Manock, commenced the autopsy within two and a half hours of the death and determined that the cause of death was massive oedema in the lungs as a result of 'status epilepticus'. An inquest was held just four days later and the Coroner, Mr Ahern, found that Highfold died from 'natural causes'.

At the hearing of the Royal Commission into Aboriginal Deaths in Custody, the Senior Director of Neurology at Flinders Medical Centre in Adelaide, who was a specialist on epilepsy, said that there was no test which could establish epilepsy as a cause of death. He said it was 'circumstantial' to conclude that Highfold had died from a seizure. He said it was quite possible that Highfold had not died from epilepsy as found by the Coroner — he had never seen anyone die from a single epileptic seizure. He said that all the major organs should have been examined and the blood should have been tested for drugs, especially Dilantin, which was being used to treat Highfold's epilepsy.[2] Dr Manock, he said, did not do that. Another doctor said that Highfold's prison medical file 'appeared to have been lost'. There was no record of it being passed to the Coroner and it was therefore doubtful if it was seen by the pathologist.[3] His clothing had also 'gone missing' and therefore it couldn't be examined.

Dr Manock told the Royal Commission that cost had been a factor in deciding not to undertake the blood tests. He said that at the time of the autopsy full toxicological testing would have cost about $2000. When asked if testing would have revealed any poisoning, Dr Manock said that he didn't do the test as Highfold didn't have access to poison. Counsel assisting the Commission told Dr Manock that this was an assumption. Testing could, however, have ruled out the possibility that Highfold had taken any drugs or that they could have been administered to him by others.

Dr Manock said that because Highfold's stomach was empty, a drug overdose was unlikely. However, there are many mechanisms by which drugs can get into someone's system. Absorption through the stomach is only one of them. Dr Manock was asked why he had not tested the level of Dilantin in the blood as the level found might help to determine if he was being properly looked after. Dr Manock said that the presence of Dilantin would not necessarily prevent a seizure, although the risk of death would have been greater without it. He said that cost was a factor here as well — $18.40 in 1983.[4]

Counsel assisting the Commission said that by regarding Highfold's death as routine, Dr Manock's approach had been 'inappropriate' as part of vital investigations into a death in custody. Counsel asked Dr Manock if he began the autopsy assuming the conclusion was to be death from epilepsy. Dr Manock said he would start every autopsy 'with an open mind'. In his report, Dr Byron Collins, a consultant pathologist retained by the lawyers for Highfold's family to evaluate Dr Manock's work, criticised the lack of thoroughness of the autopsy, saying that the only major organ that had been checked microscopically was the brain. Dr Manock claimed in court, however, that he had microscopically examined the heart and lungs as well. He produced microscope slides from his pocket to show that he had done this, even though heart and lung histology was not noted in his report.[5] Dr Collins told the Commissioner that a single section of the heart was insufficient to exclude heart disease as a cause of death.[6]

Dr Collins said that the autopsy report did not canvass all possibilities. There was no toxicological analysis of the blood, which should have been examined for both alcohol and drugs.

Counsel assisting the Commission asked Dr Manock that, where a prisoner is found in a cell with no apparent cause of death, would he not agree that a heavy responsibility is placed on the pathologist to examine and exclude all possibilities? Dr Manock replied, 'No I would not'.

He asked if it would be a failure by a pathologist not to gain access to the full medical records of a prisoner who had died in custody. Dr Manock said 'Yes'.[7]

Assisting counsel said the Coroner must be criticised for

not ensuring 'more rigorous scrutiny' of Highfold's death. No photographs were taken of Highfold's cell, his clothing was not retained and a torn shirt collar attracted no suspicion. This was not examined, nor was a damp patch that was noted to be on his pillow. The police investigations had been 'quite inadequate', the assisting counsel said. Counsel told the Commissioner that it was 'unfortunate' that the Coroner's inquiry had relied on written statements only.[8]

The lawyer for Highfold's family said that the deceased had been buried in a pauper's grave because the family had not been notified. A police officer agreed that his running sheets showed that no attempt had been made to contact Highfold's South Australian relatives. He agreed that, as the first police officer on the scene, he had a responsibility to investigate the death. He said that he did not, however, seize Highfold's clothing for examination. On the day Highfold died he had only interviewed one person, another inmate. He did not seek to examine a stain on the pillow or the collar torn from his shirt, and did not receive, or seek to obtain, a copy of the autopsy report. 'I never saw the body at all,' he said. 'To me it seemed to be a simple death in custody. I didn't see anything at all at the time to indicate that it was a death of a suspicious nature.'[9]

THE ROYAL COMMISSIONER'S FINDING

When the Royal Commissioner released his findings he was critical of both Dr Manock and the Coroner, Mr Ahern. He said that the Coroner's investigations had not been thorough and that Highfold's family had not been made aware of their right to be present at the inquiry.

He said that Dr Manock had regarded the autopsy as 'routine' once it was concluded that the death was not suspicious. He had 'relied perhaps too far on assumptions that had not been satisfactorily proven' and had not made all relevant investigations. The administration of poisons or drugs could not be excluded as a cause of death because no toxicological analyses were performed. He said that the more likely cause was heart failure due to a sudden change of heart rhythm (arrhythmia) which could have resulted from a single epileptic fit. He said that it was probable that Dr Manock's opinion as to the cause of death (status epilepticus) was incorrect.[10]

Kingsley Dixon

Kingsley Dixon was a 19-year-old Aboriginal man who was said to have been found dead in his cell in Adelaide Gaol on 9 July 1987.[11] Dr Manock performed an autopsy the next day and concluded that Dixon's death had resulted from asphyxiation due to hanging.

Dixon had a slight bruise on his head. Dr Manock said that this was consistent with his having struck his head against the cell wall while hanging. He also said that there was no injury which could not be explained by the 'mechanism of hanging'.

The Royal Commission into Aboriginal Deaths in Custody was told that Dixon's clothes had 'disappeared' after being removed from his body — just as Highfold's clothes had gone missing in 1983.[12]

Concerning the autopsy, the Commissioner noted in his report:

> Comprehensive colour photographs were taken during the autopsy procedures which enable me to accept Dr Manock's findings — particularly as to bruising or lack of bruising.[13]

This contrasts with the situation in the Keogh case discussed in Chapters 11 and 12.

The Commissioner also remarked that an issue had arisen over a request by Dixon's family to delay the initial autopsy until an independent pathologist could be present — a request that had been denied. He concluded:

> Whilst no doubt the presence of an independently appointed pathologist may be desired and may be of comfort to relatives, the critical importance of an early autopsy cannot be over-emphasised.[14]

This is a most interesting remark. It downplays the value of the presence of a second pathologist, in contrast to the principle of independent checking of observations promoted by Judge Shannon in the Splatt Royal Commission some four years earlier. Such independent corroboration would have been of assistance in the autopsies in the 'Baby Deaths' case (discussed in Chapter 10) and in the Keogh case, for example. The emphasis on the importance of an early autopsy is worth noting in the context of the Akritidis case, the Marshall case and even the Keogh case, all of which we are about to discuss.

CHAPTER NINE

'THERE BEING NOTHING SUSPICIOUS ...'

TERRY AKRITIDIS 1990
PETER MARSHALL 1992

The Akritidis and Marshall cases are discussed together as they are examples of the problems that arise when a death is considered 'not suspicious' and so the scene is not treated within the guidelines and the autopsy is not performed until the following day. In the case of Marshall, it meant that the examination of the scene was compromised because the cause of death given to the police by the pathologist attending at the scene, Dr Manock, was wrong. In the case of Akritidis, the police did not properly examine the scene or call a pathologist to it. It turned into a classic case of 'tunnel vision' created by assumptions.

Terry Akritidis
Elefterios (Terry) Akritidis was a 'troubled' person, and had been in psychiatric care spasmodically.[1] On occasions he could be verbally and physically violent. Even his parents had taken out a restraining order against him. More recently, he had turned up at the police social club and thrown a glass into the

assembled throng. He was convicted of assault and sentenced to a short period of imprisonment.

He had been out of prison for a short while, and was staying at a hostel for recently released prisoners on the coast just outside Adelaide. He was quiet and withdrawn. He spent some days working with staff and inmates from the hostel on the refurbishing of a local hall. The staff thought well of him. 'You could tell he came from a good home,' the manager said.

HIS DEATH

Akritidis's body was found late on the evening of 3 August 1987 in a fairly remote location near Yankalilla, about 65 kilometres south of Adelaide. The local milkman later said that he had seen him behaving oddly on the road in the early morning of the day on which Akritidis died. At times it appeared that he was marching along with eyes straight ahead. Some suggested that this had to do with his interest in joining the Greek army. The milkman said that Akritidis was walking along the line in the centre of the road and on occasions moved in front of his truck, making it difficult for him to get by. The milkman went back to the local shop to phone the police who came along and, as one of them said in his statement, 'conned' Akritidis into going back to the station with them.

According to the police account, Akritidis was with them from 5 am and left the station at around 7.30 am that day. The police had spoken with his parents on the phone. They could see no basis on which to arrest or detain him and said they were unaware of his previous mental problems. They had offered him money and had offered to cook breakfast for him, both of which he refused. He did however take a couple of slices of bread with him and wandered off down the road in the direction of Adelaide.

Later that day, the police said that some defect had been reported in the police radio equipment which was associated with the communications tower on a hill (appropriately named Mount Terrible) just outside Yankalilla. Police technicians were despatched and at about 6 pm they reported finding the body of a young man on the ground near to the tower. The technicians called their police colleagues to the scene. By the time they arrived it was getting dark, wet and quite cold. The tower was at a remote location at the top of the hill that could only be reached in a four-wheel-drive vehicle, and then only with some considerable difficulty. The police officers noticed that there was a hole in the roof of the hut beside which Akritidis was lying and they presumed that he had jumped off the tower, hit the roof and then landed on the ground. It was determined that there were no suspicious circumstances and Akritidis's body was put into the back of the police vehicle. A few stones were used to mark where his body lay, and his body was taken to the mortuary in Adelaide. Because the death was deemed non-suspicious it was not examined there until the next day.

The police officers said that they did not collect any forensic evidence that evening because nothing was going to be done that night to 'further contaminate the scene'. However, they did acknowledge that it was quite windy and raining slightly at the time. Relevant evidence, especially blood or other materials or stains, could either have been blown or washed away during the night.

There are no photographs of the scene that night. The police reported that they were unable to take any photographs because, even though a police photographer had attended the scene, he did not have some part of his equipment and was unable to take a picture with a flashlight.

THE INQUEST

It was not until 1990, some three years later, as a result of persistent lobbying by Akritidis's father, that a coroner's inquest was arranged. It was only at this time that the witness statements were taken and the autopsy report became available. The inquest was undertaken by a senior magistrate in Adelaide, as Deputy State Coroner.

Witnesses' observations

One farmer said that a person he presumed to be Akritidis had come into his shed as he was getting hay and asked if he could go and look at some rocks at the quarry. This farmer did have a quarry on his land, but we have no way of knowing how Akritidis knew about it. The farmer said that Akritidis climbed through the electrified fence without so much as flinching, even though the fence would give 'a fair sort of a kick'. He then walked off in the direction of the quarry.

Another man said that he saw a person he presumed to be Akritidis coming out of a field and through a fence onto the road. He only got a quick glance at him as he drove by, but thought that it must have been him as they didn't often get people just wandering about the countryside without there being a car or other people nearby. It appeared that if the witnesses' observations were correct, Akritidis had walked about 70 kilometres in the twenty-four hours prior to his death. An 'extraordinary feat' for a person in his condition, said the psychiatrist in giving evidence. Bear in mind, though, the earlier discussion about the unreliability of eye-witness evidence, and the fact that these events were being recalled some three years later.

Pathology evidence

Dr Manock gave evidence at the inquest in place of another pathologist from the Forensic Science Centre who had conducted the autopsy on Akritidis but who was no longer working in South Australia.[2] Her report showed that he had sustained significant internal injuries, the main one being a ruptured aorta, the main blood vessel leading from the heart. He also had significant fractures to both arms and to his ribs. His sternum was lacerated and he had some minor damage to the lungs. The report concluded that Akritidis had died of 'multiple injuries' and commented that the injuries were 'consistent with a fall from a very considerable height'.

It was thought that Akritidis committed suicide: it seemed that he had climbed through the barbed wire and up through the security hatch at the bottom of the tower which had been inadvertently left unlocked. Even though it was a police communications tower, nobody was able to determine who had last accessed it and left the hatch unlocked. It was suggested that Akritidis had jumped off the tower, landed on the concrete roof of the building adjacent to the tower, and then bounced off that onto the ground.

It was said at the inquest that Akritidis's body struck the concrete roof of the building with such force that it broke through the concrete, which was 5 cm thick, and caused some of it to fall into the building. The concrete was reinforced with 4 mm thick steel rods which ran through the concrete in a grid pattern 75 mm apart. It was said that the rods were bent inwards with the force of the blow.

Although Akritidis was said to have been falling 'partially inverted', there was little damage to his head and, as Dr Manock stated in his evidence, there were no 'significant' external injuries. There were no signs of bleeding when his body was found. The fact that Akritidis's body was lying there on the ground, and there was a hole in the roof of the hut, was enough for people to conclude that Akritidis had damaged the roof when falling onto it 'from a considerable height'.

When bodies and concrete collide, the normal expectation is that the body will come off worst. It is unfortunate that no one thought to seek an opinion from someone who would know about these things, such as an engineer. Dr Manock couldn't be thought to be an expert in this area. At least he produced no evidence at the hearing to that effect.

Police procedures

The police forensic procedures state that where there is a sudden or unexplained death, the scene must be treated as a crime scene and cordoned off until after the scene has been properly examined. That was not done. Crime scene examiners would have examined the ground leading to and from the tower to determine if there were any footprints or any tyre marks in the vicinity. The ground was wet at the time, and it would have been relatively simple to determine if Akritidis's footprints were there — and if they were, whether they were the only set in the vicinity of the tower that day. If he had died elsewhere, for example, and his body placed at the scene, then there could have been other prints and perhaps vehicle tyre marks as well.

Akritidis's body was fully, although quite lightly, clothed when found. He had been wearing what some said was a flannel shirt, and others described as a western style shirt, with denim jeans. Without removing his clothing the police could not determine the full extent of the injuries. The police who first attended at the scene were (on their own admission) inexperienced in crime scene examinations. They would not have been able to gauge the likelihood of a body 'bouncing' off the roof and onto the ground.

There was no forensic examination of the roof to determine whether there were traces of blood, tissue or clothing to indicate if Akritidis had in fact caused that damage. One police officer said that he had examined Akritidis's body and, on lifting his shirt, he had noticed some grazing to his back which had a white powdery material on it similar to the concrete of the roof. It appears that no samples were taken of this powder. If it was in fact concrete powder from the roof, then it is difficult to explain how that material was on Akritidis's back rather than the outside of his shirt. Unfortunately, Akritidis's clothes were destroyed within a few days of the autopsy.

The tower was not examined by crime scene examiners to determine whether Akritidis's footprints were on the steps of the ladder going up the inside of the tower, or on the cross bars of the frame of the tower itself. If he had climbed the tower, his muddy footprints would most likely have been found on the steps, and his fingerprints on the uprights. No evidence was produced to this effect. The ladder steps up the tower were thin metal rungs. Having climbed some 100 of them there would be little mud left on Akritidis's shoes, especially on the soles of his shoes, which were smooth. Yet the soles were still 'liberally coated with mud' at the time of the autopsy, according to the report.

An examination of that mud would have indicated whether it had come from the area in the vicinity of the tower or from elsewhere. That might indicate where Akritidis had died. No such evidence was given at the coronial hearing.

Neither the Deputy Coroner, nor the lawyer representing Akritidis's family, asked why these and other investigations had not been carried out. No one asked why crime scene examiners had not been called to the scene.

EXPLANATIONS TO THE INQUEST
Dr Manock reviewed the autopsy notes and then provided explanations to the inquest for most of what they contained. An expert witness is required to be well read in their area of

expertise. Dr Manock was asked if he had done some reading about the severity of injuries sustained following falls from particular heights. Dr Manock said that he had. The Deputy Coroner followed this up by asking him, 'Is there a body of material that's directed at that topic of endeavour?' He replied, 'I've been going back through some of my old post-mortem reports where people have jumped from car parks and the like …'

An expert witness would normally refer to textbooks and to peer-reviewed papers published in the medical and scientific literature.[3] But the Deputy Coroner did not press the topic.

Counsel for Akritidis's family asked Dr Manock if it was normal for there to be no external injuries on the surface of the body when it was said that it had broken through such thick reinforced concrete.

Dr Manock said, 'I wish I knew what the height was and I could estimate the speed. Are we talking about 140 feet [about 40 metres] or 200 feet [about 60 metres] or 400 feet [about 120 metres]?' The Deputy Coroner then pointed out that the height of the tower was 47 metres or 150 feet, therefore the maximum possible fall could be no more than that.

Dr Manock said that in that case, the velocity at impact would be approximately '100 feet per second' (about 30 metres per second, which is about 100 kilometres per hour), about the same as being in a moderate speed head-on car crash, he explained — except that Akritidis would not have the protection of a vehicle around him. He went on to say that there were no significant external injuries and he did not find that unusual. He said the breadth of the shoulders would have taken the major impact.

The Deputy Coroner asked Dr Manock if an impact with a hard surface would leave some abrasions or cuts of the type and nature seen on Akritidis's body. Dr Manock replied that clothing coming between the skin and the surface that the body strikes would affect the production of abrasions, and that there may be only minor marks if the clothing is relatively thick.

Yet it was an accepted part of the evidence in this case that Akritidis was wearing just a light shirt and jeans at the time of his death. His jumper was neatly folded and left on a fence that led into the field where the tower was.

Dr Manock told the Deputy Coroner that, from his reading of his old autopsy reports, Akritidis's injuries were precisely the sort of injury pattern that one would see, particularly if the person lands on the shoulders or the centre of the back. He said that the fracture of the spine at the level of the T3 and T4 vertebrae (the vertebrae near the top of the back, a little below the neck) is a classic injury of impact of the shoulders while the body is partially inverted after a fall from some considerable height. It is hard to think, though, that the shoulders could strike the concrete pad with such force without the head striking it at the same time. Yet there were no fractures to the skull.

The pathologist who conducted the autopsy had noted that there was only 'scattered bruising' of the scalp. She said that there were no fractures of the vault (the main part of the skull) or the base of the skull. The meninges (the membrane surrounding the brain) and the brain were also normal. The aorta, however, 'showed a traumatic rupture at its isthmus'. This type of injury is seen in sudden stopping, such as in car accidents where the chest is compressed against the steering wheel and the heart is forced downwards. If Akritidis were falling head down as is suggested, one would have thought that his heart would have been forced effectively upwards within his body.

Dr Manock was asked by the Deputy Coroner, 'Was the rupture of the aorta the immediate cause of death?' Dr Manock said that it was. He then went on to say that it means that the blood pressure in peripheral tissues also drops very rapidly, so there is unlikely to be external bleeding as there is no effective blood pressure to cause such bleeding. However, bleeding will occur at autopsy when the heart has stopped beating, so this comment about blood pressure does not adequately explain the lack of bleeding. If any collision were to cause damage to the tissues sufficient to cut across any of the blood vessels, then there would be bleeding — torn aorta or no torn aorta — provided that there is still fluid blood within the vessels.

As well as no photographs being taken at the scene, no photographs were taken of the body at the autopsy. Dr Manock said that in 1987 it probably wouldn't have been usual to take photographs at an autopsy. He said that in any event this autopsy was started at 8.15 am, and the photographer normally arrived at 8.30 am. It seems no one thought to start the autopsy fifteen minutes later, or to ask the photographer to get in fifteen minutes earlier.

The autopsy report had stated that death 'might have taken place about 12 hours before discovery' — that is, before the body was found. This would put the time of death at about 6 am on 3 August. We now know that at that time Akritidis was in the custody of the police at the Yankalilla police station.

Counsel for the Akritidis family asked Dr Manock to comment on the statement that death might have taken place 12 hours before discovery. Dr Manock said that he thought the word 'discovery' was in error. He said that he didn't think the word should appear there at all. He thought it to be 'more reasonable' to him that it should have been 12 hours before the body was undressed at the autopsy the following day. According to this explanation, Akritidis would then have died around 8.15 pm the previous evening. However, that time would have been some two hours *after* the police discovered his body.

Counsel asked Dr Manock about the range of accuracy in which he was able to determine a time of death. He said that in the circumstances of this case, accuracy was 'out of the window'. He explained that the pathologist has very little chance unless they are called to the scene of the death and take body temperatures. He said that from the wrinkling of the feet due to contact with water, one may be able to say '12 hours, 24 hours, 36, a week, something of that order'.

Dr Manock was then asked if he thought the pathologist who conducted the autopsy had made her calculation simply from the appearance of the feet, and he replied: 'Yes, she certainly took no temperatures, so she hasn't got a more scientific basis on which to judge time of death'.

There are, however, many ways in which time of death can be estimated. The processes of lividity and rigor mortis can be helpful indicators within the first 48 hours.

Dr Manock went on to suggest that lividity would be 'nonexistent' because of the torn aorta. This is not correct. When a person dies, the blood gradually moves through the blood vessels and, under the force of gravity, it settles at the lowest part of the body. Thus the lowest part of the body will go pink and then purple in colour as the lividity progresses. To suggest that this process would be halted because of the torn aorta is wrong. A rupture of the aorta at the aortic arch would mean that some blood could be pumped out before the heart stops. Some more blood might escape from the opening after death. However, a considerable amount of blood will remain within the blood vessels and will still settle at the lowest part of the body. Akritidis's body would have had about 4 litres of blood left within the system of blood vessels, given that the pathologist stated in her autopsy report that she had found 'approximately 1 pint' [about half a litre] of blood within the chest cavity.

The police at the scene acknowledged that Akritidis's body was cold and stiff when they found it, which means that he had in fact been dead for some time. We know that it was very cold on the mountain that day. The cold would slow down the rate of the development of rigor. This would tend to support the pathologist's view that Akritidis had been dead for some time before his body was found. The police could not have seen the pattern of lividity because the body was clothed. If that pattern had been confirmed by photographs at autopsy, then it would do much to reveal the position of Akritidis's body when he died. Without those photographs, and without any observations in relation to the pattern of lividity, we have to say that the record and procedures are seriously deficient.

For Dr Manock to observe that the pathologist had not made any comment about relating rigor mortis to the time of death, and the acceptance that it may not have been considered by her, should have given rise to questions.

FAILURE TO FOLLOW GUIDELINES
Akritidis's death was sudden, violent and unnatural, and no qualified medical practitioner was available to issue a death certificate. Therefore, the cause of death had to be established by a pathologist. In South Australia, General Order 8278 clearly instructs operational police that they must treat every unexplained death as a homicide to make sure that no vital evidence is lost. This rule was not followed.

The forensic procedures state that the scene in every such case is to be treated as if it were a crime scene. The scene must be cordoned off, access to it must be controlled and all evidence collected. This means posting a guard to control access and to record details of all the people there. Yet the Deputy Coroner had some difficulty in establishing the identity of a painter who was said to have turned up at the scene and then left. It seems that no one had bothered to record his details at the time. It might also have been expected that in addition to photographs, footprints and fingerprints would have been recorded. Nowhere in the procedures does it say that the first officer on the scene can ignore the directions of the established procedures if the answer 'appears to be obvious'. Indeed, the procedures actually state that especially where the answer appears to be obvious, one must look carefully to ensure that all of the facts are consistent with the *assumption* of what appears to be 'obvious'.

Failure of documentation

The pathologist had not filled in a body chart in her case notes. The standard body chart is pre-printed with an outline of a person, and the pathologist merely has to indicate on the diagram where injuries or marks are found. Dr Manock told the Deputy Coroner that the completion of such a document was 'a matter of choice' for each pathologist and that it was his view that it was 'not unusual' to not fill one in. He said that he preferred to 'rely on descriptions' as he had not any 'artistic ability', and he shied away from drawing charts and diagrams.

DEPUTY CORONER'S FINDING

On 22 June 1990, the Deputy Coroner handed down his findings in this case. The Deputy Coroner determined that Akritidis had taken his own life by climbing the tower and then falling to his death. While the Deputy Coroner commented that the evidence Dr Manock gave to the inquest was of considerable assistance, he was critical of the autopsy. The Deputy Coroner wrote:

> I am somewhat critical of the procedure that was adopted at autopsy. In my view, it is likely that *assumptions were made at the*

outset that the deceased had taken his own life. Ultimately I think that that assessment was correct however, in my view, that clouded the empirical taking of observations at autopsy. [Emphasis added]

Peter Marshall 1992

The police found Peter Marshall, 35, lying dead in his home unit. He was next to his bed, with blood pooling around his head. Dr Manock attended at the scene and concluded that Marshall had died by falling out of bed and hitting his head. 'There being nothing suspicious' everyone went home and Marshall's body was taken to the mortuary where nothing further was done until the following day.

During the autopsy, however, a bullet hole was found in Marshall's head, and a bullet was found lodged in his brain. The Forensic Science Centre said that the standard practice in South Australia was that unless a late afternoon death was suspicious the autopsy was done the next day. If a crime was suspected, they said, a pathologist would start immediately.

The press reports said that the police 'smarted' over the delay. The crime-scene tape was put back up.[4]

CHAPTER TEN

SEEING THINGS

THE BABY DEATHS INQUEST, 1994

Between 1994 and 1995, the Coroner in Adelaide held an inquest into the deaths of three babies who had died suddenly in separate incidents. The babies were Storm Don Deane, aged 3 months, who died on 16 October 1992 at the Adelaide Children's Hospital; William (Billy) Barnard, aged 9 months, who died on 31 July 1993 at the Adelaide Children's Hospital; and Joshua Clive Nottle, aged 9 months, who died on 17 August 1993 at the Modbury Hospital, Adelaide.

In each case Dr Manock had conducted the autopsy. The cause of death for each was given as bronchopneumonia, a basic lung infection, associated with other features.

In Storm Deane's case a congenital heart defect was also referred to. In Billy Barnard's case bone fractures of the right arm were also referred to. In Joshua Nottle's case it was noted that there were also multiple rib fractures. The police and the doctors involved thought causes of death given by Dr Manock weren't correct and may have concealed serious child abuse, or even homicide.

The police made their views known to the Coroner, Mr Wayne Chivell, who decided to hold an inquest into all three deaths. He commissioned Dr Tony Thomas as an independent pathologist to review and assess Dr Manock's autopsies. The following discussion is based on the Coroner's findings, the transcript of evidence before the Coroner, the report of Dr Tony Thomas that was accepted by the Coroner, Dr Manock's autopsy reports in each of the three deaths, and the ABC TV *4 Corners* program 'Expert Witness'.[1]

Storm Deane

Storm was born on 18 July 1992 to Craig and Heather. He lived with his parents and three siblings who were aged ten, six and four. Craig stayed at home to look after the children and Heather worked as a telemarketer. Craig said that on Thursday 15 October 1992, while he and Heather were at home, he took Storm from the baby bouncer by grabbing hold of the front of his jumpsuit without supporting his head. Craig described taking him to the master bedroom: 'I picked him up by the scruff of his clothes and carried him like a little carrying bag … I flipped him, and he went about two feet forward and then landed on the bed.'[2]

Craig told the doctors at the time that he had flipped all his children in this manner, throwing them through the air onto the bed. He had the belief that this taught the babies how to fall properly and would be helpful during their later life. In an effort to show them how to breathe from the diaphragm rather than from the chest, he had squeezed the baby around the chest on various occasions.[3]

After putting Storm on the bed, he and Heather went outside to fix his Harley Davidson motor bike. Heather later went to check on Storm and found him looking pale and not moving. Craig tried mouth-to-mouth resuscitation, but without success. Heather called an ambulance.

When the ambulance arrived, Craig was said to have run out of the house with the baby and to have fallen over. However Storm didn't hit the ground. The ambulance officers connected Storm to an electrocardiograph to measure his heart activity. They said that he was cold and grey, he had no heartbeat and he wasn't breathing. He was rushed to the Lyell McEwin hospital and then from there to the Adelaide Children's Hospital. The following morning it was agreed that Storm's life support would be terminated and Storm was pronounced dead. One of the doctors reported that at the time the life support was terminated, Craig had placed his thumb on the baby's throat saying that he did not like to see him gasping. The doctor said that while he was disturbed by this action it did not (in his view) contribute to the baby's death.

After having regarded Craig's unusual behaviour, two doctors at the hospital expressed concerns about the cause of death. The consultant paediatric pathologist at the hospital arranged for a full examination. This revealed that there was extensive bruising, a skull fracture and rib fractures, and an ulcer on the right buttock.

Storm's body was then sent to the Adelaide Forensic Science Centre for an autopsy. It was done by Dr Manock without any other doctor present. He concluded that the cause of death was bronchopneumonia. He said that there was also a heart defect, although he did not undertake any microscopical examination of the heart tissues. He noted that there was a circular mark on the buttock which was consistent with a burn. However, he said that it was probably a healing area of nappy rash. He also noted that there were bruises on the baby's back, which were consistent with finger pads. In his view, the microscopical examination of the tissues confirmed the diagnosis of bronchopneumonia.

Dr Manock reported that there were three bruises on Storm's scalp behind the left ear and that the brain was somewhat oedematous (swollen with fluid). A specialist in neuropathology subsequently examined the brain and noted that there may have been some damage to the brain stem. Dr Manock stated that he found no fracture of the skull. He saw X-rays of multiple rib fractures and said that the history of the child's birth might help to explain some of them. He took the view that a hairline fracture of the eleventh rib may have been explained by the fall on the way to the ambulance. He said that some of the rib fractures might have been caused by 'rough play', such as throwing the baby in the air and catching him again.

A detective of the Criminal Investigation Branch (CIB) who attended the autopsy told the inquest that when he suggested that the fractures could not have come about in that way, Dr Manock appeared irritated by him. He said that Dr Manock's explanation for the injuries meant that there was no evidence to suggest that the death was caused by anything other than natural causes.[4]

The detective had earlier carried out other investigations, interviewing a neighbour and Craig. Craig had suggested that he might have murdered his son at the hospital by strangling him. When the detective heard this he arrested him. However, Craig was later released when the doctor said that his actions at the hospital would not have contributed to the death. The detective said that he felt frustrated that the investigation couldn't go any further as a result of Dr Manock's autopsy report.

The Coroner said that the parents' evidence of a normal family life appeared at odds with what he described as Craig's 'rather menacing appearance' — he was dressed in black clothes, leathers and studs. Craig was said by one witness to have a 'short fuse'.[5]

Dr Terry Donald, the director of Child Protection Services at the Children's Hospital, said that the chest injuries looked as if an adult hand had been squeezing the chest. In his view, they resulted from 'serious physical abuse' on at least two occasions before death.

In the *4 Corners* program, he said:

> I'm used to working with people who have a high standard of professional practise, and I was finding it difficult to believe. These injuries were actually dismissed as being caused by somebody else. It was as though, I think, one of the children was meant to have been harmed through rough play. I mean, for heaven's sake, you know, these were babies. They're not children that would be harmed by rough play at all.

Dr Byard, a leading paediatric pathologist in Adelaide, said at the inquest that tissues from a number of areas of Storm's body should have been examined microscopically. These included the buttock lesion, which Dr Manock said he did examine and concluded from this that it was not a burn; the rib and skull fractures, which were not done; the brain, which was not done by Dr Manock before he expressed his opinion, but was later done by the neuropathologist; and the eyes, which were not done.

Dr Byard also said that there should have been a detailed examination of the waterbed because of the possibility of accidental suffocation. This had not been done either. The Coroner took the view that it was not possible to resolve the conflicting evidence with regard to the skull fracture.

One of the doctors said that Craig appeared 'enthusiastic' when the other doctor discussed the withdrawal of life support.

He described Craig as a 'violent' and 'muddle-headed' person and completely rejected the cause of death as being bronchopneumonia.

The Coroner commissioned Dr Thomas as an independent expert. He was an associate professor in anatomical pathology at the Flinders Medical Centre in Adelaide who had had forensic pathology experience in the United Kingdom and New Zealand as well as Australia. The Coroner said that 'Dr Thomas was at that stage the Senior Specialist in tissue pathology at the Institute of Medical and Veterinary Science in Adelaide. He has wide experience both in histopathology and forensic pathology and, more recently, in cardiac pathology'.

Dr Thomas prepared a report on all the matters related to Storm's death. In his report and evidence during the inquest, he stated that there were many areas where microscopical examination and weighing of organs were not done. He said even the body itself had not been weighed or measured. Some of these practices were described by Dr Thomas as 'time honoured'. He said that in his view it was clear that bronchopneumonia was not the cause of death and that the injuries were not related to birth trauma. In his view they were not accidental.

The Coroner took the view that as Dr Manock had been the head of forensic pathology in South Australia since 1968, his understanding of the criminal process, and his obligation to provide lines of inquiry to investigators, would have been second nature to him. Yet he had fundamentally failed to do that in Storm's case. The Coroner said that 'it is extraordinary' that Dr Manock did not conduct further inquiries to exclude the possibility of non-accidental injuries.[6]

Dr Manock's explanation to the Coroner was that 'It was important that the pathologist should be careful not to influence the investigation and suggest suspicion which is unwarranted'.[7]

However, the Coroner said:

> People involved in child protection agencies, police and prosecuting authorities are placed in an invidious position when they are presented with evidence which is less than completely thorough and illuminating in such cases. The courts (whether it is a coronial or a criminal court) rely upon the validity and credibility of such evidence.
>
> ... If guilt can be established, it should be established to the extent to which the system is capable. If innocent people are to be exculpated, then no questions should remain about the thoroughness of the investigation which might throw a doubt upon their innocence.[8]

At the conclusion of his examination of Storm's case, the Coroner said, 'The post-mortem examination achieved the *opposite* of what should have been its purpose — it *closed off* lines of investigation rather than opening them up'.[9]

He said that the cause of death would have to be recorded as 'undetermined'. It was his view that while a proper examination of the issues had not occurred, it was then too late to go back and put things right.

Billy Barnard

Billy was born on 29 October 1992 to Cherry and David. He lived with his parents and an older sister aged three years. Another sister had died when she had been only three weeks old. On the evening of Thursday 30 July 1993, Cherry was in a sleeping bag with Billy. The following morning, she said, she found him not breathing. She called for an ambulance and the baby was taken to the Adelaide Children's Hospital. Billy was pronounced dead shortly after arrival. One ambulance officer said he had remembered attending at that address before when the other child had died. The ambulance officers noted that

Cherry seemed 'detached', 'nonchalant', 'unconcerned' — much the same as on the first occasion. The ambulance officer conveyed his misgivings to the medical authorities on arrival at the hospital.

The physical examination of Billy by Dr Donald (the Director of Child Protection Services) revealed injuries such as bruises and fractures, that were possibly non-accidental, as well as scars which were unusual in a child that young. The body was sent to the Forensic Science Centre for an autopsy.

Dr Manock conducted the autopsy and again, no other doctor was present. His diagnosis was that Billy, too, had died of bronchopneumonia. He also had arm fractures. A detective from the CIB said that he couldn't undertake further inquiries because he was told that the cause of death was bronchopneumonia.

Cherry, when talking about Billy, admitted to having 'cracked and snapped his arm'. Billy's sister had also died while sleeping with her mother in a sleeping bag. The Coroner said that David was more articulate and careful in his answers to questions than Cherry was. The Department of Family and Community Services had had extensive involvement with the family, and there was evidence of neglect and poor parenting skills. Cherry had had a disturbed childhood, as had David, who had served a sentence for assaulting a child in an earlier relationship. The Coroner said that the Family and Community Services plan was clearly insufficient.

During the inquest, Dr Manock said he could not recall why he did not weigh the lungs. He agreed that bronchopneumonia was unlikely to have been the cause of death. He was unable to recall what he had seen in the slides that had led him to this conclusion. Dr Manock said he did not send the brain for examination because he was waiting for something from the detectives so that he could tell the specialist what to look for.

The Coroner said that he was perplexed at this statement as Dr Blumbergs (the specialist) was perfectly capable of examining the brain without being told what to look for:

> I am quite unable to accept Dr Manock's explanation as to why he did not offer this further information to the investigators immediately after the post-mortem examination concluded. It is spurious, in my opinion, to suggest that he did not offer these alternative explanations because he was waiting for further information from the detectives. Unlike Dr Blumbergs, who did not need to be told what to look for, the detectives should have received all the assistance possible so that their investigations could focus on particular issues. With a diagnosis of bronchopneumonia the investigation had no focus.[10]

The fact that the Coroner was unable to accept Dr Manock's explanation, and that he regarded Dr Manock's explanation as 'spurious', is a serious thing to say about someone in Dr Manock's position giving evidence under oath.

Dr Tony Thomas also evaluated the pathology evidence in this case for the Coroner. He said that there was no evidence of the weight of the body organs. He said that lung weights would have been invaluable. He said that there was no temperature of the body, which again he described as a time-honoured practice. He said that there was no list to identify the origin of tissues that had been taken for examination. The absence of this made interpretation of those tissue samples difficult.

The Coroner took the view that the 'bronchopneumonia' explanation had caused the death to be 'written off' as a 'natural' death. He said that the investigation was basically cut off before it began.

As in the previous case, the Coroner concluded that the autopsy in Billy's case achieved the opposite of its proper purpose, Dr Manock's report having 'closed off' lines of investigation rather than opening them up. He said that the lack of a thorough investigation was disturbing, particularly as this was the second such death in this family, and in strikingly similar circumstances.

Joshua Nottle

Joshua was born on 27 November 1992 to Julieanne and Sean. He had a brother who was about two years old. On Tuesday morning, 17 August 1993, Joshua was found dead in his cot. He was taken to Modbury Hospital where he was declared dead. Bruising and rib fractures were noted. Two detectives from the CIB attended. After an interview, Sean was arrested and charged with Joshua's murder. When the results of the autopsy were known, this was then reduced to intentionally causing grievous bodily harm.

Joshua's body was transferred to the Forensic Science Centre where Dr Manock conducted an autopsy the same day. Again, there was no other doctor present during the examination, however the CIB officers were present. Bruising was found in addition to a spine fracture and rib fractures. Yet again, the death was described as bronchopneumonia, this time associated with multiple rib fractures.

Knowing that there was evidence of spinal injury and multiple rib injuries, the detective investigating the case spoke to Dr Manock about his concerns. He said that Dr Manock explained to him that throwing the child into the air and catching him could have caused the rib injuries. Dr Manock also said that the spinal injury might have resulted from 'vigorous attempts at resuscitation' by the father. Dr Thomas took the view that this was not correct. As the Coroner said:

> Dr Manock's evidence here reflects his apparent attitude that this is an issue of credibility, that it is his word against that of

Dr Thomas, rather than an issue of scientific and professional method. Had Dr Manock done as Dr Thomas suggested he should have, this would not, and should not, have been an issue at all.

During the inquest, Dr Manock said that the baby was weighed but that the weight had been misplaced. Dr Manock said that he had expected more information from the police, however, the Coroner said that he was quite unable to understand how the police could be expected to provide that information without suggestions to help them from Dr Manock.[11]

Unhappy with Dr Manock's explanations, the detective saw the Director of Child Protection Services at the hospital (Dr Donald) who disagreed with Dr Manock's explanations. Dr Donald said that the degree of force required to cause the type of injuries sustained by Joshua would be much greater than that proposed by Dr Manock. Dr Donald said that the spinal injury in Joshua's case was typical of those seen in young children who had been involved in high-speed car accidents, particularly when a child had been thrown from the vehicle. In the *4 Corners* program, he dismissed the suggestion that it could have been caused by 'vigorous attempts at resuscitation'. He also dismissed the idea that the rib injuries in this and the other cases could have been caused by 'rough play'.

Dr Byard, the specialist in child pathology, advised the police that the rib fractures were most likely done by squeezing by an adult. He took the view that the spine fracture was most likely to be non-accidental and not as a result of resuscitation. He thought that the lung weights did not support the view of bronchopneumonia. He was 'mystified' by Dr Manock's suggestion of 'bronchospasm'. This is a twitching of the muscles — a physiological process and that could not have been seen at autopsy.[12]

Shaking babies can often cause brain damage. One of the classic signs of this is ruptured blood vessels in the eyes, which can be detected if the eyes are dissected at autopsy. The Coroner said it was 'as a result of Dr Donald's suggestion (not, as Dr Manock's report implies, on his own initiative), Dr Manock agreed to dissect the eyes for signs of severe shaking'.[13] No ruptured vessels were found.

As with the previous two cases, the independent report by Dr Thomas was critical of Dr Manock's autopsy. It showed that no body height or weights were given. There appeared to have been no microscopical examination of the bruises. Organs, other than the lungs, were not weighed. The rib fractures were noted, but not the fractures of the clavicles (collarbones), which were easily detected on the X-rays. Dr Thomas took the view that a full skeletal survey was essential and that further dissection and microscopical examination was also essential. He was quite clear in saying that further dissection and exploration of the spinal fracture would have been mandatory. Contrary to Dr Manock's view, Dr Thomas thought that bronchopneumonia was not the likely cause of death and that microscopical examination of the eyes should have been done and that the brain should also have been examined in this way. He said that the 'time-honoured practice of taking the temperature' was not done. Again, there was no list in relation to the tissues that were taken, making microscopical interpretation of those sections extremely difficult.

Dr Thomas agreed with Dr Byard that a bronchospasm would have been undetectable after death.

The detective investigating Joshua's case said that had he had the information later available in Dr Tony Thomas's report, the subsequent investigation would have been a great deal different.

The Coroner noted that Joshua's mother, in giving evidence, said that Sean was abusive to the children and to her. She said that he was violent when she became involved with another man. She would then spend nights at this other man's place, leaving the children with Sean. She then allowed Sean to move with her, the children and this other man to their new address. She said that Sean would slap or hit the baby, but that she did not report this to the authorities because she was too scared. Sean denied the abuse, however, he could not explain what the Coroner called the 'horrific injuries' to the baby, or the bite-mark on the baby's face.[14]

The Coroner said that when Joshua had been previously admitted to hospital, one had to conclude either that the bruising was not noticed, or that the notes were not acted upon. He said that 'the witnesses have been unsatisfactory, and know more than they are prepared to tell'. He agreed with Dr Thomas that the autopsy had been inadequate.[15]

Dr Manock's effect on the investigations

The Coroner concluded that, of the three deaths, that of Joshua Nottle was the most serious as the non-accidental injuries were the most evident. He said that Dr Manock's diagnosis prevented the establishment of a causative link between the non-accidental injuries and the death. In the Coroner's view, what should have been a homicide investigation became one only of serious assault. He said:

> Dr Manock's investigation, and his subsequent report, provided innocent explanations for the most serious injuries found on Joshua's body, explanations that I am now satisfied were incorrect.
>
> In those circumstances, and in common with the other two cases, the post-mortem examination basically achieved the

opposite of its proper purpose in that it closed off lines of investigation rather than opening them up.

...I consider Dr Manock's explanation that he was waiting for further information from the police to be spurious. In my view, it was incumbent upon him to provide the detectives with information so that they would know what to look for.[16]

The Coroner said that he had no hesitation in accepting Dr Thomas's opinion that there was no evidence that Joshua was suffering from bronchopneumonia to any degree sufficient to cause death. The cause of his serious physical injuries remained undetermined. The uncertainties that now surrounded his death were most disturbing, but although there were grounds for grave suspicion, nothing could be proved on the basis of the evidence as it then stood.

Of the fractures, Dr Terry Donald said in the *4 Corners* program:

> It just amazed me. That's the kind of opinion I'd expect from a relatively untrained, inexperienced, junior medical officer, not a person practising as a senior forensic pathologist. It just doesn't add up. It doesn't make any sense at all, that.

Given that the re-examination of the lungs didn't show any evidence of bronchopneumonia, Sally Neighbour asked Dr Tony Thomas on the *4 Corners* program how a pathologist could possibly come to that as the cause of death. He replied:

> I can't answer that. Given that bronchopneumonia is a basic inflammatory disease, perhaps I could answer by saying that I would have expected a first or second year trainee in anatomical pathology to be able to diagnose that down a microscope.

When asked several years later in a television interview whether he was concerned about the criticisms of Dr Manock raised in these Baby Deaths cases, the Director of Public Prosecutions, Paul Rofe QC, said:

> I mean everything concerns me. But my understanding was that those mistakes, as the coroner subsequently found, were as the result of post-mortems on babies and young children requiring a special skill which Dr Manock didn't possess and indeed didn't profess to possess.[17]

However, the Coroner found that Dr Manock had seen things which could not have been seen (such as bronchopneumonia) and that some of his answers to the Coroner's questions had been 'spurious'. It is not correct to suggest that these are the sorts of mistakes which arose because the cases involved babies and young children.

Heart attack, not heat stroke

An 18-year-old schoolboy died suddenly playing football on a rugby tour from England. The team had played in Sydney, Brisbane and Cairns before arriving in Darwin on 4 August 1999. The next day they played a game early in the evening. Towards the end of the game, the young man fell backwards and began to twitch. He was unconscious and his breathing was laboured. Resuscitation attempts failed. Dr Manock performed the autopsy and determined that the schoolboy had died as a result of heat stroke.

Once again Dr Thomas was asked to provide a second opinion on one of Dr Manock's autopsies, but this time the request was from the Coroner of the Northern Territory.

Dr Thomas determined that Dr Manock's diagnosis of heat stroke was wrong, and that the boy had in fact died as the result of a heart defect.[18] 'I have absolutely no doubt whatsoever that this is a sudden unexpected natural cardiac death and that heat stroke played no part in the causation of death.'

Dr Thomas made the following points in his report. The symptoms of sudden cardiac death and heat stroke are different, and the boy had not been playing long enough to develop heat stroke. In interpreting the heart weight, Dr Manock had failed to take into account the body weight. Also, the lungs were slightly heavy (a normal finding at autopsy), but not twice as heavy as Dr Manock stated, and Dr Manock's interpretation of 'interstitial haemorrhage' within the heart was not correct.

Dr Thomas said that the information provided in the autopsy report was grossly inadequate and that a more comprehensive examination of the heart should have been performed. He said that Dr Manock's statement that the lungs showed signs of a muscle spasm was wrong. Such a spasm cannot be detected after death; it cannot be seen either macroscopically or microscopically.

In this chapter we have seen that these cases have been based upon inadequate autopsy examinations, inadequate documentation and inappropriate interpretations of the evidence. All these issues were to be raised again in the Keogh case, as we will see in the next two chapters. The South Australian Coroner's Findings criticising Dr Manock in the Baby Deaths cases were completed by August 1995 and, as we will see, this was the time when Henry Keogh's second trial was being conducted.

CHAPTER ELEVEN

THE ONE POSITIVE INDICATION OF MURDER

HENRY KEOGH 1995
PART 1: INVESTIGATION AND TRIALS

In August 1995, Henry Keogh was convicted of the murder of his fiancee Anna-Jane Cheney, a 29-year-old solicitor. At that time Keogh had been a senior banker in Adelaide who had recently moved to a firm of financial planners. Anna had had a high profile job as the head of professional conduct at the Law Society.

Anna died on a Friday evening and, because her death was deemed 'not suspicious' by those investigating the incident, an autopsy was not conducted until the Sunday. This autopsy was done by Dr Manock at the time that his work was being subjected to the serious challenges in the Coroner's Court in the Baby Deaths cases described in the previous chapter.

Further, Anna's body was cremated shortly after the autopsy which meant that no one apart from Dr Manock was able to inspect it, or ensure that proper autopsy procedures had been undertaken and results recorded. Because the cremation took place long before Keogh was arrested and charged, it also meant that neither he nor his lawyers could do anything to check the pathology evidence or test other possible explanations.

The prosecution case, based on a scenario proposed by Dr Manock, was that when Anna was taking a bath, Keogh gripped one of her legs and raised it up, thereby forcing her head underwater, causing her to drown.

In this chapter we discuss the forensic examination of the scene and the pathology aspects of the trial. The next chapter describes information that has come to light since the trials and how the appeal process has failed to work properly in this case.[1]

Anna found dead in the bath

Henry Keogh had been married and had three daughters, but was separated. Afterwards, he met Anna and was subsequently divorced. He and Anna had become engaged and they were to be married in about two weeks' time. After work that Friday (18 March 1994) they met at a local hotel for a few drinks. They had some wine and potato wedges and then went home to Anna's house, each driving their own car. They spent a short while together at home, then Anna drove over to see her sister-in-law so that they could take their dogs for a walk at the local park. After Anna returned home, Keogh went to visit his mother for a short while.

Keogh said that he returned home at around 9.30 pm and found Anna in the bath. He said that she was sitting at the plug end with her body slumped forward to her right, with her face in the water. He said he dragged her out and tried to resuscitate her. He called the emergency number and ambulance and police officers came to the house. The ambulance officers also attempted resuscitation, but to no avail. Anna was pronounced dead. As there were 'no suspicious circumstances', her body was removed to the mortuary at the Forensic Science Centre in Adelaide.

On Sunday 20 March 1994, Dr Manock conducted the first autopsy of Anna Cheney. The coronial running sheet states that Dr Manock noticed a bruise to the top of the head and that further inquiries were to be carried out to explain this bruise, which he said was caused prior to death. The same note on the running sheet also stated that the body would be free the following day, after the laboratory technician had taken the necessary photographs in the morning.

The same day, according to the coronial running sheet, the police officer attached to the Coroner's Office contacted various police officers during the evening to raise her concerns about the case.

On Tuesday 22 March 1994, according to his autopsy report, Dr Manock conducted further autopsy procedures and two more bruises are said to have been detected at the back of the head/neck. However, when asked in evidence at trial he stated that the further procedures were completed on the Monday. This discrepancy in timing was not cleared up.

On Wednesday 23 March 1994, the police said Anna's death was a murder.

On Friday 25 March 1994, the police declared Anna's death a 'major crime'.

On Monday 28 March 1994, the Coroner, Wayne Chivell, gave written permission for Anna's body to be cremated after he received written confirmation from Dr Manock that the body would no longer be needed.[2]

On Wednesday 30 March 1994, a funeral service was held and Anna's body was cremated.

On Friday 29 April 1994, Dr Manock completed his autopsy report that mentioned bruising to Anna's left leg. He said nothing in the report about them constituting evidence of a handgrip. However, he had already indicated to the police that this was an important part of the explanation as to the cause of her death.

On Saturday 7 May 1994, Keogh was arrested while attending a basketball match with his daughters, and charged with the murder of Anna Cheney.

On Wednesday 18 May 1994, Dr Manock gave the toxicologist samples for analysis.

On Thursday 23 June 1994, the toxicologist completed his report stating that the deceased had 'no common drugs' in her system.

On Monday 27 June 1994, Dr Manock visited the scene and on 28 June produced a further report in which he described the possible murder scenario.

Keogh's committal was heard in the Adelaide Magistrates Court in August 1994 and he was committed for trial. He subsequently stood trial before Justice Duggan in the Supreme Court of South Australia in March 1995. Mr Paul Rofe QC, Director of Public Prosecutions, prosecuted. Counsel for Henry Keogh was Mr Michael David QC. The jury was unable to agree on a verdict.

A second trial took place in August 1995, before the same judge but a different jury, after there had been some delay with regard to some prejudicial publicity in the newspaper. The same defence and prosecution counsel were involved.

The case against Henry Keogh
In a criminal case, it is necessary to establish both the psychological and the physical components of the crime and the prosecution presented these two types of evidence at the Keogh trial. All of it was circumstantial. There was controversial evidence which related to insurance policies that Keogh had taken out on Anna's life. This was said to show that Keogh had a motive to murder Anna. As the prosecution said, her death

would then give him his freedom and the financial means to enjoy it. He was also said to have had affairs with other women. The prosecution also argued that at the time of Anna's death, Keogh had not ordered his suit for the wedding, nor had he arranged to take time off work for the honeymoon. This evidence was said to show that he had never had any intention of marrying Anna. There was also the pathology evidence, which they claimed was the physical proof that showed that Keogh had murdered Anna.

THE PSYCHOLOGICAL FACTORS

The prosecution led evidence that Keogh had taken out over $1 million of life insurance on Anna which he had done by signing Anna's signature on five policies. The prosecution case was that he had been planning Anna's death since the policies came into effect, that is, for about two years.

The prosecution accepted that Anna knew of at least two of the policies. It follows then, that she must have known that there were two life policies that Keogh had signed in her name. The prosecution argued that if she had known that there were in fact five policies, she would have realised that Keogh had a much greater financial interest in her demise.

Keogh said that when he was employed by the State Bank, he realised that his job was not too secure because of likely restructuring. He said that as he had agencies with five life insurance companies, he decided to put a policy through each of them to encourage the insurance companies to keep his agencies open. The five agencies therefore explained the reason for having five policies. He said that the commissions he would earn on the policies would cover their cost, and he could give the impression of doing some business without it actually costing him anything.

He said that if the prosecution case was correct, and that he had effected the policies with a view to murdering his fiancee and then claiming on them, it would have been a scheme doomed to failure.

On each of the proposals for insurance there was a question which asked if there were any other life insurances on the life to be insured. To each of those questions Keogh wrote the answer 'No'. That alone would have invalidated four of the five policies. The only way in which the scheme proposed by the prosecution could have worked would have been if Keogh could murder Anna and then claim on all five policies without any of the insurance companies realising that there were other companies who had policies on her life. If such a scheme had been attempted in a large city such as New York or London it might have had some prospect of success. Keogh argued that if he were to attempt to do such a thing in a small place such as Adelaide, he would have had no chance of getting away with it.

Keogh's former wife, Susan, supported his claims in relation to this at the trial and in a subsequent interview by Rohan Wenn for the Channel 7 *Today Tonight* program on 30 July 2002:

> ROHAN WENN: Much too was made of five insurance policies that Henry took out for Anna — by forging her signature — worth more than $1 million. And whilst on the surface it looks very suspicious, his former wife says it wasn't unusual and alone didn't make him a murderer.
> SUSAN KEOGH: Well, while we were married, as a matter of convenience, Henry always signed papers for me and he had my permission to do that and I had no problem with that, it was just a matter of convenience.[3]

Evidence was also presented to show that Keogh had recently been involved with other women. One woman said that she had sex with Keogh after he had become engaged to Anna.

Keogh agreed that this had happened. Another woman claimed that there had been some intimacy with Keogh on a number of occasions although she had never had sex with him. This evidence was strongly contested by Keogh.

THE PHYSICAL FACTORS

The pathology evidence was fundamental to the prosecution case. They produced evidence about bruising which was said to show a 'grip' mark on Anna's leg. The prosecution argued, therefore, that Anna's death was a deliberate and forced 'death by drowning', and that there were no other possibilities, such as an accident or natural causes. Dr Manock said at the committal hearing:

> I was at no time looking or thinking that the death was accidental because I could find no explanation as to why she would drown.[4]

In subsequent petitions to the Governor of South Australia on behalf of Keogh, Kevin Borick QC has claimed that Dr Manock's statement is clearly inconsistent with the most basic obligation of a pathologist — which is to consider all reasonable possibilities as to a cause of death.

Professor Stephen Cordner, the Professor of Pathology at Monash University and head of the Victorian Institute of Forensic Medicine, who gave evidence for the defence at the trial, has since reviewed the pathology material in this case and provided detailed written comments on Dr Manock's work. In his report he states: 'I think that most, if not all forensic pathologists in Australia, would have been decidedly uncomfortable proposing a murder scenario in court on the basis of the injuries present in this case'.[5]

As to the significance of the pathology evidence, the Director of Public Prosecutions, in his final address to the jury, said:

> Whereas to murder I suggest the bruising on the lower left leg, if that is a grip mark, is almost in itself conclusive, providing you accept that it was applied at or about the time of death.[6]
>
> ... you might give him the benefit of the doubt, explain away in some way, the one positive indication of murder, namely the grip mark on the bottom left leg.[7]
>
> But there are two things, you might think, that are crucial to this case. If those four bruises on her lower left leg were inflicted at the same time, and that time was just before she died in the bath, there is no other explanation for them, other than a grip. If it was a grip, it must have been the grip of the accused. If it was the grip of the accused, it must have been part of the act of murder.[8]

In other words, the jury were told that Dr Manock's evidence about the grip mark was the one positive indication of murder and crucial to the prosecution case.

This should be contrasted with what the DPP said in an interview recorded for the *Today Tonight* program in June 2002 when he was asked how important was the pathology evidence:

> I said in my final address to the jury that the forensic pathology wasn't going to provide the answer. I mean it was necessary and important background.
>
> ... a fit and healthy 29-year-old girl doesn't drown in the bath.[9]

Also, the Attorney-General, in his statement to the South Australian Legislative Council on 20 February 2003, stated:

> Dr Manock's evidence as to how the bruises came to be on the victim's leg in the Keogh case had marginal weight and relevance to the prosecution case.
>
> ... the verdict did not depend on Dr Manock's evidence.

Mr Borick has argued in Keogh's petitions that the jury, on the evidence presented to them, had no option but to consider the pathology evidence significant, and they made their decision accordingly.

At the scene

The police took some colour photographs at the scene that night. The implications arising from them were not brought out at the trial, but they have proved since to be most useful in developing an understanding of what occurred that night. We can now see that they disclose important information about the condition of the body, and the way in which the scene was altered. This information has now become crucial to establishing a more informed understanding of what really happened that night.

RESUSCITATION FAILED

The statements of the ambulance officers indicate that they arrived at the house at 9.38 pm in response to Keogh's call for help. After waiting for a moment or two for the dog to be removed from the hallway, they commenced CPR but found that Anna's airway was full of fluid and they could not get air into her lungs. They stopped resuscitation attempts at 9.55 pm after working on her for ten minutes.

One of the ambulance officers made a statement that night but did not appear to express in it any concerns about the situation as they found it. After all, the police were to conclude that night that there were no suspicious circumstances. Some months later, however, the ambulance officer made another statement to the police in which he listed a series of observations, apparently reflecting some concerns which he says he had on the night. These were: there was no vomit near the body or on it; the hair, body and towel were not wet; and there was no water on the floor in the bedroom or in the bathroom. He thought the explanation about Keogh doing CPR was unusual, saying that any attempt at manual compression would cause vomit and water to spill out. In evidence at the trial he said that whatever he tried to do as he worked on her, Anna's airway filled with water. They could not get it clear and this indicated to him that CPR had not been attempted.

The second ambulance officer also made a statement around the time of Anna's death and noted that they found Anna to be asystolic (clinically dead). The officer said that doing CPR caused water and vomit to come from her mouth. She said that Anna's hair was damp (but not wet) and the bathroom floor was dry. As with her colleague, the second officer also made another statement some months later and likewise referred to apparent observations which she thought *then* to be significant, but which were not included as part of her previous statement — that there had been no water or vomit on the carpet, and the airway was *clear* — indicating that she thought that Keogh did not attempt resuscitation.

This is confusing. Both officers agree that Keogh could not have done CPR. Yet the facts on which they base their inferences that led each of them to the conclusion that Keogh had not done CPR as he had claimed — the presence of water in the upper airway on one hand and the absence of it on the other — are diametrically opposed.

Had these concerns been stated at the outset instead of months later, the police would have been alerted to potential problems and could have secured the scene. The fact that the observations of the second officer were at odds with that of the first officer would indicate that their recall of these matters was unreliable. The ambulance officers do not appear to have made any notes of their observations that evening — their evidence in court was given without reference to such notes.

Keogh gave evidence at his trial that he tried to resuscitate Anna and that in doing so, he saw that she had mucous around her mouth. He said that he had wiped this away using some track pants lying nearby in order to get a seal so that he could inflate her lungs. It was part of the prosecution case that he had not done so, because he would hardly be trying to save her if he had in fact just tried to murder her. However, a police photograph taken at the scene shows the presence on the track pants of what appears to be mucous material.

CONTAMINATED SCENE

The police did not at any time cordon off the scene of the death to avoid contamination, as they should have done. An officer was placed at the door, but when people arrived and said that they were family or friends they were allowed in. In all, about 20 people were allowed into the house, and from the various reports it seems that many of them went to the bathroom and the bedroom where the events had occurred. Anna's body was lying naked on the floor of the bedroom adjacent to the bathroom, with her feet just level with the bathroom door.

When Mr Rofe was asked in an interview later whether he was concerned that the scene wasn't cordoned off, given the impact that it could have on evidence, he replied, 'No. I can't think off-hand of any evidence that might have been lost by the lack of it cordoned'.[10] The bath water, however, was evidence and this was lost as a direct result of the failure to properly secure and examine the scene. It may well have provided significant information about what occurred that night, but it was never sampled or tested. If there was something in the water that night, it might be important to know whether it was just bath salts, bodily fluids or vomit, for example. If testing had shown that there was biological material present, it might be an important clue to know whom it belonged to. However, the reports about the bath water are conflicting and confused.

Anna's father said that the water was clear, but that there were flecks of amorphous material on the bottom of bath. The first ambulance officer said that he examined the bathroom area and that the bath water was slightly cloudy but there was no sign of vomit in the bath. Yet how could he have known that the cloudiness had nothing to do with vomitus material? One of the police officers reported that the bath was three-quarters full — with 'almost clear' water. The second ambulance officer said that the bath was three-quarters full and the water was still warm, but not as warm as she would use for a bath. But no one recorded the temperature or took a sample of water for analysis for diatoms or for anything else. Substances such as vomit, bodily fluids or bath salts could have caused the 'cloudiness' or 'amorphous material' in the water. One might have thought it to be important to determine which, if any, it was. Anna's father said (in his statement) that he let the water out after the police had left the house that night.

THE FLOORS WERE WET AND DRY
Evidence about the state of the floors was also lost because of the failure to secure and examine the scene, and to record the information at the time. The condition of the floors is important with regard to Keogh's actions on the night. He claimed to have found Anna in the bath and pulled her out and attempted resuscitation. If this was the case, one might expect that the floors would be wet, but the evidence about the floors is as confusing as that about the CPR. The first ambulance officer said in his statement months later that he examined the bathroom area and could see no sign of vomit or water on the floor. The second ambulance officer said that she could remember that when they arrived the floor in the

bathroom was dry and the bathroom mat was dry. Anna's father said the fact that the floor was not wet in the bathroom seemed strange. However, other witnesses that evening stated that the floor was wet, and that the bathroom mat was very wet. The police officer from the Coroner's Office even stated that she picked the bath mat up and it was 'heavy with water'.

The second ambulance officer recalled that there was no water or vomit on the bedroom carpet. This was taken to be a further indication that Keogh did not attempt to resuscitate Anna. The photographs taken at the scene, however, show that the carpet under the body appears to be wet.

WAS THE BODY TIDIED UP?
Some of the photographs, taken by the police shortly after their arrival at the scene, show Anna's body with her face swollen and with vomit in her hair. They also show the patches where the pads for the monitoring equipment had been attached. In one photograph, Anna's left leg, below the knee, can be seen pressed against the door frame. In later photographs, the swelling in Anna's face has reduced, and most surprisingly, her hair has been combed and her make-up has been reapplied. The photographs show a mark on her forehead that was not evident in the earlier photographs. This was not recorded in the autopsy report, but it is commented upon in the coronial running sheet. None of the witness statements taken that evening say anything about her body being tidied up at the scene, even though the evidence is plainly visible in the police photographs.

WHAT HAPPENED TO ANNA'S CAR?
A police photograph taken of the outside of the house that night shows that Anna's car was not where it should have been. The coroner's van can be seen on the road and police

officers can be seen standing on the doorstep. Keogh's car is in the driveway, but Anna's car is not in the carport, nor is it on the road outside the house. Another photograph taken at the house two days later shows Anna's car parked beside the house. None of the witness statements refer either to the fact that the car was missing, or to the fact of its being returned by someone. Evidence of this, though, could indicate that after Keogh went to his mother's house that evening, Anna either left the house in her car and walked back home, or else someone had been to the house while Keogh was away and then left using Anna's car. This matter was not raised at the trial. The DPP now says that the explanation could be an innocent one.[11] However, if that were so, one would think it would have been explained in the witness statements. The lack of a simple explanation where one might be expected should be cause for concern.

NO SUSPICIOUS CIRCUMSTANCES

At the end of the evening the police present determined that there were no suspicious circumstances. Anna's body was then picked up and carried out of the house before being placed on a stretcher. This handling of the body is significant because, as it turned out, one of the most important signs said to indicate murder was stated by Dr Manock to be bruising to the legs. However, no one was questioned about this at the trial, not even those who carried the body out of the house, to see if they could have caused any of the bruising to the legs.

Death by drowning

At the trial, the prosecution's case was that Anna's death was a 'death by drowning'. But death by drowning is a diagnosis of exclusion. This means that death by drowning cannot be proved conclusively. To reach such a diagnosis all other possibilities, such as accident or natural causes, must first be examined and excluded.

Dr Manock had ruled out other possibilities. However, other possibilities *do* exist and have not been eliminated by proper examination or testing.

SUDDEN DEATH IN APPARENTLY FIT AND HEALTHY PEOPLE

The DPP made it clear in his opening and closing addresses to the jury that death by natural causes, or a death contributed to by natural causes, should be ruled out. It was said on many occasions throughout the trial that Anna was a fit and healthy person, and that fit and healthy people do not just fall over and die. Dr Manock gave evidence that he regarded Anna as having been 'fit and healthy'. However, Anna's full medical history was never produced in court. The only evidence at the trial in this regard was that of her general practitioner. However, it is now known that Anna had some 37 consultations with a number of different medical practitioners over the previous five years, but the details of these visits have not been revealed.

In an interview with the Channel 7 *Today Tonight* program in 2002, Mr Rofe stated that:

> As indeed we said, you know, a 29-year-old girl doesn't drown in the bath. And Dr James [another forensic pathologist from the Forensic Science Centre in Adelaide], for example, had never come across such a case.[12]

But fit and healthy young people do die suddenly and unexpectedly in all sorts of circumstances. Professor Tony Thomas, the expert pathologist used by the Coroner in the Baby Deaths cases, is highly respected as an expert on the subject of sudden death in young people. He has about ten to twelve cases of sudden death in a young person referred to him each year. As no cause of death has been found at autopsy, he is requested to examine the heart.[13]

Shortly after Keogh's trial but prior to his appeals, *The Advertiser*, Adelaide's main newspaper, reported a similar bath death in Sydney. The article of 18 June 1996 stated, 'A healthy young woman drowned while taking an early morning bath when she fell asleep'. It went on to say that the woman, who was 22 years old and 'was fit and healthy, a former State champion swimmer and runner', had been found immersed in lukewarm water in the bath at her home in May 1995. However, the Coroner said that he 'was satisfied there was no foul play involved'. So it does happen.

ANAPHYLACTIC DEATH A POSSIBILITY

Another possible cause of Anna's death, again based on evidence available at the time, is that of a severe allergic or anaphylactic reaction. This was not tested for at autopsy and the possibility was not put before the court.

The photographs taken at the house show that Anna had some general swelling of the face, and that there was what looked like some streaking or blistering on her body in the upper left-hand side. She also had what appeared to be a dark red blister or sore behind her ear. These are classic signs of anaphylaxis, a severe allergic reaction to certain foods, medications or other substances. It is quite possible that Anna went into anaphylactic shock, especially as it appears that she may have suffered from allergies. While no evidence with regard to this was provided to the court, there is some information to suggest that she bought cosmetics specially designed for people with allergic sensitivities.

Haemolysis, an indicator of possible anaphylaxis, was found in the aorta at autopsy, although it was explained by Dr

Manock only as part of a process of 'drowning'. No other possible causes were mentioned. Dr Manock said that the lungs were heavier than normal. His autopsy report stated that there was 'massive oedema' in the lungs and that when the lungs were cut, 'water' flowed from them. However, water and oedema are not the same thing. The former would indicate drowning. The latter could result from anaphylaxis or cardiac failure. But it would seem that the possibility of anaphylaxis was not even considered at autopsy, and certainly no test was made for it.

It is worth noting that anaphylaxis often causes difficulty with breathing. The muscles and tissues of the airways can expand, narrowing the airways, and this can lead to fainting or unconsciousness. If this had occurred it may well have been undetectable by the time of the autopsy. Mucous plugging, which could also have been undetectable at autopsy, could also have caused a blockage.

However, Dr Manock said that Anna's airway was blocked. The inability to obtain an airway could have been caused by a narrowing of the airway as the result of an anaphylactic reaction. When combined with the regurgitation of food, if inhaled into the airway, it would have caused a blockage of the airway. The initial muscular spasms or narrowing of the airway may have been undetectable at autopsy, although the blockage by the regurgitated food would still be present as Dr Manock found.

In fact, Dr Manock's autopsy report stated: 'Larynx, trachea and main bronchi were packed with fluid and gastric contents but it was difficult to ascertain whether this was an ante mortem phenomenon … '

It is worth noting that if it had been ante mortem, which means 'prior to death', this would have meant that Anna would have choked to death.

The photographs taken at the scene also show that Anna had what appears to be a mark with some redness around it on her upper left leg. It is the sort of mark that can result from an injection or an insect bite or sting, any of which could cause an anaphylactic reaction. None of the witnesses at the scene mentioned this mark. Nor is there any mention of it in the autopsy report. As the body was not examined until two days later, it's possible that the symptoms had disappeared by that time. There are no colour photographs from the autopsy, so it is not possible to confirm this one way or the other. However, it is expected that the pathologist would review all the available evidence, and the photographs taken at the scene would be important to that assessment.

'It must be a grip'

Dr Manock said that he could identify three bruises to the outside of Anna's left leg, and a single bruise on the inside of the left leg. He said that this particular combination of bruises was the classic sign of a grip and he couldn't think of anything else that it could be. This led him to hypothesise that Keogh had gripped Anna's left calf to force her legs over her head and then to drown her by pushing her head under the water. This scenario, he said, would explain the bruising to the top of the head. It would, he said, have the effect of trapping the arms by the sides of the bath but leave the right leg free to thrash around and bang itself against the edge of the bath and so produce bruising along the border. A later re-enactment that disproved this hypothesis is discussed in the next chapter.

Dr Manock asserted that his own hand 'fitted the pattern of bruising' on Anna's left leg. Neither he nor the police made any proper attempt to determine if Keogh's hand also fitted that pattern of bruising. Dr Manock said that while he was able to explain the grip theory to the police as soon as he saw the body, he could not write it in his report until he had been to the scene some three months later. It is difficult to understand why that should be so.

The autopsy

PHOTOGRAPHY INADEQUATE

None of the photographs which were said to have been taken at the autopsy and tendered in court actually *identify* the person in the photographs. One set is of a person's legs from just above the knees to the feet. The other set is of bruising to the head, but the angle of the photograph is such that it does not show the face or any other distinguishing features.

Interestingly, these photographs are all in black and white. They were accepted into evidence at the trial without any explanation being provided as to why colour photographs weren't taken. In relation to this case, the Attorney-General made the following statement in the South Australian Parliament:

> In 1994 it was the policy of the State Forensic Science Centre to take only black and white photographs. For the purposes of examining suspected bruises, black and white photographs are useful because they can be enhanced better than can colour photographs to help with the examination.[14]

But, in his evidence in the Baby Deaths inquest in 1994, Dr Manock said that 'currently it [the photography] would be in colour'.[15] There are also on record many cases in which the Forensic Science Centre has used colour autopsy photographs prior to 1994. For example, in the 1987 case of Kingsley Dixon, the Commissioner into Aboriginal Deaths in Custody specifically commented on how useful the colour autopsy photographs were, particularly with respect to bruising. Indeed, as Professor Derrick Pounder has said, 'We would never take a black and white photograph *instead* of a colour photograph'.[16]

In the Keogh trial in 1995, however, the only photographic evidence before the court of bruises to the legs consisted of two black and white photographs. The most important of these was the one said to show a bruise on the inside of the left leg — the supposed thumb mark of the grip. In court, the photograph was first shown to Dr Manock for him to confirm that the photograph showed a bruise on the leg. Before the photograph was shown to the jury, he was asked to mark a circle with a red pen around where the bruise was said to be. This meant that the jury only got to see the photograph with the red circle marked on it. When another copy of the photograph (without the red circle) was shown later to an expert in forensic photography, he said that it was impossible for him to see any mark in that location which could be said to be a bruise.

Police crime scene examiners were not present at the autopsy as required by the police forensic procedures manual. If they had been present, they would have taken sufficient and suitable colour photographs, as the police manual instructs. The DPP stated since the trial that he did not know of the existence of this manual, and that he had never seen it.[17]

In an affidavit filed before the Medical Board in June 2004, Dr Manock stated:

> Coloured photographs were taken later on 21 March 1994 by a police crime scene photographer.

After all of the trials, appeals and petitions, this is the first time that the existence of such photographs has been revealed.

EXAMINATION OF THE HEAD
Dr Manock stated that he peeled back part of the scalp to check for bruising. He said that he returned to further peel

back the scalp some 24 hours later and found some further bruising. The obvious thing to watch out for in such a situation is that the bruising (which is really just bleeding under the skin) found at the second stage was not caused by the earlier autopsy procedures. Yet there was no discussion at the trial or in any of the notes of this possibility. This was critical to the understanding of the whole situation. It was said that the two sets of bruises to the head made it less likely that Anna had simply fainted and hit her head as she fell. But if the pathologist had caused at least one of the sets of bruises, then this simple explanation is perfectly plausible.

HISTOLOGY SAMPLES INADEQUATE
Dr Manock took just two tissue samples of the heart, one of kidney, one of lung, and four of bruising. He did not conduct appropriate testing for the presence of diatoms in Anna's system. He said that the presence of diatoms in the lungs would have been evidence of drowning, just as he had said years before in the Van Beelen case. As we have already shown, this is not necessarily correct. If Anna had died and then fallen into the water she might still have had diatoms in her lungs. Diatom testing of bone marrow samples may have been able to confirm or exclude drowning.

NO SPECIALIST EXAMINATION OF HEART OR BRAIN
Dr Manock did not get specialist opinions regarding the heart and brain, in spite of the Coroner saying in relation to the Baby Deaths cases that such expert assistance would be absolutely essential in cases of sudden and otherwise unexplained deaths.

Throughout the trial the prosecution repeatedly stated that Anna was a fit and healthy person, but we cannot possibly know if she was unless a proper examination was undertaken at autopsy. Detailed examination of the brain and heart are absolutely essential, even if only to rule out other possible causes of sudden death. Without detailed examination of the brain and heart at least, the autopsy examination is fundamentally incomplete.

TOXICOLOGY INADEQUATE

Dr Manock's autopsy report states that a blood sample was taken for alcohol analysis, which yielded a result of 0.08g per cent, 'which is about the level achieved in normal social drinking'. It also states that the only sample taken for drug testing was a urine sample. This was tested by a screening method, with negative results. However, just as in the Highfold case, in giving evidence Dr Manock stated that other work had been done but not recorded in his report. Toxicology tests had been done on blood and liver tissue for chloroform and a whole range of drugs, and had given negative results.

There is no specific statement in Dr Manock's autopsy report, or his evidence, that tests were done to determine if Anna had taken medications that were known to be present at the house that evening. The police took a drug container from the house on 23 March 1994 (five days after her death). The container can be seen in photographs of bookshelves in the study/office taken on the night she died. The drug was a non-steroid anti-inflammatory drug (NSAID) commonly used to relieve pain and reduce inflammation, swelling, redness and soreness which may occur in different types of arthritis and in muscle and bone injuries. The drug comes with a manufacturer's warning that the medicine is not to be taken if there is an allergy to it, or if one has taken aspirin or any other NSAID medicine. The warning describes the symptoms of an allergic reaction, which may include asthma, wheezing or shortness of breath, swelling of the face, lips or tongue, which may give difficulty in swallowing or breathing, hives (urticaria), oedema, itching or skin rash, and fainting. Symptoms which may occur include drowsiness, stomach upset, vomiting, nausea, dizziness or light-headedness. Given that there is a specific warning that a known side-effect of this drug is an allergic reaction which could cause swelling of the face, such as can be seen in the photographs of Anna's body, one would have thought it would be important to undertake appropriate tests to determine if Anna had this drug in her system before determining the cause of death. However, the toxicology samples were not submitted for testing until some three weeks after Dr Manock had *completed* his autopsy report, and nearly two weeks after Keogh had been arrested. The results were not known until five weeks after that.

RECORDS INADEQUATE
The police running sheets indicate that it was just before the second trial that the police reported to the DPP that Dr Manock did not have his original notes. The DPP is said (in the running sheet) to have responded that the matter should be left with *him* (the DPP) to deal with. But as Professor Cordner stated in his report after the trial, Dr Manock failed to make or keep sufficient written records of his observations and findings. As indicated earlier in the discussion of the Splatt Royal Commission, proper procedures would require observations to be recorded in writing and signed by the person making them. They should then be checked by another qualified person and initialled by them also.

Dr Manock also failed to establish or maintain proper photographic records of Anna's condition before the autopsy or of the procedures that he said he undertook. As Professor Cordner has said, 'The autopsy pathologist who fails to adequately describe and record his or her findings runs the risk that s/he may not be able to substantiate a particular observation if it is queried'.[18]

PEER REVIEW INADEQUATE

Dr Ross James was another forensic pathologist at the Adelaide Forensic Science Centre at the time. He gave evidence that he was asked by the DPP, before the trials, to check the work of Dr Manock in this case. The explanation given as to why it was necessary to have Dr James check the work of his then director was that Dr Manock was away on leave. Dr James was provided with Dr Manock's autopsy report, a number of black and white autopsy photographs, a toxicology report and ten microscope slides, four of which were of samples from areas of bruising on Anna's body.

Dr James indicated to the court that he had checked the work. But this could only have been in a limited way. He could not have, for example, confirmed the observations of the body or the procedures that had been made. No one, not even Dr James, had checked any of Dr Manock's observations throughout the investigation stage of this case. They could not. Anna's body had been cremated before anyone else could examine it and, given the lack of photographic records, it was impossible for anyone later to see what was said to have been seen by Dr Manock. Indeed, in so far as the cause of death was, according to Dr Manock, fresh water drowning, Dr James said he had to take the appearance of the lungs as described by Dr Manock 'on face value by his report only'. As to the previous medical history of the deceased, Dr James had to base his opinion solely on Dr Manock's autopsy report. He said that he had to rely on Dr Manock's body chart for his information about the bruises.

A grip inferred

Dr James gave evidence concerning the bruise on the *inside* of the left leg — the supposed 'thumb' mark of the grip — the one Dr Manock circled in red on the photograph. While Dr James said he saw photographs of three bruises on the outer side of the left leg, he said that he did not see a photograph of the bruise on the inner side. He agreed that he had only a small portion of the tissue to look at but stated that if the small section was representative of the bruise as a whole, then it could be inferred that it could be used as assessment of that bruise. In relation to this alleged bruise, Dr James said, 'If it was present as he [Dr Manock] suggests then a grip mark is an obvious explanation'.

In other words, Dr James was unable to confirm the presence of that bruise. He merely stated that *if* it were present, then certain inferences might be drawn. Kevin Borick QC, as counsel for Keogh, has stated in his second petition to the Governor that Dr James, however, was not legally entitled to make these inferences. Mr Borick argued that an expression of opinion can be based on a fact, or a combination of facts, but never on an assumption that is based on an earlier assumption.

In June 2004, however, Dr James stated in his affidavit to the Medical Board that he and Dr Manock differed about the bruise on the inside left ankle. He said:

> When I looked at the histological section purported to have been taken from this area, I would not have described what I saw in the sample as a bruise.

Professor Cordner makes the observation that it is hard to assert that Dr Manock's opinions are inconsistent with the evidence because he has preserved so little of that evidence. He says, 'Once one approaches the autopsy of Anna Cheney wishing to scrutinize it, one finds this a difficult exercise to do objectively because of the paucity of the record'.[19]

Keogh convicted

Keogh was convicted of murder on 23 August 1995. He was sentenced to a minimum period of 25 years' imprisonment.

CHAPTER TWELVE

NO BRUISE, NO GRIP, NO CRIME

HENRY KEOGH 1995
PART 2: FURTHER INVESTIGATIONS AND THE APPEALS

Henry Keogh has always maintained that he is innocent of the crime for which he was convicted. Several attempts have been made by his lawyers to establish this through the appeal process of the courts, but without success. In the meantime, a large amount of research has taken place into the events on the night of Anna Cheney's death, the police investigation, the pathology (particularly Dr Manock's expertise, his diagnosis of drowning and his grip theory) and the conduct of the trials.

This second chapter on the Keogh case looks in more detail at the scenario proposed by Dr Manock for the drowning of Anna, and at some of the work which has been done since the trial to test the theory, including a re-enactment. It then discusses the problems Keogh has had in appealing his conviction.

The pathology evidence

Professor Stephen Cordner was called by the defence to give evidence at Keogh's trials. He was extremely critical of Dr Manock's evidence. During the second trial, to elicit the professor's response, Mr David QC read out to him the questions which had been put to Dr Manock at the first trial and the answers which Dr Manock gave to them. The first extract that was read to the professor covered two pages of transcript and included a series of eight questions and answers. The next extract (which was read to him shortly after) covered three pages and a series of 27 questions and answers. Professor Cordner has since provided a report containing further and more detailed comments on Dr Manock's evidence.[1]

WRONG OPINIONS

Professor Cordner concludes his analysis of Dr Manock's work in this case by stating:

> I believe Dr Manock has expressed opinions in this case which are wrong. These wrong views are then combined with other rather speculative propositions to support a reconstruction of this death as a murder. Dr Manock has, in my view, wrongly dismissed an accidental explanation for this death as, at least, a reasonable proposition
>
> One of my objections to Dr Manock's putting his proposition is that it was not refutable by enquiry or testing and therefore he should have surrounded it with caution. I believe no other forensic pathologist in Australia would be of the view that murder is the only explanation of the findings in this case.

In spite of Professor Cordner's concern about the difficulty of refuting Dr Manock's opinions, it has been possible to test some aspects of the scenario.

HISTOLOGY SHOWS NO BRUISE

Microscopical examination of histology sections will determine if what looks like a bruise really is a bruise.

The tissue remaining from the sample said to have been removed from the alleged bruise on the inside of the left leg — the supposed thumb mark of the grip — has been examined by pathologist Dr Tony Thomas as an independent expert. He was the expert called by the Coroner in the Baby Deaths inquest. He has stated that the tissue sample showed no sign of a bruise at all.[2]

If in fact there was no thumb bruise, then, with only the three bruises on the left side of the leg, there was no basis for the suggestion that they were part of a grip mark. Without the grip mark, 'the one positive indication of murder' (according to Mr Rofe[3]), the prosecution case is seriously weakened.

However, when we look in more detail at the three bruises on the outside of the left leg, further questions arise. According to an affidavit of Dr Tony Thomas, Dr Manock said that a sample of tissue was taken from only one of the three marks on the outside of this leg. These are the marks which Dr Manock had attributed to finger marks. Dr Thomas says that his histological examination of the one sample taken from those three bruises does show some leakage of blood into the tissues. However, he says, there is no cellular reaction present related to this leaked blood. Therefore, he concludes that it may be inferred that the blood could have got there at any time within the twenty-four hours prior to death or in the immediate post-mortem period.[4]

Dr Thomas then goes on to state in his affidavit that, in his opinion, the leakage of blood runs more along the lines between the fatty tissues rather than diffusely within the fatty tissue. Therefore the cause of this type of leakage may have been artifactual; that is, it may have been caused by the manner of taking the tissue sample at the time of the autopsy. Dr Thomas also points out that because there are so few red blood cells in the tissues, they would not have been able to be seen through the skin. Therefore, they would not have constituted a 'bruise' as a bruise had been defined by Dr Manock in his evidence:

> Bruising is bleeding which has occurred in tissues, and any pressure or blow or tearing of the tissues can cause small blood vessels to be torn and to leak, and that's what we call a bruise when we can view this blood *through the skin*.[5]

Dr James's opinion on this matter was in accordance with Dr Manock's:

> Bruising is simply bleeding beneath the skin as a result of crushing of the tissues by some external factor such that *it can be seen from outside the body*.[6]

Dr Manock said that he had not sampled all of the bruises on the left leg because, to him, they all looked the same. Therefore, Dr Thomas concludes in his affidavit, that:

> … it follows that there is no scientific evidence available to me to conclude that any of the marks seen by Dr Manock on the left leg represent bruises.[7]

A RE-ENACTMENT
Dr Manock proposed his scenario as follows:

> If the person is sitting at the plug end of the bath and an arm is put underneath both legs to grip the left calf, either by simply lifting or lifting the leg and pushing the head, then the head

could slide under the water. At this time, the edge of the bath could cause bruising to the back of the neck or the muscles attached to the base of the skull. If the movement is then continued and the legs are folded over entirely, this would have the effect of trapping the arms by the sides of the bath and the top of the head would then be against the top of the bath and that would give a flat surface that could cause the bruising to the top of the head. The left leg has been gripped. However, the right leg is merely encompassed by the arc of the arm and can move. If it thrashes around, it will bang itself against the edge of the bath and may produce bruising along the border.[8]

On this theory, Keogh put an arm underneath both legs to grip Anna's left calf. The left leg is the leg nearest the wall and is just beneath the taps on the wall, halfway along the bath. Then Anna's head slides under the water either by simply lifting the left leg, or by lifting the left leg with Keogh using his other arm to push Anna's head under the water. Her legs are then folded over entirely, supposedly trapping her arms by the sides of the bath. Her left leg is gripped, but the right leg (which would have been closest to Keogh) is free to thrash around causing bruising to the front of the right leg.

In putting this scenario Dr Manock did not specify which hand he thought it was that had been used to grab Anna's left leg.

Professor Maciej Henneberg, the Professor of Anatomy at the University of Adelaide, has stated that this scenario propounded by Dr Manock is inconsistent with a proper understanding of the science of anatomy and biomechanics. Contrary to the view expressed by Dr Manock that such a scenario would be 'relatively easy', Professor Henneberg takes the view that it would be entirely implausible. The power of the flexor and extensor muscles in a woman's leg would always be greater than the power which a man could exert through a fingertip grip of a woman's calf. Dr Manock claimed that he had been involved in a number of drowning cases. Even so, it would not make him an expert on drowning scenarios or on biomechanics.

In a television interview some time after the trial, the DPP said he did not recall that there were any intentions to undertake a re-enactment of the scenario.[9] However, the police running sheets show that such a re-enactment was planned. They also note that the DPP instructed the police not to go ahead with it. This was perhaps unfortunate, as the re-enactment subsequently undertaken by Mr Borick QC has provided some important insights regarding the shortcomings of the prosecution theory.

Kevin Borick QC has put the proposed scenario to a practical test. Using the actual bath at Anna's former home, an actress of similar proportions to Anna and an investigator of similar size to Keogh, a re-enactment was filmed. All of those involved were convinced afterwards that the scenario which Dr Manock had proposed did not make sense.

It could be seen that it would not be at all difficult for 'the victim' to use the free right leg to kick any possible assailant, and to kick him in the face. Given that the taps and the waterspout were located on the wall, halfway along the bath, such a victim could easily take hold of those to help her keep her head above the water. Also, her arms would clearly have been injured from hitting against the taps if there had been any real struggle. When she lay down with her head on the bottom of the bath there was only two or three centimetres of water over her nose and mouth, and it would be quite impossible for someone to hold her head under with one hand. If there had been a fight, it would have been inevitable that the assailant and the victim would both be injured from hitting against the taps and waterspout. At no time was there any possibility that the victim's arms could be 'trapped by the sides of the bath' as Dr Manock said that they would be. It was not possible for the victim to bang the crown of her head against the end of the bath, as Dr Manock said would be done.

WHICH HAND?

In the scenario quoted above from Dr Manock's evidence, he did not indicate which hand it was he thought had been used to grip Anna's left leg. However, in the first trial he said that his own left hand fitted the marks, but then immediately said that a right hand had been used.

As part of their analysis of this case, the Channel 7 *Today Tonight* program produced a series of computer-generated images to help viewers understand the proposed scenario and its limitations.[10] It was effectively a *virtual* re-enactment to demonstrate the grip theory and its limitations and to examine the situation using either hand.

The computer images show the position of the alleged bruises on Anna's left leg — the three bruises which are supposed to be on the outside of the leg and the single bruise on the inside. With a *left* hand gripping the leg, the thumb is covering the mark on the inside of the leg and it is possible for three fingers to occupy the other positions, although it is difficult to position the middle finger to properly cover the centre mark.

Further images show the position Keogh's arm would have had to be in to be under both of Anna's legs with his left hand gripping her left leg, in accordance with the theory. With the left arm being used like this, it is apparent that it would be impossible for the right arm to have reached Anna's head to hold it under the water. Keogh would have to have reached across his body with his right arm, crossing over his left arm, to have reached Anna's head, which would have been to the left of him.

Images depicting the position that Anna would have been in if she had been sitting at the sloping end of the bath, rather than the plug end as proposed by Dr Manock, show that the theory is impossible in that scenario too. To have done what was alleged, in accordance with the marks and the theory, Keogh's arms would have to have been coming out of the wall.

Dr Manock's theory, as eventually given at the second trial, involved the alleged use by Keogh of his *right* hand on Anna's left leg and his left arm on her head.

The computer-generated images of a right hand gripping the left leg show that it is impossible for the right thumb to fit the pattern of marks. With a right hand (as opposed to a left hand) the thumb cannot match up with the supposed bruise on the inside of the leg. The only way in which this could be done would be if the leg had been gripped from above with the right hand. It would, of course, be impossible to force the legs up and over in this scenario. It was one that was never proposed by Dr Manock.

In every description of his theory, the action required a hand to be placed beneath the calf of the leg. Whether it was said to have been the left hand or the right hand that was used, the theory is demonstrably impossible.

Keogh's appeals

The DPP has stated that both he and the defence were aware that, at the time of the first trial, Dr Manock's credibility and expertise had been subjected to serious challenge in the Baby Deaths inquest in the Adelaide Coroner's Court between 1993 and 1995.[11] The Coroner completed his Findings in that matter during the time the second Keogh trial was proceeding. His report, as we have seen in Chapter 10, revealed the true extent of Dr Manock's shortcomings. The Findings, however, were not published until two days *after* the verdict in the second Keogh trial. The Coroner has stated to Keogh's solicitor that he deliberately delayed releasing them because he was sensitive to the fact that Dr Manock was a principal prosecution witness in the trial, and he was concerned that publishing the report may have resulted in a mistrial.[12]

One cannot know if this would have been so, but what *is* known is that the Coroner's decision meant that the jury in the second Keogh trial had to choose between the credibility of the evidence given by Dr Manock, the principal prosecution witness, and that given by Professors Ansford and Cordner for the defence, unaware of matters which cast severe doubt on the competence and professional integrity of Dr Manock. It can be argued that the holding back of the report was an error of judgment by the Coroner. In the United Kingdom, similar circumstances have been used to overturn convictions on the basis that they constitute miscarriages of justice.

THE COURT OF CRIMINAL APPEAL

Keogh appealed his conviction, without success, to the Court of Criminal Appeal, in December 1995. Unusually, the solicitor retained by Keogh lodged a further application to reopen the appeal with the Court of Criminal Appeal in May 1997. This is unusual because normally once an appeal is heard one either goes to the High Court or one accepts the decision. It is not usual procedure to go back to the same court of appeal for another hearing of an appeal in the same case. In Keogh's case, when he applied to reopen the appeal, an application for special leave to appeal to the High Court had been filed, but the court had not heard the matter.

The further application to the Court of Criminal Appeal was heard by the same judges who had heard the first appeal.

The application was to the effect that the trial miscarried by reason of the unavailability at trial of evidence which would establish that no reliance could be placed on the opinions and evidence of Dr Manock. The court determined that as the order of the Court of Criminal Appeal had been perfected (that is, it had been signed and recorded), it was no longer possible to approach that court to reopen the appeal.

The only procedures then left to Keogh's legal advisers were to proceed with an appeal to the High Court, or to seek a reference under section 369 of the *Criminal Law Consolidation Act 1935*, of South Australia, which is the petition procedure. The High Court would not be able to hear any new evidence (about the findings of the Coroner concerning Dr Manock, for example) so Keogh's lawyer decided to approach the Governor with a petition on behalf of Keogh.

THE FIRST PETITION

In December 1996, during the appeal process, Keogh lodged a petition to the then Governor of South Australia, requesting that the Attorney-General refer the whole case to the Appeal Court to be heard by the court as if it were an appeal against the conviction. As there had already been one appeal, to allow a new appeal there had to be some 'new evidence'. Keogh claimed that fresh evidence had emerged subsequent to his trial that went to the issue of the competence of Dr Manock, the expert witness who had propounded the 'deliberate drowning' theory. The Governor replied by letter in March 1997 stating that, on the advice of his ministers, it would not be appropriate for him to take any action in respect of the petition because Keogh still had an application for leave to appeal to the High Court which had not been pursued. This meant that the only avenue open to Keogh was to proceed with the High Court appeal, even though his lawyers knew that the High Court could not consider new evidence concerning Dr Manock's role in the case.

In October 1997, the application for special leave to appeal was heard by the High Court. The application was refused. This meant that the issues that Keogh had wanted to raise relating to Dr Manock had not been considered in *any* of the legal proceedings.

QUESTIONS ASKED IN PARLIAMENT

In October 2001, the ABC *4 Corners* program investigated a number of the issues which we have discussed in this book. In particular, they discussed the nature of Dr Manock's qualifications and his evidence in a number of cases. In the State Parliament, the Hon. Nick Xenophon, an independent member of the Legislative Council, asked the South Australian Attorney-General to look into the issues raised by the program.[13] The Attorney-General asked the DPP's office and the Forensic Science Centre to comment. The Attorney-General reported to the Parliament that his advice was that there was no need for an inquiry.

A SECOND PETITION

In August 2002, a further petition on behalf of Keogh was prepared by his lawyers and presented to the Governor of South Australia. This covered the issues raised in the *4 Corners* program together with a number of other cases and issues, many of which have been included in this book. On the last working day before Christmas 2002, the Attorney-General, Michael Atkinson, posted a letter to Keogh's lawyers to inform them that the petition had been rejected. The following day, Mr Borick QC said on the Channel 7 *Today Tonight* program that he thought the decision and its timing were 'cowardly'. He said that if the government and the DPP thought that the people of South Australia had confidence in the justice system, then (if they did) their confidence was seriously mistaken. He said, 'I think the decision is a reflection on our justice system; it's a disgrace.'[14]

The Attorney-General subsequently provided two detailed statements to the South Australian Parliament to explain why the second petition was rejected. The first statement was made to the Legislative Council on 20 February 2003; the second was made to the House of Assembly on 1 April 2003. He questioned the credibility of the *4 Corners* program and the Channel 7 *Today Tonight* programs. He said he had acted after being contacted by Anna Cheney's family.[15]

A THIRD PETITION

A third petition was then lodged with the Governor in September 2003. It claimed that much of the information relied upon by the Attorney-General in his statements to the Parliament was provided to the Attorney-General by the DPP and by the South Australian Forensic Science Centre. Both the DPP and the Forensic Science Centre were the subject of complaints in the second petition, and it was claimed that it was therefore inappropriate for the Attorney-General to seek advice about whether to have an inquiry from persons or organisations that would be the subject of the inquiry.

The petition further claimed that much of the information provided to the Parliament of South Australia in the statements by the Attorney-General was in error, listing some 29 topics. It claimed that this indicated that, as a result, the Governor had acted on information that was misleading or unsatisfactory and as a consequence the second petition had not been properly considered.

In November 2003, the Attorney-General referred the second and third petitions to the Solicitor-General for further investigation and consideration. The lawyers for Keogh submitted affidavits in support of the petitions to the Solicitor-General in February 2004. In May 2004, the Premier publicly announced the inquiry which was being undertaken by the Solicitor-General into the Keogh case.

Summary

Keogh's situation highlights some of the deficiencies of the appeals process.

In his book, *The Stuart Affair*, Sir Roderic Chamberlain, a former Crown prosecutor and Supreme Court judge in South Australia, wrote: 'Under the system of justice that prevails in South Australia, no person is ever denied assistance in disproving a charge against him if he, or his legal advisers, takes the trouble to ask for it'.[16]

Keogh might well find this a bit hard to believe.

CHAPTER THIRTEEN

NO MATCH

MICHAEL PENNEY 1996

In 1996, Michael Penney was convicted of the attempted murder of his wife.[1] It was said that he had set fire to the boot of her car just before she drove away in it. The case against him was entirely circumstantial, based on what turned out to be a less than adequate examination of the scene by the police and a less than adequate investigation into the events by the investigating officer and a forensic scientist. As in the Keogh case, evidence was destroyed before the defence had an opportunity to examine it. The case provides another example of the legal issues involved in cases based on circumstantial evidence and in the decision to prosecute.

Attempted murder

Julie married Michael Penney in January 1989. They were both schoolteachers. They had two children and in 1993 they took out insurance policies — $250,000 on her life and $150,000 on his. During 1994 they had some problems with their marriage and went to a marriage counsellor in July that year.

Mr Penney left home twice during the year: first for six weeks, and then for seventeen weeks but returned home in late September 1994. The Penney's had two cars: Julie drove a Magna and Michael drove a Torana. Julie Penney said that she hardly ever used the Torana because the boot leaked because the seal had become damaged, but she had driven it about a week before the incident which gave rise to the charge of attempted murder. She said that there was a petrol cap on the car then. The petrol filler on this model car is in the centre of the back, just below the boot lid.

It was said that while Julie Penny's car was parked by the side of the road, Michael Penney threw a lighted match into a tin of methylated spirits which was in the boot and this started a fire. Their five-year-old son said that his dad had bought a petrol can about two weeks before the incident, and Mr Penney agreed that this was so. The family had a large lawn mower and Mr Penney had decided to get a larger petrol can for it so that he didn't have to go to the service station so often. The can was found, full of petrol, in the boot of the Torana after the incident.

Mrs Penney said that on the morning of the incident, she was going to take the Magna to work but Mr Penney said that he wanted to take it because the indicators on it weren't working properly. She said her husband would have gone outside and she thought he would have changed some things around with the cars, making sure that he had his briefcase and papers for school in his car. On the way to work, they both went to an automatic teller to get some cash, then went their different ways.

After a while, Mrs Penney noticed her husband driving behind her. She stopped and he parked behind her, with the boot of the Magna facing the boot of her car. He said that he had left his briefcase in the Torana's boot. She said she thought that it was strange, as he wouldn't have put his briefcase in the Torana because he knew that the boot leaked. She said that while he was at the boot, she could feel the car moving and things being moved around in the boot. She didn't hear the boot close, but she heard him tap the boot and saw him put his hand up. She said that she drove off wondering why he had been at the boot for so long.

After she had driven a short way, she saw a driver flashing his lights at her and sounding the horn. The man had seen smoke and fire coming from the boot of her car, and a rag in the fuel filler pipe was burning, with white smoke coming from it. Both cars stopped and the man yelled at her that her car was on fire. She leapt from the car and could then see that there were flames coming from the boot.

The man sprayed the burning rag with a fire extinguisher. One end of the rag was in the boot and the other wedged into the filler pipe of the petrol tank, which, he noticed, had no petrol cap. He pulled the rag out, stamped on it and kicked it to beside the rear wheel. He sprayed the extinguisher across the back and around the boot as he said the seal of the boot lid was alight, and he also sprayed through a gap (where the seal should have been) underneath the boot lid where the flames were coming out. He got the keys and opened the boot.

Mrs Penney said she saw that there were containers with fluid in them and rags in the boot of the car, and that the petrol cap was missing. She hadn't noticed the missing cap before, or the can of petrol. The man grabbed the can to see if there was anything in it. The boot also contained a partially melted plastic ice cream container with some rags in it. The man said there was the smell of methylated spirits, and that the rags smelled of petrol.

Mrs Penney and the man went and rang the police, and met them back at the car.

A circumstantial case

The prosecution's case against Mr Penney was entirely circumstantial. This means that the special legal rules relating to circumstantial evidence apply. These rules state that a person can only be convicted on circumstantial evidence where the facts, as alleged by the prosecution, lead inescapably to an inference of guilt. If there is a rational hypothesis that is inconsistent with the guilt of the accused, then the evidence should not be admitted, as was pointed out in the earlier discussions of the judgments in the Van Beelen and Perry cases. Once the prosecution accepts that the facts as alleged are consistent with an interpretation *other than guilt*, they should discontinue the prosecution. It is not acceptable for the prosecution to say that while guilt and innocence are possibilities, they prefer the guilty story and then urge the jury to agree with them.

Another way of putting this is to say that unless the prosecution can positively assert that an interpretation of the facts consistent with innocence can be excluded, then they have not really done their job properly. It would not be satisfactory, for example, for the prosecution to say that they had not investigated theories consistent with innocence, that is, that they had only looked at the reasons for guilt and ignored the rest.

It is the responsibility of the prosecution, in the form of the Director of Public Prosecutions, to make strategic decisions about whether charges are to be laid. The police may present a brief of evidence but if it is not convincing in terms of the applicable legal rules, then charges should not be laid. The police cannot insist upon a prosecution if it is not supported by the DPP. The job of the police is to investigate. The DPP's job is to prosecute. If, however, an over zealous prosecutor were to lay charges where the rules did not support that decision, then a motion from the defence to discontinue the case would be expected.

The first opportunity to do this would be at the committal hearing, but if a motion to discontinue at that stage was unsuccessful, and the case was set down for trial, the next main opportunity would be at the close of the prosecution case at the trial, that is, after they have brought forward all their witnesses, and before the defence brings their witnesses. If the prosecution has not established guilt beyond reasonable doubt by this stage, then the defence can apply to have the case struck out. If the judge disagrees and takes the view that the prosecution has the possibility of establishing guilt beyond reasonable doubt, then the defence will open their case and see if, through the witnesses they bring forward, they can establish such doubt to the satisfaction of the jury by the time they complete it.

In a properly operating legal system, a circumstantial case that does not accord with the rules of circumstantial evidence really should not be put to a jury decision. We take the view that Mr Penney's case should have been struck out at the committal stage. This did not happen although such an application was made. A further application was made to have it struck out at the close of the prosecution case, but that too was not successful.

The committal proceedings

At the committal proceedings, the police investigating officer revealed that he did not know that there was an eye-witness to the fire or that the witness had made a statement. This man was the only independent eye-witness at the scene, and one would have thought that his evidence would be crucial. In fact, it was another constable involved in the case who, just a day or two before the hearing, realised the investigating officer didn't know of the eye-witness or his statement and told him about it. When questioned by defence counsel, Kevin Borick QC, as to what his reaction was to discovering that there was an important eye-witness statement that he had not seen, the investigating officer said he was 'surprised and alarmed' by it.[2] Asked what he did as a result of finding out about it, the officer replied that he spoke to the prosecutor and was shown a copy of the witness statement. He confirmed that this was the first time that he had seen what the eye-witness had to say.

The officer was also unaware at the time of the committal proceedings of what Julie Penney had had to say about the rags, or what the first policeman on the scene had had to say about them. He was also unaware that Mrs Penney or her helper had picked up the rags and put them behind the rear wheel of the car. He was unaware that she had subsequently picked them up again and handed them to the first policeman. He was unaware that it was this policeman who had placed them in the boot of the car.[3] The importance of all this is that these are crucial elements in piecing together the story of what had happened (the chain-of-evidence). If the investigating officer is attempting to determine what the scene was like at the time of the events, it is clear that he must reconstruct any changes to the scene since these events occurred. Without interviewing the key eye-witness, and without determining the ways in which the witnesses had themselves altered the scene, the officer can hardly draw any sensible inferences about what may have happened initially. The man and Mrs Penney had taken things from the boot and the first policeman had placed rags in it. Without asking the people who were there, it would be impossible to know what the scene was like at the time of the incident.

Evidence discarded
It appeared that after the fire had been put out, two blackened tin cans,[4] one inside the other, were found in the boot. The cans were photographed at the scene. The investigating officer

said that the photograph showed that there was liquid in one of these cans. When asked what had happened to the liquid, he explained that it was tipped out: 'I'd already taken a sample of the liquid, and the small quantity left inside it, we just tipped that out on the side of the road'.

The officer hadn't measured how much liquid there was before he tipped it out. Knowledge of the original volume would have been crucial to both the defence and the prosecution to be able to precisely reconstruct the scene. To be able to reconstruct a scene effectively, an investigator has to preserve all the evidence and to investigate *everything* thoroughly. Mr Penney said that he did not place the can with methylated spirits in the boot of the car. He said it was possible that one of the children may have put the cans there without his noticing it while they were tidying the garage. He also said he had been cleaning his large mower in the garage during the previous few days and had used petrol and some rags to do this.

The trial

Michael Penney was tried in the Supreme Court before a judge and jury. Mr Paul Rofe QC, Director of Public Prosecutions, prosecuted and Mr Kevin Borick QC appeared for Penney.

At the committal hearing, the police investigating officer had been presented as an expert witness, giving opinion evidence, but he did not appear in this capacity at the trial. He did give evidence, but the role of expert witness was taken by the forensic scientist.

THE 'MURDER WEAPON' ALSO DISCARDED

The sequence of events put forward by the prosecution was that Michael Penney had gone to the boot of the car and, knowing that there were flammable liquids and vapours in the boot, had thrown a lighted match into the boot before he made off. The investigating officer said that he had found a broken match in the liquid in the cans in the boot. However, the photograph taken to show the match in the cans in the boot was shot at such an angle that the match is not visible. It was found that only part of the red head of the match had been burned. However, it was clear that the match was considered to be the 'murder weapon'. The officer was then asked to look at the photograph of the pieces of the match that he had spoken about. For the photograph they had been placed on the side of the blackened can which had been laid on its side for the purpose of the photograph.

Defence counsel asked the officer in cross-examination what had happened to the pieces of match since the photograph was taken. The police officer said that after he had examined them on the day he 'threw them away'.

> COUNSEL: Did it not occur to you that they could be important exhibits at any subsequent trial?
> POLICE OFFICER: I photographed them, and the photographs show the match, and I considered that was sufficient to bring to court.
> COUNSEL: Did it occur to you that it might be important to have someone with a knowledge of match heads, [and] chemistry, to have an opportunity to have examined that match?
> POLICE OFFICER: No.[5]

A charge of attempted murder should not have been laid or prosecuted in such a situation as this in which the investigator destroys the evidence before the defence, or anyone else, has any chance to examine it.

UNPRINTED FILM
Even at the trial, which was five months after the committal hearing, it appears that the investigating officer was not fully

prepared. He was asked whether the photographs presented in court were the only photographs that were taken at the scene.

> POLICE OFFICER: No.
> COUNSEL: Where are the others?
> POLICE OFFICER: I haven't had them printed. They are still in their negative form.[6]

So not only had evidence been destroyed before the defence could examine it, but photographs had not been developed and made available to the defence. The following points made by the defence at the trial show just how important photographs can be.

HOW LONG HAD THE RAGS BEEN IN THE BOOT?

The rags in the boot were to be of considerable importance to the prosecution case. They were produced in court; still dripping wet with petrol, when they were taken from the container in which they had been kept in the meantime. Defence counsel asked the officer if he had questioned anyone as to how long they had been in the boot before the fire. He said he did not recall doing so and agreed that it would be important information to know. It would 'show how long those particular petrol-soaked rags had been in that boot compartment to allow for evaporation of the petrol vapour and spread of the odour through the vehicle'.

Indeed, as the rags were still wet with petrol when produced in court, it would seem unlikely they could have been in the boot for very long, otherwise the petrol would have evaporated. Mrs Penney said that her husband had been moving things around in the boot just before the fire so, if the rags had been wet when he had been at the boot, it would be surprising if he hadn't arrived at school smelling of petrol. We also know that the rags had been removed from the boot by one of the police officers, and then placed back there by another officer. The defence claimed that Mr Penney's clothes were not properly tested, nor was his briefcase, which was said to have been in the boot.

NO PROPER EXAMINATION OF THE BOOT
There were two holes in the metal bulkhead at the back of the boot through which the felt backing of the rear seats could be seen. The officer said that on his visual inspection, he saw smoke staining to the surface of the felt behind those two holes. He was asked if he had conducted any other examination of the felt and he said that he had not.

The carpet in the boot had been covered with white powder from the extinguisher. Mr Borick asked the officer if he had inspected the carpet to see whether there was soot staining underneath the white powder. He said that he did not. However, he did say that it could have been done, just that he did not think to do it. He also said that he had never investigated a fire in the boot of a car before.

The officer then went on to say that when he examined the vehicle on 30 October he did not find any other holes in the bodywork. When calculating the possible rate of evaporation of the petrol on the rags, or of the methylated spirits, and the build up of fumes, it would be important to know all the facts about the ventilation of the boot. To calculate the progress of a fire, it would be important to know the amount of oxygen available to feed it. Earlier, at the committal hearing, when the officer was shown the photos of the vehicle, he had admitted that he had 'completely missed' other holes which were in the lower area of the left rear mudguard and which went through to the boot.[7]

THE WIRING AND THE BOOT LIGHT SWITCH

The line of questioning then moved to the wiring in the boot to see if that had been examined properly. This questioning was aimed at ascertaining possible ignition sources, such as from a fault in the wiring. When he was asked in cross-examination if he had examined the whole of the wiring in and around the boot, the police officer said that he had 'conducted an examination of the visible wiring to the boot compartment, yes'. However he said that he had not examined any wiring not visible (such as that which went behind the bulkhead), nor had he examined the fuses.

> COUNSEL: Did you look for a boot light switch in this vehicle when you were conducting your examination on 30 October?
> POLICE OFFICER: No, I did not.
> COUNSEL: Did you in fact see a boot light switch?
> POLICE OFFICER: No.
> COUNSEL: Can you tell us now as a result of information you have gained at other times, whether or not there is a boot light switch there?
> POLICE OFFICER: Yes, there was.
> COUNSEL: And when did you first see the boot light switch?
> POLICE OFFICER: When I uncovered it underneath a number [on a sticker] that I placed on one of my photographs.[8]

It seems that the officer failed to see the boot light switch when he examined the car, then later, when the photographs were developed and he was numbering them, he accidentally covered the switch, which appeared in the photograph, with one of his numbering stickers. Because of this he failed to notice the switch in the photographs for some time.

The officer and other witnesses said that the switch was made of metal plates which came together to complete the circuit. Each time the plates opened and closed they created a spark.

Interestingly, it would appear that a key point about this issue, which had been examined in some detail at the committal proceeding, was not pressed quite so far during the trial. Defence counsel had put it to the police officer in the committal that the boot light switch might have been a possible cause of the ignition in the boot. He had agreed that this might have been so. Indeed, he said that it could have been a probable cause of the ignition. Some of the answers repay careful attention:

> COUNSEL: Your observations were somewhat flawed, weren't they; I give you two examples why: one is that you didn't see the hole, and two, you didn't see the switch.
> POLICE OFFICER: I'll agree to those areas, yes.
> COUNSEL: If there was a light globe there, it would have been vital to look at the switch, do you agree?
> POLICE OFFICER: Yes.
> COUNSEL: Why would it be vital?
> POLICE OFFICER: To eliminate that as a cause of the ignition.
> COUNSEL: So you can't eliminate that as a cause of ignition, can you; you didn't inspect the switch and you don't know if there is a light globe there or not?
> POLICE OFFICER: No, there wasn't a light globe because I didn't see it and I cannot eliminate that as a probable cause.
> LAST ANSWER READ [BACK] BY REPORTER.
> COUNSEL: You can't eliminate what as a probable cause or possible cause?
> POLICE OFFICER: The light, the rear boot compartment light as an ignition source.[9]

At the trial the officer merely stated that he was not qualified to discuss whether or not the switch would give rise to a spark.

The re-enactment

The forensic scientist giving evidence at the trial said that he and the investigating officer had conducted certain experiments to reconstruct the scene, and these were shown to the court on video. The first experiment was the lighting by a match of a rag placed in the fuel filler pipe of a Torana wreck, said to be 'similar' to the Torana in the incident. However, there were some important differences: the wreck was a two-door model, not a four-door model like the Penney's car, and it had no wheels, no windows or windscreen, and many other parts were missing. To simulate the original incident, the wreck was put onto a trailer and towed up and down the road with various fires in the boot. The police officer admitted that with the wreck being towed behind another car, with it having no windows, and the back seat not fitting properly, the aerodynamics around the boot might have been different in the reconstruction. The contrast to the re-enactment conducted by the defence in the Keogh case, in which they used the original bath in its original location, could not be more marked.

The scientist acknowledged in answers to questions by the prosecutor that the circumstances were not ideal in terms of trying to re-create what had supposedly occurred in this case. He said that the wreck, for example, did not have any indicators in place, so there were some large holes on that part of the body not present on the original vehicle. He said that he tried to fill those up as much as possible, but that 'one would not achieve a perfect seal like an indicator would do'. In addition, the rear seat didn't fit as a normal seat would and therefore, he agreed, more air might get through that opening.

NO EXAMINATION OF THE CAR OR WIRING

Under cross-examination by defence counsel, the forensic scientist agreed that during the investigation it would be important to know how airtight the boot was, but admitted that he had not even examined the seal of the boot of the Penney's Torana. He accepted that if there were quite large holes in the body of the car which allowed air into the boot, then that would be an important factor to take into account, but he did not explain in what way.

He also accepted that as he had never seen the burned seal on the Penney's Torana boot, it would be 'basically impossible' to make a comparison with the seal on the model used in the 'experiment'.

On the topic of the wiring, the scientist agreed that as a matter of proper forensic procedure, it would have been important to examine all the wiring in the boot that could be a possible source of ignition. However, he had not examined it himself. He also agreed that it would be very important to examine the fuses as they could indicate that something was wrong with the car. He said that he did not have any basic knowledge of what the wiring system would be like in the boot of such a vehicle — his electrical expertise, he said, was 'pretty limited'. He agreed that an auto-electrician, or someone who has had a lot of experience in that field, would be needed to give some assistance on that.

Proper procedures not followed

The forensic scientist said that, in the world of forensic science generally, one of the most important things for the scientist is that all relevant data, information and exhibits are properly collected and stored before they go for examination. This is, he said, because one has to exclude the possibility of contamination — material from one item getting onto another item. It is also important, he said, for the chain-of-custody to be recorded so that one knows, from photographs for example or from markings, where those items were taken from.

He also agreed that it is very important to keep all relevant items and that it is not good practice to throw away a broken match found in a tin of methylated spirits 'if it's going to have a bearing on the proceedings'. As he said, 'I guess it's a fairly simple item to keep, yes'.[10]

He said in this case that it was fairly difficult to say whether it was an explosion or a rolling fire. He said that it was clear that at least some things had burned inside the boot, and there was something on the outside of the boot that had been on fire at some stage. However, he said, 'the exact course of events, for example, whether it was started by an explosion, or whether it was just a flame, I think is difficult to come to'.

> COUNSEL: Certainly one real possibility that exists is that petrol vapour in the car, in the boot, could have been set on fire by a spark from the electrical switch, the rear boot light switch?
> SCIENTIST: I think that is a possibility, yes.[11]

The rules of circumstantial evidence ignored

The forensic scientist was *the* expert witness for the prosecution. He readily accepted that a naturally occurring set of events (a spark from a switch) could well explain the sequence of events, and these events could have occurred without any human intervention. What he has said here means that, because this is a circumstantial case, subject to the rules explained earlier in the chapter, the case should have been ended at this point.

The judge, however, appeared to be of the view that unless the defence could *rule out* human agency, then the case should proceed. This seems to put the cart before the horse. The proper approach should be that unless the prosecution can rule out naturally occurring factors — that is, without human agency — then the case should not proceed. Up until the close of the prosecution case, it is not for the defence to prove anything. At that point, with a circumstantial case, as this was, the prosecution should have established that the facts on which it based its case were consistent with the guilt of Mr Penney — *and not with anything else*. Yet the prosecution witnesses agreed that the fire could well have been an accident. In those circumstances, it was, in our opinion, inappropriate for the judge to allow the case to proceed beyond the close of the prosecution case.

In this particular case, the original investigator had failed to examine crucial aspects of the scene, and the expert witness had not examined them at all. Yet, by getting together to tow a shell of a car up and down the road, they felt that they could provide the court with useful information which could lead to a conviction 'beyond reasonable doubt'.

Michael Penney convicted

Mr Penney was convicted by a majority verdict and sentenced to ten years' imprisonment.

He appealed to the Court of Criminal Appeal of South Australia, which included the Chief Justice. The appeal was dismissed.[12] His appeal to the High Court was refused.[13] This would appear to be one of those examples, such as those we discuss in Chapter 16, where a problem in the trial process was not picked up as part of the appellate process.

Although Michael Penney was sentenced to ten years' imprisonment, as far as he is concerned it might as well have been for life — as a convicted attempted murderer he is not allowed to know the whereabouts of his children.

CHAPTER FOURTEEN

JUSTICE FOR SOME OR FOR ALL?

PLEA-BARGAINING

Plea-bargaining is an important part of the criminal justice system and one that has aroused considerable controversy in South Australia. The DPP has said that by using such negotiation processes, the department has been able to ensure one of the shortest backlogs in Australia of criminal offences waiting to be dealt with. However, he said the arrangements that are reached in each case are based on justice, not expediency. He also said that although his prosecutors may each be dealing with as many as 100 cases at a time, any plea-bargaining reflects the evidence in the particular case and the charges which the prosecutor thinks are appropriate.[1]

Defence lawyers say that there would be little point in the DPP prosecuting on a more serious charge only to end in an acquittal. The argument in some of the cases in this chapter is that the prosecutor accepted a plea to a serious assault charge, instead of going ahead with a murder charge, because if he had proceeded on the more serious charge and was unsuccessful, then the person accused could walk free without any punishment.

In South Australia, the DPP has said that about 80 per cent of the total workload is dealt with by plea-bargaining.[2] Given that the average cost of a criminal trial in South Australia is about $10,000 per day, it is said to be in the interest of all if matters can be resolved without the necessity for a trial.

Generally, it would seem, plea-bargaining works satisfactorily, but cases such as those discussed here have caused considerable public concern. Some have said that there is no community involvement and that the way in which the process is conducted seems to lack justice. While victims have a right to an explanation afterwards, they have no say in the process and if they do not agree with the decision to drop or reduce the charges, they have no legal avenue to insist on the original charges proceeding.[3] It has been suggested that a community commissioner be appointed to represent the views of the public.[4] How this would work is not clear. What is clear, though, is that the way in which plea-bargaining has been used in South Australia has seriously eroded the community's confidence in the criminal justice system.

The difficulty with the cases in this chapter is that while the prosecutor said that lesser charges were accepted, because a prosecution for more serious charges may not succeed, there are those who think that his judgment in this respect was not correct. After looking at some of the more recent cases, we will discuss the review by the Solicitor-General of South Australia which examined some of the more contentious cases. It was that review which led to the resignation of the then Director of Public Prosecutions, Mr Paul Rofe QC.

Scott Aitken (January 2000)

Scott Aitken, 43, was driving his four-wheel-drive vehicle when it went over an embankment (a 27-metre drop) onto a freeway under construction, killing two of his four children.[5]

It was alleged that he had a container of petrol with him in the vehicle, and he was smoking a cigarette at the time of the incident, although he did not normally smoke. His daughter Hayley, 17, who survived the crash, said that she believed that he crashed the car deliberately and that he intended to kill himself and all his children. Her brother Hayden, 11, also survived. Lauren, 8, and Callum, 10, were killed in the crash. Aitken was originally charged with two counts of murder and two of attempted murder, which would have carried a possible sentence of life imprisonment upon conviction.

Mr Aitken's case never went to trial. Following negotiations between the DPP, Mr Rofe QC, and defence counsel, the charges were reduced to causing death by dangerous driving and grievous bodily harm. Mr Aitken pleaded guilty to those charges.

Mr Aitken had claimed that he had swerved to avoid a dog which had run across the road. A key witness was another member of Aitken's law firm who said that he had seen a dog in the area after the time of the crash.[6] Surprisingly, the witness did not come forward to give that evidence until some twelve months after the crash. He said that the delay in coming forward was on legal advice.

Mr Aitken was given a two-year suspended sentence with a one-year non-parole period. The sentence was suspended on condition that he enter into a two-year good behaviour bond. He was ordered to undertake 120 hours of community service and disqualified from driving for six years. He was able to continue his legal practice without interruption, although he did move with his firm from Adelaide to Sydney.

In an unusual move, the Coroner, who had commenced an inquiry before the initiation of the criminal proceedings, reopened his inquiry into the crash, after the criminal proceedings had been concluded. By law, the coronial inquiry is not allowed to continue while there are criminal proceedings pending. The Coroner received a report from an American crash expert (by email) regarding the circumstances of the crash. In his reconstruction of events however, the expert used a Ford Explorer. Aitken had been driving a Mitsubishi Pajero.[7] It has been argued that the performance capabilities of the two vehicles differ significantly.

The Coroner concluded that the circumstances were consistent with the crash resulting from an accident. Channel 7 *Today Tonight* subsequently broadcast a number of programs dealing with this matter.[8] Aitken's case was subsequently referred to the Solicitor-General for further consideration.

Andrew Priestly (December 2002)

Mr Priestley, aged 32, had been out drinking one night and hit a cyclist as he was driving home. He dragged the man for over 6 kilometres. He was originally charged with manslaughter, which carried a possible sentence of life imprisonment. Priestley said that he would plead guilty if the prosecution reduced the charge to one of death by dangerous driving, which they did. He was sentenced to four years' imprisonment, with a non-parole period of two years. The prosecution appealed against the sentence and, in December 2002, the Court of Criminal Appeal increased the sentence to six years and three months, and doubled the non-parole period to four years.[9]

Darren Schmidt (June 2003)

Mr Schmidt, 29, killed a young woman by shooting her in the head with a handgun. He disappeared from the scene and reappeared some days later in the company of his solicitor. He said that it was a horrible accident. He said he had the loaded gun in his apartment, and it went off accidentally when the woman was handing it to him. He was originally charged with murder, which carried a possible life sentence. He said that he would plead guilty if the prosecution reduced the charge to one of manslaughter, which they did. The prosecution and defence tendered an agreed statement of facts which said that it was accepted to be an accident, and that Schmidt, who was a member of one of the 'bikie gangs', was remorseful about what had happened. He was sentenced to three years and nine months, with a non-parole period of fifteen months. As he had already been in custody for twelve months, he only had another three months to serve.

According to the media report, the gun was never recovered, which was strange. Surely the accused would have known where the gun was and, if it had the young woman's fingerprints on it, then this would have provided important confirmation for his story. However, without the gun, there is only his word to substantiate the claim that it was an accident.[10]

Paul Nemer (July 2003)

Mr Nemer, aged 19, said he was telephoned by a female friend in the early hours of the morning one day in August 2001. She was calling from her mobile phone and sounded quite hysterical. She said that she and her girlfriend had been walking along the street after going to a nightclub and now she was scared that they were being stalked by a rapist and that she feared for her safety.[11] Nemer took a loaded gun from his house and went to find her. When he met up with the young women, both of them were fairly hysterical. They pointed in the direction of a white van. Nemer ran over to the van and fired his gun. It so happened that the driver was a Mr Williams who was a newspaper delivery-man going about his rounds. He had not noticed the girls walking along the road. He was shot in the face, with the bullet only narrowly missing his brain. He lost an eye, but not his life.

Nemer was initially charged with attempted murder but, in return for a guilty plea, the charge was subsequently reduced to one of endangering life. The DPP and defence counsel tendered an agreed statement of facts to the court, which included the recitals that Nemer was very distressed and remorseful about what had happened. He said that he only meant to fire in the general direction of the van, and that it had not been his intention to shoot the driver. The judge told Nemer, 'You must consider yourself very fortunate because the Director of Public Prosecutions has deemed to accept your pleas to a lesser charge'. He went on to say:

> If it had not been for your plea of guilty, I would have sentenced you to four years imprisonment. I take into account your plea, and I reduce the sentence to three years, three months imprisonment. I set a non-parole period of two years. I suspend the sentence upon you entering into a bond in the sum of $100 to be of good behaviour for three years, and during a period of two years, to be under the supervision of a community corrections officer.[12]

A bond differs from a fine in that the amount specified in the bond has to be paid only if the terms of the bond are broken. A suspended sentence does not have to be served, and a bond does not have to be paid, if the person continues to be of good behaviour for the specified period.

There was public outrage at what was perceived to be the very lenient sentence imposed upon Nemer.[13] He came from a wealthy family and there was much media debate about whether or not he was being treated more favourably than someone from less affluent circumstances would be. The DPP said that he would be reluctant to lodge an appeal because he accepted the sentence handed down and he took the view that an appeal would have no reasonable prospects of success. The Premier immediately announced that he would have the matter re-examined by the Solicitor-General, who would also advise the government on its ability to lodge an appeal against the ruling. The Solicitor-General found that there were in fact 'good grounds' for an appeal.[14]

One of the points raised in the appeal was that the psychiatric report on Nemer, although it had been lodged in court, was not brought to the attention of the judge by counsel. The account of the incident in this report was 'plainly inconsistent' with the statement of facts put before the judge.

A second point was that the gun which was handed in by Nemer was not the same one that was used in the assault. At least, it was said, the barrel on the gun handed in did not match the one that fired the bullet at Mr Williams.[15] This is important, for if the gun had been changed or adapted, it would indicate that the accused was not being straightforward with the authorities. No charges were brought with regard to firearms offences.

The Attorney-General took advice from the Solicitor-General who advised that the Attorney-General had the power to direct the DPP to lodge an appeal. The Attorney-General then instructed the DPP to appeal the matter on sentence. The appeal, although formally applied for by the DPP, was to be argued by the Solicitor-General. Just before the appeal was due to be heard, Nemer asked his legal counsel to bring a case for judicial review of the Attorney-General's decision. They argued that the DPP was statutorily independent and that any purported direction to him by the Attorney-General undermined his independence and was, therefore, an invalid exercise of power by the Attorney-General.

Three Supreme Court judges sat as the Full Court of the Supreme Court to hear the judicial review argument (a civil matter), and then in the same sitting, they sat as the Court of Criminal Appeal to hear the appeal against the sentence. Of the three Supreme Court judges, two thought that the judicial review argument should be rejected, and then they determined that the appeal against the sentence should be allowed. The suspension of Nemer's sentence was cancelled and he was required to serve a prison sentence of four years and nine months, with a 21-month non-parole period.

An application by Mr Nemer for special leave to appeal to the High Court was refused. The High Court said:

> We are not persuaded that it is arguable that there has been any miscarriage of justice in this matter or that it is in the interests of justice in the particular case, or more generally, that there be a grant of special leave in this matter.[16]

The Premier, Mr Rann, in commenting on the Nemer case, told the South Australian Parliament that this was 'an important outcome for justice in this state'. He went on to say, 'It maintains the accountability of the criminal justice system ultimately to this Parliament'.[17]

At least we now know where to look to for the answers to the questions raised by this book.

Parliamentary accountability

In April 2004 the Solicitor-General submitted to the Attorney-General a further report as part of the original request to advise on the Nemer case and associated issues in the process of plea-bargaining.[18] The Solicitor-General found that although 'Mr Rofe QC at all times acted in good faith and in accordance with what he believed to be his duty, overall the conduct of the prosecution of Mr Nemer was inept'. According to the Solicitor-General the prosecution case was 'overwhelming' and the 'error of the sentencing judge was contributed to by the confused submissions put by the DPP', submissions which were 'the product of his imperfect assessment of the prosecution case'. He found that it was 'inappropriate' for Mr Rofe not to have disputed the version of the facts put forward by the defence, and that Mr Rofe's reasons for not doing so were 'unpersuasive'. He said that the DPP had failed 'to properly record and confirm the terms of the arrangement' between the prosecution and the defence — neither Ms Powell QC nor Mr Rofe had made notes of their discussions. He further pointed out that the 'errors made by Mr Rofe QC might not have been made if he had properly conferred with other members of the prosecution team, and if he had meaningfully consulted the police and Mr Williams'.

The Solicitor-General also looked at the plea-bargaining in the case of Schmidt. He concluded that Schmidt 'was sentenced on a particularly favourable version appearing in the agreed facts'. Further, it was his view that 'the agreed facts were inconsistent with the evidence of Dr James [the pathologist]'. Again, there was 'no record on the file of the reasons for deciding that the public interest was better served by accepting a plea to manslaughter than by proceeding to trial on murder'.

The Solicitor-General made it clear in his report that prosecutors 'must serve the public interest and not any private, individual or sectional interest'. It is their duty 'to serve the public interest by acting fairly and to assist the court to reach a just resolution of the proceedings'.

He recommended a number of improvements in the prosecutorial practices in plea-bargaining, including more prescriptive requirements as to consultation with victims and police and the recording thereof, and a Statement of Facts to be provided to the sentencing judge.

In commenting on the Solicitor-General's report, the Premier said that he was 'seriously concerned' by it. 'There were very serious and scathing criticisms of the DPP', he said.[19]

On 3 May 2004, Mr Paul Rofe QC announced that he had resigned although there was still two years before his contract was due to end. He said that given the nature of the Solicitor-General's report, it was better for the office that he 'went now'.[20]

The Attorney-General told Parliament that in addition to his entitlements, Mr Rofe would 'be paid $188,068 [equivalent to nine months' salary], on account of his extensive period of service to the state, and the uncertainty of his health'.[21]

The Premier then announced that he would be looking for a new prosecutor — one who would be like Eliot Ness, the American crime fighter in the television series *The Untouchables* — a 'fearless prosecutor' who 'wants to knock off the bad guys and has a hide as tough as a rhinoceros'.[22]

PART

3

WHERE TO FROM HERE?

CHAPTER FIFTEEN

THIS IS NOT GOOD ENOUGH

RESPONSES TO MISCARRIAGES OF JUSTICE

The desired result of a criminal trial is that justice be done; that is, that the accused should receive a fair trial according to law. A miscarriage of justice occurs when there is a failure to achieve that result.[1] And every time there is a miscarriage of justice our legal system loses credibility as a finder of truth, and each of us may become that little bit more insecure. Each time it happens, the system can become weaker and more vulnerable unless the issues are tackled and resolved.

In this book we have looked at a range of cases that have occurred in South Australia over a number of years — cases which we believe, based on the issues that we have touched on, give cause for concern as to the justice of the outcome. These cases go back some 30 years and must lead us to wonder, 'Is this good enough?'

Our analysis of the cases in question shows that unreliable pathology evidence was significant in a proportion of them, and one must ask, 'Why is this so?' In 1993, in a paper entitled 'Is this the best we can do?', the Honourable Gordon Samuels

AC, QC, then a judge of the Court of Appeal, Supreme Court of New South Wales, said:

> In cases ... in which a conviction has been obtained in circumstances where it must be assumed that the jury were strongly influenced in their conclusion by scientific evidence which appeared to be beyond rebuttal, but later turns out to be seriously flawed, there are, plainly enough, two problems which call for solution. The first is how, and how quickly, can we establish that a miscarriage of justice has occurred and correct its consequences? The second is how do we prevent such a thing from happening?[2]

This, in our view, aptly describes the situation in South Australia. It raises the two questions with which this book is concerned. This chapter looks at the question, 'How, and how quickly, can we establish that a miscarriage of justice has occurred and correct its consequences?' We will do so particularly in relation to the cases involving pathology evidence.

The next chapter, addresses the question, 'How do we prevent such a thing from happening?'

As discussed earlier, the cases we are concerned about involving pathology cover some 30 years, and a common factor in them is the work of Dr Colin Manock. In these cases he was put forward as a person with substantial experience, and even as an expert witness who was highly qualified. Although his evidence did not go unchallenged — for example, in the Van Beelen case his position on time of death based on stomach contents was vigorously contested — this was often regarded as just the normal clash of opinion between experts. However, on a proper analysis, it can be seen that the problems went deeper than that.

It is possible that if the pathology and investigation procedures had been properly examined in the early 1970s, then the situations which later occurred in the Akritidis case, in the Niewdach and Ellis case, in the Highfold, Dixon and Marshall cases, in the Baby Deaths cases, and in the Keogh case in particular, might have been averted.

It is instructive to compare the situation with that of Dr Clift, a forensic biologist in the United Kingdom. At about the same time that concerns were beginning to be raised about pathology and investigation procedures in South Australia, similar issues were being raised about Dr Clift. Yet while Dr Clift was suspended and an inquiry was held into his work, no similar inquiries were conducted into the problems in South Australia.

Dr Alan Clift was an experienced biologist at a Home Office forensic science laboratory. He was a founder member of The Forensic Science Society (UK) and its treasurer. In 1977 he was suspended after a routine internal check and a case in which he was due to give evidence was suddenly dropped.[3] The Home Office asked the police to investigate. Their report went to the Director of Public Prosecutions, who decided to take no action. In 1979 Dr Clift was asked to provide comments on six of his cases. His replies were considered to be unsatisfactory.

Following another case in which Dr Clift's evidence was successfully challenged in court, the Home Office asked another forensic scientist to investigate. Margaret Pereira, a director of one of the Home Office forensic science laboratories, produced a report in November 1979. It concluded:

> In many ways Dr Clift's attitudes reflect those of the very early forensic scientists who saw their function as one of 'helping the police' and not as I believe a modern forensic scientist would see it (a) to assist police in their investigations and (b) to assist in the cause of justice in the courts.[4]

Ms Pereira said that it was incumbent on forensic scientists to be totally honest about their findings and not to edit them in a way that might be prejudicial to either the prosecution or the defence. Dr Clift, on the other hand, had said that police officers were the scientists' customers and that it was the view of some senior police officers that the job of the scientists was to find evidence which might contribute to police inquiries.

The most high profile of the cases which led to concerns about Dr Clift's work was that of Mr Preece, who had been convicted in the High Court in Edinburgh in June 1973 for the murder of Mrs Will. An important aspect of the evidence given by Dr Clift was based on his analysis of a stain containing semen found on the victim's underwear. He said it pointed to the killer being a person who was a blood group A secretor (as Preece was). A secretor is a person that secretes detectable levels of their ABO blood group substances in their bodily fluids, such as saliva, semen or vaginal secretions, and this allows their blood group to be identified. However, Dr Clift failed to mention that Mrs Will also had the same blood group and thus it was not possible to definitively determine that the blood grouping in the stain came from the semen.

In March 1981, the Scottish Secretary (equivalent to the Attorney-General in Australia) referred the Preece case to the Scottish Court of Criminal Appeal for review. The court spent four days re-examining the crucial forensic evidence. The court said that 'Dr Clift expressed his confident opinion that the donor of semen was an A secretor in a wholly misleading way'. The court also said that Clift did not disclose the victim's blood group, or possible secretor status, and that he knew that it was impossible for the defence to discover this for themselves.

Dr Clift's justification for the failure to disclose these important matters was that he took them into account in employing a theory, born of his own experience, in interpreting the results on mixed stains. That theory did not at the time, and it still does not, have support from any reputable scientific authority. The Lord Justice General said of Dr Clift:

> This was conduct on the part of an expert witness which demonstrated a complete misunderstanding of scientific witnesses in our courts and a lack of the essential qualities of accuracy and scientific objectivity which are normally to be taken for granted.[5]

The court reached the conclusion that Dr Clift was discredited as a scientist. The prosecution conceded as much. The judge went on to say: 'We are convinced, beyond all reasonable doubt, that no reasonable jury would have convicted once it had become clear ... that Dr Clift was discredited not only as a scientist but as a witness'.[6]

The court allowed Mr Preece's appeal and quashed his conviction. By that stage, he had been imprisoned for eight years for killing a woman that he said he had never met. He had lost his marriage, his home and his job.

The Ombudsman was critical of the time it took to review Mr Preece's case. He was also critical of the fact that there had not been a review of Dr Clift's cases when the issue of his incompetence was first raised. A senior civil servant at the time said that there was no onus on them to take the initiative to trawl through his cases.

There was, however, a subsequent inquiry that lasted two years and looked into 1500 cases in which Dr Clift had given evidence. Sixteen convicted people, including four serving life sentences, one of whom had been in prison for sixteen years, were to have their cases reopened because of serious doubts about the evidence of Dr Clift.

A Member of Parliament said that he found the whole thing very disturbing. Dr Clift, he said, had worked for the forensic service for 24 years and gave evidence in some 5000 cases.

There were at least two very important outcomes from the Preece inquiry as far as lawyers and expert witnesses were concerned. For expert witnesses (be they scientists or pathologists) it was made clear that everything relevant must be disclosed in their *written reports*, and that they should refer to the weakness as well as the strength of the evidence, whether asked or not. Their reports must be sufficiently comprehensive as to convey a fair understanding of the evidence.

As for lawyers, the important lesson to be learned is that they must carry out their function diligently and grapple with the scientific evidence. It is vital that they be alert to both what is said and what is *not* said. If lawyers fail to understand the importance and the consequences of the expert evidence, and fail to have it thoroughly tested, all sorts of injustices may follow for their clients.[7]

The Royal Commission into the Splatt case concluded in South Australia in 1984, only a few years after the Preece appeal in the United Kingdom. Like Preece, the Splatt Commission had significant outcomes for lawyers and expert witnesses. We have already referred to some of these outcomes (the proper role of expert witnesses, the proper role of lawyers) in the chapter on the criminal justice system, and they are quite similar to those of Preece. The ramifications of the Splatt Commission resulted in the formation of a single integrated Forensic Science Centre in Adelaide. The Commissioner's recommendations were adopted — checking of observations, good documentation and peer review — and in 1990 the scientific operations of the centre became the first non-United States laboratory to gain accreditation through the American Society of Crime Laboratory Directors — Laboratory Accreditation Board quality assurance program.

However, the Splatt inquiry was seen to be only about how forensic *science* was done, and the principles were not applied to forensic *pathology*. Thus, later, there was to be no checking of the autopsy observations in the Baby Deaths cases and no peer review of the interpretations of the observations. In the Keogh case, no pathologist other than Dr Manock had the chance to view the body of Anna Cheney and confirm his findings before it was cremated.

Another example that shows preparedness to tackle difficult cases and problems with witnesses involves the doctors, Professor Sir Roy Meadow and Dr Alan Williams in the United Kingdom. Dr Williams was the original pathologist in the case of Sally Clark. He initially diagnosed that Mrs Clark's first child died naturally of a lung infection. When her second child died, Dr Williams determined that the child had been killed. He then changed his mind regarding the first child, saying that it too had been killed. Mrs Clark was tried for double murder. Sir Roy Meadow, a professor of child health with some 25 years' experience, was called as an expert in child deaths. He gave persuasive evidence, as he had in the past, that given the statistics on such deaths, the deaths had to be murder. Mrs Clark was convicted and imprisoned.

However, she was subsequently released following an appeal in which it was demonstrated that Sir Roy Meadow was wrong and that his theory concerning the deaths was not supported by any scientific evidence. It was also established that Dr Williams did not disclose to the court evidence that the second child had a deadly bacterial infection and most likely died from natural causes. Sir Roy Meadow gave evidence in another baby death trial which resulted in the imprisonment of the mother, but she too was acquitted on appeal. He also provided an opinion in another case that resulted in a mother's second baby being taken from her at birth and adopted out because her first child had died in mysterious circumstances. He did this without any contact with the parents — they did not see him until he gave his evidence in court.[8]

The General Medical Council, which registers United Kingdom doctors, is reported to be investigating Sir Roy Meadow. Their Preliminary Procedures Committee has determined that the allegations against him, if proved, would raise a question of serious professional misconduct which would affect his fitness to practise.[9] It has also been reported that the British government is considering undertaking a review of all cases involving evidence from Sir Roy Meadow and from Dr Williams.[10]

The Criminal Cases Review Commission

In the period following the Preece appeal, there were a number of notorious cases in the United Kingdom in which there were concerns about the justice of the outcome. Some were cases relating to apparent terrorist activities. In 1991, after the overturning of the convictions in the cases of the Birmingham Six and the Guildford Four, the government set up a Royal Commission (The Runciman Commission) charged with examining the effectiveness of the criminal justice system in securing the conviction of the guilty and the acquittal of the innocent. One of the Commission's key recommendations was the creation of an independent body, the Criminal Cases Review Commission (CCRC), to take on the responsibilities to investigate alleged miscarriages of justice in England, Wales and Northern Ireland.[11]

The principal role of the CCRC is to review the convictions and sentences of those who claim to be victims of a miscarriage of justice, and to determine whether or not the cases brought before it should be referred back to the appropriate appeal court. The CCRC started casework at the beginning of April 1997. Since then it has reviewed allegations of some of the most serious miscarriages of justice going back to the 1950s. Prior to the formation of the CCRC, applications for the review of criminal convictions were made to the Home Secretary, who could refer cases to the Court of Appeal.

The Commission is a last resort. It cannot normally consider any case until it has been through the appeal system. This means that applicants should have already filled in a notice of appeal. If that appeal fails, or if leave to appeal is refused, the CCRC can become involved.

The task is to examine each case impartially and decide whether it would have a real possibility of succeeding if it were given a further hearing in an appeal court. Sometimes a decision can be reached based on the information given in the application form or other correspondence. More often, it may be necessary to call for further information or carry out an investigation. Some cases are dealt with entirely by members of the CCRC and caseworkers. If a case calls for special knowledge — for example, about engineering, medicine or video analysis — the CCRC can instruct an expert to examine the evidence and report on it. If the case depends on materials held by a public body, the CCRC can instruct that body to keep the materials safe and to allow the CCRC to inspect them.

The CCRC has no powers to carry out searches of premises, to check criminal records, to use police computers or to make an arrest. However, it can appoint an investigating officer, such as a senior police officer, who has those powers. By regular monitoring and review, it keeps strict control over whoever is appointed and how they conduct the investigation.

Once the investigations are complete, the CCRC informs the applicants of what it has learned so that they have an opportunity to comment before it makes its decision.

The CCRC's involvement in the matter ends once the case is referred back to the Court of Appeal. From that point it is up to the applicants and their legal representatives to present a persuasive case to convince the court. If an application is not referred to the court and more evidence is later uncovered, or a new line of argument appears, there is nothing to prevent a further application to the CCRC.

For a case to be referred to the Court of Appeal there must generally be evidence or arguments that were not considered at the original trial or appeal. Convictions and sentences are referred if the CCRC believes that there is a real possibility that they will be found to be unsafe or unsatisfactory. A high proportion of the applications involve only simple points of fact or law, and can be reviewed within a month or two. Where there are complex issues to investigate, the review may take a year or more. Final decisions about referrals are made by the Commission members, either singly, or in three-member committees.

The CCRC members include people with high-level experience in business, industry and government, as well as those with legal and forensic experience. It is of particular interest that one of the members has been David Jessel, the investigative reporter who is probably best known for his work since 1985 as the presenter of *Rough Justice* (BBC) and *Trial and Error* (Channel 4). Many of the cases featured in his programs have been referred to the Court of Appeal, with the result that convictions have been set aside.

The necessity of having a body such as the CCRC as part of the criminal justice system can be seen from the fact that 64 of the first 94 cases the Commission referred to the Court of Appeal for reconsideration were upheld as constituting miscarriages of justice. There have been four cases where those convicted were hanged after conviction, but have subsequently had their convictions overturned. In the first two years, more than 4000 applications were made to the CCRC for it to consider. By the end of the third year of operation, some two thirds of the cases referred back to the courts were found to be miscarriages of justice.

The following is a small selection of cases that have been overturned by the United Kingdom Court of Appeal through this process. They indicate the sorts of reasons that have resulted in convictions being quashed. What is interesting is that they reflect the types of issues which are raised by the South Australian cases discussed in this book.

Mahmood Mattan was convicted of murder in 1952 and was hanged. After a reference by the CCRC, the conviction was quashed by the Court of Appeal in 1998. The judges ruled that the conviction was unsafe because the evidence of the main prosecution witness was unreliable. There was a serious concern that it was the witness and not Mattan who had committed the original offence.

Derek Bentley was 19 years old and educationally subnormal. In 1952 he was convicted of the murder of Constable Sidney Miles and was hanged. In 1993 the Queen granted a posthumous pardon to Bentley, limited to sentence. The CCRC referred the case to the Court of Appeal and the conviction was quashed in 1998. In his judgment, the Lord Chief Justice ruled that there had been a number of significant misdirections to the jury by the trial judge.

John Taylor was convicted of burglary and given a five-year sentence after a trial in 1962. The Court of Appeal quashed the conviction on the grounds that Taylor had been inadequately represented at the original trial.

Patrick Nicholls was convicted in 1975 of robbery and murder, and sentenced to life imprisonment. The Court of Appeal quashed the conviction on the basis of new pathology evidence which indicated that the 'victim' had died from natural causes.

John Kamara was convicted of the murder of the manager of a betting shop which occurred in 1981. A Home Office review of his case, conducted with the assistance of the police, failed to discover any new evidence. The case was transferred to the CCRC and during their review it was discovered that 201 documents, some of which could have been used by defence counsel at the trial, had not been disclosed by the prosecution. Additionally, some of the volunteers on the identity parade at which Kamara was picked out provided new evidence which suggested that the process had been deeply flawed. Following a three-day hearing, the Court of Appeal allowed the appeal in 2000, declaring that it had been a 'difficult, worrying and complex' case.

Trevor Campbell was convicted in 1985 of murder and sentenced to life imprisonment. The Court of Appeal ruled that the conviction was unsafe on the basis that the trial jury was required to make a choice between the credibility of evidence given by Campbell and that given by three police officers. The jury had been unaware of matters which cast severe doubt on the honesty and professional integrity of those officers.

Danny McNamee was convicted in 1987 of conspiracy to cause explosions. The prosecution case linked McNamee by fingerprints to caches of IRA arms and explosives, to an explosion in Hyde Park in 1982 and to a bomb found in London in 1983. The case was eventually transferred to the CCRC which referred it to the Court of Appeal. The conviction was quashed in 1998, the court ruling that the verdict was unsafe because there had been a failure to disclose relevant evidence, even though the impact of the fresh evidence was not conclusive.

Michael O'Brien, Ellis Sherwood and Darren Hall were convicted in 1988 of murder and robbery. All three were sentenced to life imprisonment for the murder, with additional custody for the robbery. In 1999 the Court of Appeal ruled that the convictions were unsafe and overturned them. At the trial, Hall had given evidence that implicated all three men. The Court of Appeal was satisfied that a jury might have taken a different view of the reliability of Hall's evidence if they had heard the new medical evidence and the unsatisfactory way in which the police interviews were conducted.

Mary Druhan was convicted in 1989 of the murders of two men who died in a fire at a house used by squatters. She was sentenced to life imprisonment for each count, to run concurrently. The case was passed to the CCRC in 1997 and referred to the Court of Appeal in 1998. The convictions were quashed because the evidence of a main prosecution witness was unreliable.

Our legal system

The English trial system enjoys an enviable reputation for integrity and fairness and it has even been said that this system of justice is the finest in the world.[12] However, the situation we have just described regarding the CCRC would suggest that the system has had significant problems, particularly with regard to criminal matters involving expert witnesses. The Australian legal system is based closely on that of England and Wales so it could also be expected to suffer from many of the same difficulties. Many authors have considered this matter.[13] Many feel that the problems stem from the adversarial (or accusatorial) nature of the system, and that justice would be better served in an inquisitorial legal system.[14]

The inquisitorial or 'civil' systems of law are based on Roman law and tend to be used in one form or another by continental European countries (and are therefore sometimes referred to as 'Continental' systems). In contrast, the adversarial system of English law with its jury is a more recent invention, going back only 300 years or so.[15]

It is argued that an inquisitorial system is more appropriate in determining the *truth* in matters involving scientific evidence. This may well be so; an adversarial trial is not a pursuit of truth in the fullest sense.[16] This in part is because it asks a very limited question; it asks, for example, '*Did* this particular person murder this other person?' While it is a practical inquiry into truth, it inquires only into the truth of particular facets of a whole problem. An inquisitorial system asks the more general question, '*Who* murdered the person?' This is not an unfamiliar approach in Australia as this type of inquiry already operates in the Coroner's Court, where it seems to work well. Professional conduct tribunals and medical boards have similar powers. Royal Commissions are also of this nature. Inquiries of this type in cases such as Chamberlain and Splatt (in which the case effectively has been retried) have proved their worth.

A survey of the ministries of justice and/or leading newspapers in eleven countries of Western Europe, all of which operate some form of an inquisitorial legal system, found that none of these countries seemed to have frequent and ongoing campaigns concerning alleged miscarriages of justice. The survey arose out of a concern that these seemed to be a recurrent feature in Britain, even after the introduction of the CCRC.[17] Not only that, they seemed to be a feature too in other major countries which have an adversarial system. Australia has had high-profile and drawn out cases such as Chamberlain and Splatt. In Canada they have even formed an organization called the Association in Aid of the Wrongly Convicted.[18]

The advent of DNA typing has revealed many miscarriages of justice in the United States where a number of Innocence Projects have been formed to pursue this type of case. Between

1992 and March 2003, 124 people were exonerated in this way.[19] Similar groups in Canada have also achieved exonerations. Innocence Projects are run in Australia by Griffith University Law School in Queensland, Newcastle University Law School and the University of Technology in Sydney.[20]

The French inquisitorial system is seen by some to have particular advantages.[21] However, to radically change a fundamental and entrenched system such as that of the criminal law in Australia in that direction would be no easy task. No one state on its own could make the change and much discussion and debate would be necessary. It would not happen overnight. In the meantime, we need remedies that work sooner rather than later, and to that end it would be better to adapt rather than adopt. Some ideas for this are explored in the next chapter, but first the miscarriages which we believe already exist in South Australia must be properly and fully examined.

The problems in South Australia

In many of the cases we have looked at, the science did not and does not support the conclusions. In the pathology cases using Dr Manock's evidence, Dr Manock *did* support the conclusions. In a number of instances, however, Dr Manock's theories were not in accordance with the scientific literature, nor, as some say, would they be held by other people professionally engaged in these areas of scientific interest.[22] His calculations of the time of death in the Van Beelen and Szach cases, the cause of death in the Baby Deaths cases and his scenario of the death in the Keogh case are some examples. As the Preece case shows, one cannot have scientific theories that exist just on the basis of one person's say-so.

In the Baby Deaths inquest, the Coroner accepted that Dr Manock had seen things which could not have been seen and that his answers to some of the questions were 'spurious'.

Without any independent witnesses and without any photographs in some of the cases, it may have been inappropriate to accept Dr Manock's explanations of what he saw. Yet the Director of Public Prosecutions could still not see that there was something fundamentally wrong with Dr Manock's continued involvement in the Keogh case. He said that the criticisms by the Coroner in the Baby Deaths inquest only related to Dr Manock's shortcomings in respect of baby deaths, for which special skills are required.[23] Yet Dr Tony Thomas has stated that the errors that occurred there, such as the interpretation of X-rays, bruising or bronchopneumonia, were not matters which required any special paediatric skills.

> VOICE OVER ATTORNEY-GENERAL: The Coroner did not find Dr Manock incompetent to conduct adult autopsies.
> GRAHAM ARCHER: Correct? Totally wrong. While the subjects were babies Manock failed to diagnose injury and infection common in both infants and adults. No specialised skills were required for that?
> DR TONY THOMAS: Not in that particular context — of the interpretation of bronchopneumonia or even as I said fractured bones which one would expect a forensic pathologist to deal with in adults as well as in children.[24]

A Melbourne QC has commented that the Baby Deaths inquest was like the thirteenth chime of the crazy clock — it should have brought into question 'all prior utterances'. The DPP acknowledged in a television interview that he had confidence in Dr Manock in the Keogh case because Dr Manock had done some 9000 previous autopsies.[25] But as Rohan Wenn said in the interview (and the DPP accepted), just because you do a job often, doesn't necessarily mean that you are doing it well. In this analogy, it could be said the 9000 autopsy reports might be the equivalent of '9000 prior utterances'. We take the view that the Baby Deaths cases alone should have justified a serious inquiry into Dr Manock's other cases. However, we can now see that *all* of the cases which we have looked at in this book give rise to concerns that need to be addressed

Serious inquiries are therefore warranted. To be effective, two inquiries are needed and they must be established promptly.

The first inquiry should be set up to investigate whether the verdict in the Keogh case is safe and satisfactory. Of all the cases mentioned in this book, he is the only person who is still — perhaps inappropriately — currently serving a prison sentence.

The second inquiry, with the scope and powers of a Royal Commission, should examine the cases that we have discussed in this book. The inquiry must look not only at those particular cases we have raised, but also at the systemic problems which they represent and at the criminal justice system itself.

We can appreciate that the task of reviewing a considerable number of cases will be neither easy nor pleasant. It will reawaken interest in some of the most sordid aspects of our social history. It will bring great pain to the families and friends of those who have been caught up in those cases. The financial cost, as well as the social cost, will be considerable. It will take up money, time and expertise which could well be spent on current investigations and trials, or on other pressing social needs such as health and education. But this must not deter people. If the health of our criminal justice system is to be restored, it is imperative that it is known if there are yet more problems to be resolved.

Each inquiry's investigations must be followed by corrective action. Just knowing is not enough — we have to be prepared to make the hard decisions.

CHAPTER SIXTEEN

WE CAN'T FACE THE FUTURE IF WE CAN'T FACE THE TRUTH

We now come to examine our second question: how to prevent the type of miscarriages of justice discussed in this book from occurring in the future. To do this, there needs to be a review of past cases and an analysis of what was done, what went wrong and why it happened that way. If those factors can be understood, then, provided there is the will, we can all change and improve our situation.

Review the failures to implement current procedures
Any review should be focussed on the real issues of reform. It might be tempting to imagine that some new procedural code to fix the problems could just be implemented. The danger, though, is that this code too could be ignored. Therefore, it must first be determined why the procedures that are already in place have not been fully implemented. There must be a way to ensure that the current safeguards and procedures are adhered to before extending their range.

In order to do that, the current institutional safeguards will have to be scrutinised, and an attempt made to determine why and how they have failed to work. This will require an examination of the role of prosecution and defence lawyers, of judges at both the trial and appellate levels, and the Coroner's Office. It was their job to ensure that the current procedures were properly adhered to. The awkward questions will have to be asked — and answered.

In the cases that we have looked at, a number of coronial and judicial hearings have accepted evidence that is deficient. In the Perry case, for example, why did the South Australian judges not reveal the problems with the evidence when the case was first taken to the Court of Criminal Appeal in South Australia? As one of the High Court judges said, parts of the scientific evidence revealed an appalling departure from proper standards. It should not have been left to the High Court of Australia to expose the true state of affairs. How can that be properly explained? And why was insufficient action taken about it even after the comments by some of the High Court judges?

Questions now need to be asked about why the situation of the Baby Deaths cases was allowed to develop and how was it that the criticisms of Dr Manock revealed in the inquest were not brought to the attention of the jury in the Keogh trial? Why was Dr Manock allowed to conduct the autopsy in the Keogh case, and why was disposal of the body permitted without his work being properly checked?

In tackling some of these problems it could well be useful to look at the way court proceedings are conducted in South Australia. Perhaps changes in the way expert witnesses are handled and scientific evidence is processed, or the way in which the court and the jury interact, could be beneficial.

THE DANGERS OF ASSUMPTIONS

We have referred to the danger of making *assumptions*, and examples of errors caused by assumptions are provided in some of the cases we have discussed. For example, as Robertson points out in his discussion of the Splatt Commission:

> Shannon found that many things had gone wrong in the case. Some of these included: tunnel vision on the part of the police, the investigation quickly focussed on Splatt, and other possible scenarios were not taken seriously.[1]

Another example was the Highfold case where the investigating police officer did not even look at the body. He and the other officers seem to have assumed that the cause of death was 'not suspicious' and did not seriously examine alternative explanations. They merely set out to substantiate the explanation which appeared to be the most obvious. In the Akritidis case, there was no questioning of what had happened. Everyone seemed to assume from the time of finding the body that Akritidis had committed suicide. Indeed, the Deputy Coroner even commented in his Finding about the 'assumptions' which had been made at the autopsy. But it is the pathologists who should be alert to the perils of assumptions and should be working to provide objective scientific evidence. Yet in the Keogh case, Dr Manock assumed that Anna Cheney was murdered ('I was at no time looking or thinking that the death was accidental') and did not explore other possibilities such as an anaphylactic reaction.

The Office of the Director of Public Prosecutions

In South Australia the role of the Director of Public Prosecutions has come under increasing scrutiny, largely as a result of the plea-bargaining cases that we discussed in Chapter 14, and which caused a public outcry in the media. These cases brought condemnation from the Premier of South Australia. Editorials in the *Advertiser* were strident in their criticism. One noted:

> People are rightly concerned. The legal fraternity can send up smoke screens fuelled by academic arguments but the inescapable, bedrock conclusion is that, in the Nemer case, the legal system has failed.[2]

Another said, 'It also prompts questions about confidence in the office of the DPP and Mr Rofe himself'.[3] Another claimed that 'the Nemer case, without any shadow of a doubt, has eroded the public's confidence in the justice system to such an extent that Mr Rofe's position is untenable'.[4]

In addition to the plea-bargaining issues, there has also been concern that in 2001 and 2002, the South Australian DPP's office had the highest number of dropped prosecutions in the country with 23.4 per cent, almost double the national average. These are cases in which people have been charged but then the DPP has decided not to proceed with a prosecution because in his view there was 'no reasonable prospect of conviction'. Mr Borick QC has queried if this was because there was something wrong with the investigations, or something wrong with the evaluations of those investigations, that led to the charges being laid in the first place.[5]

When assessing the suitability of evidence for prosecutions, a number of issues need to be considered. Did the police secure the scene and ensure that the evidence was not contaminated or destroyed? Have they provided the best possible evidence of what occurred (the 'best evidence' rule)? Are there other possible explanations? To assess the adequacy of any police investigation, it is essential to refer to the police forensic procedures manual. However, in a televised interview relating to the Keogh case, Mr Rofe revealed that he did not know of the existence of such a manual:[6]

> ROHAN WENN: The next and more critical breakdown in procedures occurred with the autopsy. Dr Manock was the only pathologist to examine the body. It's a breach that is further amplified by this amazing admission from our DPP when questioned by *Today Tonight*.
>
> Was it unfortunate that Manock was the only one to see the body?
> MR ROFE: No, as I said that was the established procedure at the time, in my experience.
> ROHAN WENN: But it goes against the Police Forensic Guidelines?
> MR ROFE: Well I haven't seen those, and I'm not aware of them.
> ROHAN WENN: Well, here they are. Paul Rofe later called us to say that no one has heard of the Police Forensic Guidelines. But when we offered to send him our copy, he declined.[7]

If he (as the DPP) did not know about the procedures, about what *ought* to be done, then the system of checks and balances cannot be expected to work properly.

ANYTHING NEW

In the televised interview, Mr Rofe said he would look at anything new with regard to the adequacy of a conviction. He admitted during the interview that there were many things that the interviewer was putting to him about the Keogh case which were new to him. He acknowledged that he had been unaware of them, or that they had not been brought to his attention before. However, on being asked about them, he was able to determine immediately that they were 'not of concern' to him and did not require any further examination or consideration. He said that this was because there *could be* 'innocent explanations' for such things. Just as there could be innocent explanations for other things in the case.

It is, of course, correct to say that an injection mark or bee sting *could* provide an innocent explanation for the cause of death of Anna Cheney. However, if that were so, it would mean that Keogh should not have been charged, let alone convicted.

However, by saying that there *could be* 'innocent explanations', Mr Rofe indicated that the correct explanation is still in doubt. This means that there could also be explanations which are not so innocent and which had not been ruled out. If that were so, then it is still possible that others may have been involved. After all, if someone had been to the house while Keogh was away that night, and drove Anna's car away, it is *possible* that they could have done other things before they left. For someone to have been sentenced to a minimum of 25 years' imprisonment, as Keogh has, one would have thought that any outstanding 'could be' would have been resolved. If this has not been done, then we are still left with reasonable doubt. And the presumption of innocence prevails unless guilt can be proven *beyond* reasonable doubt.

THE ROLE OF THE PROSECUTION

It is the role of the prosecution to *determine the truth*, rather than just to obtain a conviction. We argue, therefore, as Mr Borick QC has done for many years, that it is the duty of the prosecution to examine all reasonable alternatives to guilt. How can guilt be established beyond reasonable doubt if reasonable doubts are not even examined? This was the situation that occurred in the Penney case, for example, in relation to the examination of the wiring, the boot light switch or a possible spark from the muffler.

Determining the truth implies that the prosecution will fulfil its duty of informing the defence lawyers of any doubts which arise during the investigation. For example, in our view it is not acceptable that the defence lawyers in the Van Beelen case only learned at a social function, some time after the trials, that someone had 'confessed' to the crime.

United States Supreme Court decisions hold that the prosecuting authorities cannot constitutionally withhold evidence that is exculpatory or favourable to the accused.[8] In Canada, the role of the prosecutor specifically excludes any notion of winning or losing; it is made clear that the purpose of a criminal prosecution is not to obtain a conviction, but rather it is the duty of the prosecutor to present credible evidence, firmly but fairly.[9] In Australia the duty of the prosecutor has been defined succinctly as follows:

> The duty of the prosecutor, as I see it, is to present to the Tribunal a precisely formulated case for the Crown against the accused and call evidence in support of it ... I consider it the duty of prosecuting counsel to assist the defence in every way.[10]

The South Australian Solicitor-General, Chris Kourakis QC, has more recently stated the duty of the prosecutor as follows:

> ... the prosecutorial duty [is] to serve the public interest by acting fairly and to assist the court to reach a just resolution of the proceedings. Transparency in and accountability for the conduct of prosecutions are necessary elements in maintaining public confidence in the discharge of that duty.[11]

Given the cases we have discussed in this book, there is clearly much more that could be done in pursuit of that standard.

It is important that prosecutors ensure that all relevant evidence and information has not only been collected, but also preserved. The match was thrown away in the Penney case. Clothing went missing in the Dixon and Akritidis cases; and both clothing and medical files went missing in the

Highfold case. Temperatures were not taken in the Baby Deaths cases, nor in the Van Beelen, Akritidis, Dixon, Highfold, Niewdach and Ellis and Keogh cases, even though a forensic pathologist was present in some cases or at least always on call. Photographs, or at least *sufficient and suitable* photographs, were not taken in Akritidis, Highfold and Keogh. The 'wet patch' on the body of Warren on a hot day in the middle of nowhere was not sampled. If even a small sample of Anna Cheney's blood had been retained, tests could now be undertaken to establish conclusively the presence or absence of the anaphylactic reaction that may have occurred. The role of prosecutors in ensuring that evidence is preserved must be reassessed.

De-institutionalise prosecutions and scientific support

We also take the view that the existing situation, which is that much of the scientific, technical and prosecutorial work is essentially done by publicly funded departments, must be re-examined.

We see no reason why the work of prosecutions should necessarily be restricted to lawyers employed by a publicly funded department. Private sector lawyers now undertake much of the work previously undertaken by the federal Attorney-General's office, for example. In South Australia we already have systems of independent legal chambers where lawyers with ability could be found to undertake the work of prosecutions.

There are obvious advantages in having a system in which all lawyers are able to prosecute as well as defend. It would discourage the 'us and them' attitudes. It could help generate an understanding of the problems and difficulties of each side. It could contribute to better understanding and relationships between police and lawyers. Further, it would give all lawyers better access to and understanding of the expert witnesses and their evidence.

Capable and independent forensic science specialists should be encouraged to compete for the work of the police. Independent forensic science services such as Forensic Alliance Ltd, for example, have achieved this in the United Kingdom. However, because of the infrastructure costs involved, in Australia something like this would need to be organised on a national basis.

There is a need to ensure that forensic science services are impartial and transparent in all their operations. We see no reason why those engaged in scientific work should not be required to service both prosecution and defence clients. Having to work on both sides might well encourage a more sensible and balanced view of things.[12] The normal rules concerning conflict of interest could work to prevent the same individual or organisation from having multiple involvements in the same issue or case. There should be no impossibility or impropriety in two experts of an independent forensic service adopting different views about some forensic science problem.[13] All forensic science and forensic pathology organisations must involve themselves in external peer review.

The conduct of trials

We have already alluded to the fact that the adversarial nature of our legal system can be the cause of some of the problems that are arising. The confrontational approach of the trial process makes it less easy for a witness to concede a point, as it can be seen as weakening their credibility.[14] This sometimes makes it harder to determine the truth and may even mislead the court.

THE JURY

We do not want there to be any suggestion that the responsibility for any of the alleged miscarriages of justice that we refer to in this book can be attributed to the juries which convicted the accused. They could make their decisions only on the facts and information the court provided them.

Equally, one cannot generally lay the blame with any of the specific individuals or lawyers involved. Without knowing more details about the instructions they were given, or the constraints under which they were working, one cannot attribute individual blame for any perceived shortcomings without further and proper inquiry. Natural justice also requires that before adverse judgments are made about a person's conduct, that person has the right to be fully informed about the nature of the concern, and the right to give a full response to the issues that have been raised. The failure to adhere to this simple requirement has itself been the cause of much injustice in South Australia over the years.

We believe that the jury is a useful and valuable aspect of the trial process because it represents the community. Trial by jury ensures that the criminal law will conform to the ordinary person's idea of what is fair and just.[15] We appreciate, however, that their job is not an easy one. There have been moves to assist them in their task — practicalities such as providing adequate numbers of photographs and copies of documents, and also projectors and display screens for viewing exhibits and witness demonstrations are basic but important issues. However, there are more fundamental things about the process of the courts that could be done to assist.

In long and complex trials it may be helpful to change the practice whereby the prosecution presents its entire case first and then the defence follows. Rather, the evidence could be presented by topic: for example, the prosecution would put their pathology evidence, it would be cross-examined in the normal way, then the defence would call their pathology evidence for examination and cross-examination. The next topic, say, document examination, would then be dealt with in the same way, and so on. An advantage of this approach would be that it brings together for the jury at the one time all aspects of a complex topic, yet still retains the adversarial nature of the proceedings. In conjunction with this, one might expect the experts to confer or to engage in a joint conference before the trial to settle or at least narrow the issues involved.[16] A more innovative approach would be to have the evidence presented, still by topic, but more in the form of a debate with the judge acting as chairman.[17] In a rational forum, one might think that the ability of the decision-makers (the jury members) to ask questions of the expert advisers would be no bad thing.

It could well be helpful to develop ways in which the jury could interact more with the witnesses and evidence presented. It can be seen from some of the cases that sometimes the evidence given by experts and investigators has missed the point or has been incomprehensible and confusing, as we saw, for example, in the Niewdach and Ellis case and in the Penney case. In situations such as this, in which for whatever reason 'the court does not rise in indignation' and 'opposing counsel does not retaliate with the obvious retort, nor ask the revealing, searching question'[18], the jury, by bringing their 'average commonsense to bear'[19] in asking questions, might get closer to the truth. It has traditionally been considered dangerous to encourage the jury to interact directly with witnesses and counsel. This is a phenomenon of the adversarial nature of the system. There is concern that the wrong sort of questions will be asked.[20] By changing to a more inquisitorial procedure, this concern could be addressed. There is of course the possibility that more interaction with the jurors during the course of the trial would enable them to expose to the court any misunderstandings under which they are labouring.

Even if jurors have doubts or concerns about the evidence, they are not allowed to do their own research to resolve them.

This is because they are only allowed to consider evidence which has been presented and tested in court. Judges go to great lengths to explain this to jurors. If a juror should choose to ignore those directions, then there is a great likelihood that the trial will be declared a mistrial and will have to start afresh, as happened in a case in New South Wales.[21]

It might be that in some instances the test of deciding between 'guilty' and 'not guilty' is too hard for the jury. We know from information published about the juror who spoke out in the Van Beelen case that this can be so. Several jurors in the Splatt case also voiced similar concerns in a newspaper article.[22] In some cases, a more appropriate verdict might be 'not proven', as is available in Scottish courts. The introduction of this verdict could provide useful feedback to the court and it can provide community comment on the standard of the investigation and the prosecution.

Such an option would have the additional benefit of avoiding the undesirable consequences in what are called the 'double jeopardy' cases. In present circumstances, once a person has been found not guilty, they can't be charged again for the crime that has been dealt with at that trial, even if further and compelling evidence is discovered. A not-proven verdict has the potential advantage of allowing another prosecution to proceed later if more evidence becomes available.

EXPERT WITNESSES

There is a particular onus on prosecution witnesses to be correct and fair. Because they give their evidence first, juries will tend to believe them. This is a natural reaction. It is especially so if the witness is prominent and works for the government. It is very important that such witnesses be cautious. It is easy for pseudo-science to pass as evidence in these circumstances because of the status that is accorded the witness.[23]

They are more likely to be believed than an independent expert who may well be better qualified but who may rarely work in that particular field.[24]

In 1972, the British judge Sir Roger Ormrod wrote:

> The one essential of all expert evidence is a frank statement by the expert of the limits of accuracy within which they are speaking, and a readiness to indicate, whether asked to or not, what their evidence does not prove or suggest as likely. Just as counsel is under an obligation to call the judge's attention to points of law which are against their case, so the expert should be under an obligation to make sure that the court does not, unwittingly, use their evidence without realising its scientific limitations.[25]

This is the position now confirmed and strengthened by the Preece inquiry in Scotland and the Splatt Commission in South Australia. To some extent it removes the expert witness from the extremes of the adversarial nature of the trial by emphasising their responsibility to the *court*, rather than to the party they were called by.

CROSS-EXAMINATION

Cross-examination is the means the legal system uses to test the validity of the evidence. It is a powerful technique and is relied upon to reveal the truth. It is generally considered to be effective, but lawyers are becoming increasingly aware of its limitations with regard to expert witnesses. It is of course essential for forensic experts to come to the correct conclusions in the first place. Medical evidence especially needs to be expressed with care and constraint. But it is not sufficient to trust that cross-examination or other experts will always, or even often, reveal errors.[26] The proper examination of an expert should explore their qualifications, knowledge and experience, the facts upon which their opinion is based and the logic of the arguments expressed in the opinion.[27] Some knowledge and reading in the subject by the lawyers involved is important, and there is an argument for a different approach in the training of law students in this regard. Nevertheless, to get an intelligent answer, one must ask an intelligent question.[28] This often requires the assistance of an expert with the necessary qualifications and experience, and the intellectual courage to risk upsetting colleagues.[29]

If not detected and corrected by cross-examination, mistaken or misleading expert evidence effectively reverses the onus of proof. It does not take long for the evidence to be given, but it may take many years for an accused to refute it.[30] It may even need a book like this to do so.

If cross-examination cannot be relied on to reveal problems with expert evidence, what can? Often it needs other experts in the particular field who read reports of the case or who have a particular interest in the outcome.[31] Trials may well be open to the public, but busy professional people do not have the time to sit through the proceedings to hear the parts of the evidence in which they may have some expertise and interest. A suggestion from the United States to overcome this problem is peer review facilitated by publication of expert testimony, or synopses of such testimony, in professional journals.[32] Judge Weinstein takes the view that 'If medical journals routinely published excerpts from scientific testimony, "rogue" scientists would quickly come to the attention of their peers and the legal profession'. Likewise, sound and correct evidence would be available which would be a valuable asset in the training of pathologists, scientists and lawyers.

Judges now make most of their judgments (explaining what they do and what they say about why they do it) available to the public on the internet. In South Australia reasons for sentencing are also available in this way. Why should the forensic scientists or pathologists be any different? What they say and do is done on behalf of the public and the public need to know more about this. Publication in professional journals (or on-line) would achieve this.

WHEN AND HOW TO INVOLVE THE EXPERT

A practical problem with our trial process is the effectiveness or otherwise of asking a forensic pathologist or scientific specialist to look at slides, photos or documents only shortly before they are to be called as a witness. Most complex cases require some period of assimilation and analysis. It may be that to do the job properly a specialist would need to look at the whole of the file, or at the full range of processes and issues involved. Yet in some cases, witnesses have not been asked to look at certain aspects of the case until they are in the witness box. If a period of reflection and reasoning is required, then it would make sense to give such expert witnesses prior notice of the questions which they will be required to address.[33] It is important that when the specialist is in the witness box they should be questioned in a manner which will bring out all of the significant aspects of the evidence. If the specialist is depending on a scientifically untrained lawyer to point them in the right direction, this might prove to be inadequate.

The examination and analysis of different procedures and processes takes time and involves particular skills and knowledge, and it involves some cost. However, the failure to pick up on errors early in the process can prove to be far more costly. Professionals must be allowed sufficient time to properly conduct a peer review process.

A national appeal court

In South Australia, unlike the other mainland states in Australia, it is the trial judges who collectively make up the Court of

Criminal Appeal. The Chief Justice of South Australia has recently stated that South Australia is not a large enough jurisdiction to be able to have a separate court of appeal.[34] This means that a person who is an appeal judge one day will be acting as trial judge the next. Given that all of the education, legal experience and job opportunities are invariably based on the one city of Adelaide, one can see the pressures that might lead to conformity. It is interesting also to note that, at present, all the judges of the Supreme Court of South Australia were educated at just one law school — Adelaide University.[35]

In contrast, in England the judges will be drawn from a more diverse background and range of educational experiences. The work of trial judges is also assessed by a separate court, the Court of Appeal. Appointments to the Court of Appeal in England are full-time appointments, which means these judges do not have to mix up their function at the Court of Appeal with the conduct of trials. They do not have to consider that if they overturn the decisions of some of their fellow judges today, those judges might overturn their decisions tomorrow. Also, in England the Court of Appeal is a national court. Appellate judges are selected from practising judges across all the towns and cities of England and Wales — not just from the equivalent of one small city, as Adelaide is. The United Kingdom judges have not spent the whole of their professional life in one city, where they may have practised as a lawyer for 20 years before becoming a judge, and then conducting both trials and appeals. They would also have had some time as a trial court judge, before being given the chance to sit on appeals.

We take the view that appeal court judges should not feel beholden in any way to those whose judgments are being appealed. One way in which this can be done would be for the appeal court in Australia to also work on a national basis. Each state and territory could appoint a judge to a national appeal court and have the appeals heard by any of the judges who are not from the state or territory of the decision being appealed. In this way the government could afford to have a permanent appeal court. This would lead to a more consistent set of legal principles, and would also overcome the problem of the smaller jurisdictions not having sufficient work to justify the establishment of a full-time appeal court.

COMPETITION FOR THE TOP JOBS
Likewise at the state level, jobs at the level of judges and magistrates should be filled by applicants from anywhere within the national boundary. It should be accepted that a lawyer couldn't expect to become a judge in the same town where they have been in practice. Otherwise there may be too many potential conflicts of interest. It is commendable that there has already been a move towards this sort of approach: magistrates' positions in South Australia and judicial officers of the Supreme Court in Victoria are now advertised for nationally.[36]

Perhaps it is time to introduce 'career judges' — people who train specifically to be a judge from the time of their graduation, and operate only as judges — as happens in civil law systems in the continental countries.[37]

The appeal system must be improved

We can see from the Keogh case that the appeal system is deficient. If after two appeals, a special leave application to the High Court and two petitions, the problems with the case have still not even been *addressed*, there must be something wrong with the system. And it is not as though Keogh is the first such case. The Splatt case, where problems with the trial were not addressed in the course of the appeal processes, is an earlier well-known example of a similar situation. In the Splatt case, however, these problems were recognised eventually by a commission, an inquiry established outside of the normal process, as seen in Chapter 1.

As a community we must accept that our criminal justice system is fallible, as all human systems are. Indeed, the law allows for the fact that a trial may miscarry for legal reasons, such as an error on the part of the judge or jury. The appeal process is designed to handle such errors. But trials will miscarry from time to time because of inadequacies in scientific evidence.[38] As we have shown, the appeal system cannot cope with these and therefore there should be some arrangement in place to address the problems quickly and effectively when they arise. The public should not have to rely on the efforts of a few people with faith in the innocence of the accused or the support and influence of the media, as in the case of Edward Splatt, to cause governments to address these situations. They occur, and a mechanism to resolve them should be part of our criminal justice system.

A PROPOSAL FOR A JUDICIAL REVIEW SYSTEM

It is apparent that the Criminal Cases Review Commission performs a useful and much needed addition to the criminal justice system in the United Kingdom. A sensible first step for Australia therefore would be the expeditious establishment of an equivalent — a judicial review system.

We envisage that an appropriate system would consist of three linked organizations.

A Judicial Review Inquiry (JRI) would be the first stage in the reinvestigation of alleged miscarriages of justice. It would have the power to require people to attend interviews and to demand the attendance of witnesses and the production of documents. It must have the power to require witnesses to give evidence under oath. It should have the power to direct the retention of documents or evidence held by or on behalf of any public authority, and to commission independent reports by appropriate experts. It should have an independent chairperson who had no prior involvement in the legal system of the state or territory concerned, and a senior and experienced investigator with the powers of a senior police officer and subject to the direction of the JRI. It would only deal with alleged miscarriages of justice where the normal appeal procedures have been exhausted.

After the reinvestigation, the JRI would prepare a brief with the intention that it be put before a Judicial Review Commission (JRC). The mechanism for doing this would be to present the report to the legal representatives of the parties concerned. It would then be the representatives' decision to put the matter in the hands of the Commission if they so desired. In that eventuality, the JRI would then make a formal reference of the matter to the JRC.

The Commission would comprise three Supreme Court judges from outside the particular state. They would have the ability to examine all aspects of the case and to make a determination as to whether the verdict arrived at was reliable. They would not be hampered by the technical rules relating to whether or not matters arising constituted 'fresh evidence' as might be the case with an appeal.

The Commission would have the power to overturn convictions and to formally refer matters to a Judicial Review Tribunal (JRT) to determine the matter of compensation for those who have been victims of miscarriages of justice. These matters would be determined in accordance with the normal principles of compensation.

We are aware that to establish and operate such a system will require legislation and funding, but these practicalities shouldn't be allowed to delay proceeding with this initiative.

The need should be apparent to all. Eventually, this review system should operate on a national basis. However, South Australians may not want to wait for that to happen, and so South Australia could set up the system and become a model for the rest of the country. The judicial review system would reconsider the type of cases that have been looked at in this book, thereby helping restore public confidence in our criminal justice system.

On several occasions we have referred to the importance of an effective system of peer review in the context of forensic science and forensic pathology. If peer review is suitable to scientists, then it should also be suitable for lawyers and judges, and a judicial review system such as the one we propose will provide that.

It would be appropriate at the same time to establish a Law Reform Institute in South Australia as called for by the Law Society.[39] As a body that would examine legal issues to ensure that the system reflected community values, it may well be a suitable vehicle through which some of the recommended changes could be implemented.

The legal and political issues

It is our understanding that the adequacy of the convictions referred to in this book has now become far more of a political issue than a legal issue. Yet the doctrine of the separation of powers means that these respective areas of activity should be examined separately. The judges should be looking to the legal principles and their fair and consistent application to all of the cases which come before them. The Attorney-General, as the senior law officer, should be looking to ensure that the relevant legal procedures have been properly applied. Of course, the Attorney-General is part of the government and has a political role to play. However, in seeking to advise the governor of the day on the adequacy or otherwise of convictions, the Attorney-General must put those political considerations to one side and ensure that the advice which is given is soundly based in law.

The issues we have raised are not about any one individual's performance. We deal with a much broader and more important question. It was neatly stated by Sally Neighbour at the conclusion of the *4 Corners* 'Expert Witness' program:

> What is clear is that there is much more in question than one man's competence. The much bigger question is how an entire system has let so many doubts go unresolved in so many cases for so many years.[40]

We take the view that we cannot adequately face the future if we cannot bring ourselves to face the truth.

Moving forward

The proper functioning of the criminal justice system is an essential safeguard for the liberty of each and every one of us. The cases we have discussed in this book give rise to significant areas of concern. Undoubtedly, the problems arise in part because the system is confrontational and designed to win. It is not directed at critical engagement designed to seek the truth. Some changes to the system are required.

But changes in approach are also required. Even though they represent different aspects of the system, police, prosecutors, defence counsel, forensic scientists and pathologists need to improve their attitude to teamwork and to begin working with a common goal of justice in each case.

The cornerstone of the criminal justice system is the principle that the search for truth is fundamental to the administration of justice. The focus must be on the truth, not on winning the case. Justice fails when the goal of winning a case unnecessarily eclipses the need to find the truth.[41] The aim is not merely justice in a single case for a single individual, but justice for all. Without the precepts of justice, the truth will not emerge. Without truth, justice cannot prevail.[42]

It must never be forgotten that money cannot compensate for the damage to the lives of people who have been convicted of crimes they did not commit.

To move forward, alliances of convenience must be replaced by critical engagement. There must be a proper culture of peer review. Peer review must operate at and between all levels of the justice system — police, pathologists, scientists, lawyers and judges must be subject to it as part of the way things are done.

Accountability must be assured, and it must be democratic. This will require a change of attitude and approach — but it can be done.

Provided there is a genuine desire for justice.

GLOSSARY

abdominal
>the stomach region of the body

ABO
>the ABO blood group substances are the determinants that define the ABO group of the blood (A, B, AB or O). About 80 per cent of the population secrete their blood group substances in their bodily fluids such as semen and saliva. These people are known as 'secretors'.

actus reus
>a completed physical act that forms the basis of a criminal offence

adrenaline
>a hormone produced in the adrenal glands. It is released into the bloodstream when faced with an emergency, shock or fear, and speeds up the heart rate and breathing to make the muscles work faster. It is used in the treatment of severe allergic reaction.

adversarial legal system
>the legal system practised in Australia, where each side puts its version of events to a jury by calling witnesses and taking them through their evidence by asking questions, with the witness's testimony being tested by the other side through cross-examination. In this system the role of the jury after hearing the evidence is to determine what the facts are. The judge acts as an umpire to ensure that both sides play by the rules.

algor mortis
>cooling of the body after death

allergen
> any substance which might produce an allergic reaction. An example is pollen, which may cause the allergic reaction of hay fever.

alveoli
> air cells of the lungs, attached to the bronchial tubes, like little branches of brocolli

ambient conditions
> surrounding conditions; e.g. temperature of the room, air or water near where a body was found

amphetamines
> drugs used as stimulants

anaphylactic shock
> a systemic or whole body reaction to the presence of an allergen in the bloodstream

aneurism
> a swelling like a small 'balloon' in an artery

angio-oedema
> swelling of the lips, tongue, neck and face

antibodies
> molecules which arise in response to the invasion of the body by foreign material such as bacteria, viruses and allergens. They work to destroy the foreign material and remove it from the system.

antigen
> a substance that stimulates the production of antibodies in the body

antihistamine
> blocks the effect of the histamine that has been released into the system in an allergic reaction

aorta
> the main artery of the body, conveying blood from the left ventricle of the heart to all of the body except the lungs

aortic arch
: also known as the isthmus, the bend of the large artery coming from the top of the heart and firmly fixed to the surrounding tissues of the body

arrhythmia
: an irregular heartbeat

artifactual bleeding/bruising
: bleeding/bruising caused during the procedures of an autopsy

asphyxiation
: suffocation

aspire
: inhale, breathe in

asystolic
: also known as straightline, where there is no heartbeat as shown on an electrocardiogram monitor that is recording electrical activity associated with the heartbeat

ATP
: adenosine triphosphate, a chemical that keeps muscles flexible. Its absence causes rigor mortis or stiffening in a dead body.

autopsy
: also known as post-mortem examination, post-mortem or PM, procedure of examining a dead body to determine the cause of death. *See also* hospital autopsy and forensic autopsy.

Birmingham Six
: one of the major IRA terrorist cases in the United Kingdom in which the convictions were overturned many years later

blood spattering
: provides information about the location and movements of a person during an attack

CCRC
: Criminal Cases Review Commission in the United Kingdom

chain-of-causation
 establishes the order of events leading to death

chain-of-evidence
 the complete and unbroken linking of all relevant evidence to the source from which it arises

Chamberlain case
 the famous Australian case in which a mother was convicted of murdering her baby while on a camping holiday near Uluru. She had claimed that a dingo had taken the baby. The conviction was subsequently overturned by a Royal Commission.

civil case
 an action between individuals, companies or public entities

committal hearing
 also known as the preliminary hearing, a hearing held to review the evidence against the accused and to satisfy the magistrate that there is a sufficient case to go for trial. The Magistrates Court is also referred to as the Local Court in some states.

contamination of scene
 the alteration or interference with the scene after a criminal event that makes reconstruction of the scene difficult

contamination/destruction of evidence
 see destruction/contamination of evidence

corticosteroids
 synthetic hormones, used to treat certain diseases. Examples are cortisone and dexamethasone.

CPR
 cardiopulmonary resuscitation

criminal case
 an action between the state on the one hand and an individual or group on the other

defence counsel
 the lawyer representing the accused person in court

defibrillator
: a machine used to apply an electric shock across the chest when fibrillation of the heart occurs

destruction/contamination of evidence
: evidence that has been lost, removed or transformed in some way as to make it unavailable or unusable

diagnostic reagent
: a chemical used in a series of reactions or tests to identify (diagnose) a medical condition

diatoms
: microscopic unicellular algae found in fresh and salt water

Dietrich principle
: the prosecution cannot proceed with a case if a person is unable to pay for their legal representation on serious criminal charges, and the State will not pay for their defence

double jeopardy
: where a person has been tried and acquitted of a criminal offence, they cannot subsequently be tried again for the same offence or any other offence arising principally from the same circumstances.

DPP
: Director of Public Prosecution

drowning
: *see* wet and dry drowning

dry drowning
: death where water has not reached the lungs while alive. This may happen when a spasm of the larynx, for example, blocks the passage of air (and hence water) into the lungs while the person is alive. *See also* wet drowning.

endocrine
: Relating to the edocrine gland or organ or their secretions in the body

entomology
: study of insects

epinephrine
> a biological chemical produced in the adrenal glands. It can dilate (expand) some blood vessels and can also increase the force and rate of contraction of the heart.

evidence-in-chief
> information provided by witnesses through their written statements made and signed before the trial and presented to the jury via questioning of the witnesses

exculpate
> tending to acquit, clear of a criminal charge

expert witness
> witness with credentials upon which their expertise is based who gives evidence about what they have seen (e.g. a pathologist reporting on observations at an autopsy), as well as providing an opinion on what inferences may be drawn from the facts as they are or may be established. The only type of witness allowed to give an opinion.

fibrillation
> caused when the heart muscle is twitching but not moving enough to pump blood

fibrin
> a highly insoluble protein which forms the structural network of a blood clot. It is formed from a soluble blood protein (fibrinogen) in the clotting process.

forensic autopsy
> differs from a hospital autopsy in that the forensic pathologist doesn't only look for disease, but also for signs of trauma, injury or foreign objects such as bullets, as well as clues to a suspect, to try to determine how and when the death occurred

forensic scientist
> a scientist who uses their science training for the investigation of crime

formalin
> an aqueous solution of formaldehyde which is used to harden and preserve tissues

Guildford Four
> another of the famous United Kingdom IRA terrorist cases where those convicted subsequently had their convictions overturned, many years later

haemoglobin
> an iron-containing substance that gives blood its red colour

haemolysis
> the breakdown of red blood cells, releasing free haemoglobin into the blood. This can be caused by drugs and infections, and also by dilution of the blood with water.

haemopoietic
> the making of blood cells

hand-up committal
> committal proceedings handled in written form involving an exchange of relevant statements and reports rather than the accused appearing in person before a magistrate

histamine
> a biological chemical formed in the mast cells in response to the presence of an allergen. Too much histamine will cause an allergic reaction. Antihistamine drugs can help control the amount of histamine and give relief in allergies such as hay fever.

histology
> the microscopic study of tissue

histopathology
> the study of minute changes in body tissue caused by disease

hives
> also known as urticaria, localised swelling involving itching caused by allergen exposure

hospital autopsy
> an internal examination of a body for disease to try to determine why the death occurred

hyper-peristalsis
> over-contraction of the muscles

hypostasis
see lividity

IgE
immunoglobulin E, antibodies arising as part of an allergic reaction

IMVS
Institute of Medical and Veterinary Science (Adelaide, SA)

inculpate
tending to prove guilt in relation to a criminal charge

inferior vena cava
one of the two veins discharging into the right auricle or chamber of the heart

inquisitorial legal system
the legal system practised in Europe, where the judges and magistrate take an active part in the investigations and the proceedings in court. Judges are entitled to engage actively in asking questions and in seeking the truth of what happened.

interstitial haemorrhage
haemorrhage (bleeding) which occurs in the small spaces between cells

intubation
see tracheotomy tube

ischaemic disease
damage caused by inadequate supply of blood

isthmus
see aortic arch

latent evidence
invisible evidence until it is enhanced in some way, e.g. fingerprints that cannot be seen until treated with powder or light

lividity
also known as livor mortis or hypostasis, the way in which the blood settles in the body after death — a valuable indicator of the timing and circumstances of death

livor mortis
see lividity

Locard's principle of interchange (or transference)
when a person commits a crime they leave at the scene something that was not there before, and carry away with them something that was not on them previously

mast cells
millions of cells found in the tissues lining the surfaces of the body in the skin, ears, lips, eyes, nose, mouth, lungs and intestines which attract IgE antibodies which react with allergens that enter the body

mens rea
an awareness that an act was unlawful and that the accused was aware of doing it

microtome
a machine used in pathology to cut very fine slices (or sections) of tissue to enable examination using a microscope

molecular biology
the study of the interaction of biological and biochemical molecules (such as DNA and proteins)

myocardial infarction
also know as heart attack, occurs where the muscle of the heart is irreversibly damaged due to a loss of blood supply

NATA
National Association of Testing Authorities, the body responsible for laboratory accreditation

neurone
nerve cell

neutrophil
a type of white blood cell that scavenges for bacteria and dead tissue

nomogram
graphical presentation of relations between quantities whereby

the value of one may be found by simple geometric construction from those of others. A nomogram may be used to relate times and body weights to help determine time of death.

odontology
the study of teeth

oedema
excess fluid dispersed in the tissues, occurring when the plasma separates from the rest of the blood under certain conditions and cannot be returned to the veins and arteries. Oedema can affect all organs and may give rise to swelling or a weal-like blister.

pericardium
the membrane surrounding the heart

physical evidence
anything physical in nature that can be seen by the naked eye; e.g. vehicles, buildings, fibres, footprints

plasma
a straw-coloured liquid that makes up approximately half the average adult's blood volume

plea-bargaining
an attempt to negotiate the lowest reasonable charges in return for a guilty plea

PM
see autopsy

post-mortem examination
see autopsy

prima facie
literally 'on the face of it', sufficient evidence to provide a reasonable prospect of securing a conviction should a case go to trial

pupate
a stage in the development of an insect when a larva becomes a pupa; a dormant or inactive phase

QC (Queen's Counsel)
a senior lawyer (barrister) who has received a commission to act for the State as recognition of their eminence. In more recent times and in some states they are known as SC (Senior Counsel).

renal arteries
blood vessels leading to the kidneys

rhinitis
a runny nose and sneezing caused by an allergic reaction

rigor mortis
stiffening of the muscles after death

RCPA
Royal College of Pathologists of Australasia

septal plane
area between tissue surfaces where blood may collect in bleeding

status epilepticus
a condition where epileptic convulsive fits occur in rapid succession without intervals of consciousness. It may terminate in death.

straightline
see asystolic

subarachnoid haemorrhage
bleeding under the arachnoid membrane which surrounds the brain

thoracic
relating to the thorax (chest), the part of the body between the neck and the abdomen. In humans it is enclosed by the ribs and contains the heart, lungs, etc. Vertebrae in this area of the spine are referred to as thoracic vertebrae, such as T3 or T4, for example.

thrombus
blood clot

tryptase
   an enzyme that is released from the mast cells at the same time as histamine during an anaphylactic reaction

toxicology
   the study of poisons and their effects. Used in forensic science to detect drugs and poisons.

trachea
   windpipe

tracheotomy tube
   also known as intubation, a hollow tube or needle inserted through an incision into the trachea below a blockage to allow air into the windpipe and hence to the lungs

ureter
   tube conducting urine from the kidney to the bladder

urticaria
   see hives

vagal inhibition
   a condition where the nervous system stops sending the electrical signals that keep the heart and lungs functioning.

variable wavelength light source
   a light source that can produce a range of different coloured visible light as well as infra-red and ultraviolet light. It can be useful in detecting fingerprints, for example, or stains of bodily fluids.

virtopsy
   created from 'virtual' and 'autopsy' to describe a virtual autopsy or an autopsy performed without dissecting the body, using computerised imaging and radiology technology

voir dire
   often called a 'trial within a trial', this is the hearing of argument about admissibility of evidence. The jury is sent out of the courtroom while such argument is heard by the judge and the jury is not informed what the issue was or what the judge's ruling was.

wet drowning
> when water has been taken into the system while the person was alive, and the water in the lungs and stomach has been carried into the bloodstream. *See also* dry drowning.

ENDNOTES

Introduction
1 The law and procedures are based on those in South Australia. Although the names may vary from one place to another, the basic procedures and issues we refer to are part of all common law systems.
2 'Expert Witness', *4 Corners*, television program, ABC TV, 22 October 2001. <http://www.abc.net.au/4corners/stories/s397448.htm>

Chapter 1
1 Information on this case is taken from the *Royal Commission Report concerning the conviction of Edward Charles Splatt* (1984), Government Printer, South Australia.
2 *Re: Request to advise on matter of Paul Nemer and associated issues.* Report to the Attorney-General, by Mr Chris Kourakis QC, Solicitor-General of South Australia, 7 April 2004, pp. 4, 29.
3 *Dietrich v. The Queen* [1992] HCA 57; (1992) 177 CLR 292 (13 November 1992).
4 The comments and quotes are taken from the *Royal Commission Report concerning the conviction of Edward Charles Splatt* (1984), Government Printer, South Australia, pp. 43–52.

Chapter 2
1 *The Times* (London), 19 July 2003.
2 S Kind & M Overman, *Science against crime*, Aldus, London, 1972, p. 23.
3 *South Australian Police Crime Scene and Forensic Procedures Manual*, General Order 8278, '5. Death', 1996.
4 B Bass & J Jefferson, *Death's Acre*, Time Warner Books, 2003, p. 185.

Chapter 3
1 JS Sexton & GR Hennigar, 'Forensic pathology — the hidden speciality: a survey of forensic pathology training available to medical students and residents', *Journal of Forensic Sciences*, vol. 24, 1979, pp. 275–81.
VJ DiMaio & D DiMaio, *Forensic pathology*, 2nd edn, CRC Press, Boca Raton, Florida, 2001, p. 547.

2 VD Plueckhahn, *Lectures on forensic medicine and pathology*, 5th edn, University of Melbourne, 1982, p. 118.
3 C Capper, 'The language of forensic medicine: the meaning of some terms employed', *Medicine, Science and the Law*, vol. 41, 2001, pp. 256–9.
4 MJ Thali, K Yen, W Schweitzer, WP Vock, C Boesch, C Ozdoba, G Schroth, M Ith, M Sonnenschein, T Doernhoefer, E Scheurer, T Plattner & R Dirnhofer, 'Virtopsy, a new imaging horizon in forensic pathology: virtual autopsy by postmortem multislice computed tomography (MSCT) and magnetic resonance imaging (MRI) — a feasibility study', *Journal of Forensic Sciences*, vol. 48, 2003, pp. 386–403.
5 AA Moenssens, RE Moses & FE Inbau, *Scientific evidence in criminal cases*, Foundation Press, New York, 1973, pp. 174–6, 212–21 (example of report).
6 VJ DiMaio & D DiMaio, *Forensic pathology*, 2nd edn, CRC Press, Boca Raton, Florida, 2001, p. 549.

Chapter 4

1 AJ Peabody, 'Diatoms and drowning — a review', *Medicine, Science and the Law*, vol. 20, 1980, pp. 254–61.
AJ Peabody, 'Diatoms in forensic science', *Journal of the Forensic Science Society*, vol. 17, 1977, pp. 81–7.
2 NI Hendrey, 'Diatoms and drowning — a review' (letter), *Medicine, Science and the Law*, vol. 20, 1980, p. 289.
3 VD Plueckhahn, *Lectures on forensic medicine and pathology*, 5th edn, University of Melbourne, 1982, p. 204.
4 FH Martini, *Fundamentals of anatomy and physiology*, 5th edn, Prentice-Hall, New Jersey, 2001, pp. 788–9.
5 JW Yunginger, DR Nelson, DL Squillace, RT Jones, KE Holley, BA Hyma, L Biedrzycki, KG Sweeney, WQ Sturner & LB Schwartz, 'Laboratory investigation of deaths due to anaphylaxis', *Journal of Forensic Sciences*, vol. 36, 1991, pp. 857–65.
6 See Martini, ref. 4.
7 Ibid.
C Delage & NS Irey, 'Anaphylactic deaths: a clinicopathological study of 43 cases', *Journal of Forensic Sciences*, vol. 17, 1972, pp. 525–40.
8 AT Bennett & KA Collins, 'An unusual case of anaphylaxis', *American Journal of Forensic Medicine and Pathology*, vol. 22, 2001, pp. 292–5.
9 Ibid.

10 LB Schwartz, DD Metcalfe, JS Miller, H Earl & T Sullivan, 'Tryptase levels as an indicator of mast-cell activation in systemic anaphylaxis and mastocytosis', *New England Journal of Medicine*, vol. 316, 1987, pp. 1622–6.
11 See Delage & Irey, ref. 7.
12 VW Weedn, 'Anaphylactic deaths', *Journal of Forensic Sciences*, vol. 33, 1988, pp. 1108–9.
B Randall, J Butts & JF Halsey, 'Elevated post-mortem tryptase in the absence of anaphylaxis', *Journal of Forensic Sciences*, vol. 40, 1995, pp. 208–11.
13 See Bennett & Collins, ref. 8.
14 See Schwartz *et al*, ref. 10.
15 See Yunginger *et al*, ref. 5.
16 RSH Pumphrey & IS Roberts, 'Postmortem findings after fatal anaphylactic reactions', *Journal of Clinical Pathology*, vol. 53, 2000, pp. 273–6.
17 VJ DiMaio & D DiMaio, *Forensic pathology*, 2nd edn, CRC Press, Boca Raton, Florida, 2001, pp. 28–30.
18 TK Marshall, 'The use of body temperature in estimating the time of death and its limitations', *Medicine, Science and the Law*, vol. 9, 1969, pp. 178–82, 184–5 (figures).
19 C Henssge, 'Death time estimation in case work: I. The rectal temperature time of death nomogram', *Forensic Science International*, vol. 38, 1988, pp. 209–36.
20 See Marshall, ref. 18.
21 University of Dundee, Forensic Medicine, <www.dundee.ac.uk/forensicmedicine/llb/timedeath.htm>
22 See DiMaio, ref. 17, pp. 21–5.
J Dix & M Graham, *Time of death, decomposition and identification: An atlas*, CRC Press, Boca Raton, Florida, 2000, pp. 4–6.
23 See Plueckhahn, ref. 3, p. 117.
24 See DiMaio, ref. 17, pp. 26–8.
See Dix & Graham, ref. pp. 2–4.
25 See DiMaio, ref. 17, pp. 26–8.
See also Dix & Graham, ref. 22, pp. 2–4.
26 See DiMaio, ref. 17, p. 37.
EF Rose, 'Factors influencing gastric emptying', *Journal of Forensic Sciences*, vol. 24, 1979, pp. 200–6.
27 See DiMaio, ref. 17, pp. 37–9.
See also Rose, ref. 26 above and Horowitz & Pounder, refs. 28 and 30 below.

TH Howells, T Khanam, L Kreel, Seymour, B Oliver & JAH Davies, 'Pharmacological emptying of the stomach with metoclopramide', *British Medical Journal*, vol. 2, 1970, pp. 558–60.

28 M Horowitz & DJ Pounder, 'Gastric emptying: forensic implications of current concepts', *Medicine, Science and the Law*, vol. 25, 1985, pp. 201–14.

29 FA Jaffe, 'Stomach contents and the time of death. Reexamination of a persistent question', *American Journal of Forensic Medicine and Pathology*, vol. 10, 1989, pp. 37–41.

30 M Horowitz & DJ Pounder, 'Is the stomach a useful forensic clock?', *Australian and New Zealand Journal of Medicine*, vol. 15, 1985, pp. 273–6.

Chapter 5

1 Statements by the Hon. Nick Xenophon and the Hon. Sandra Kanck to the South Australian Legislative Council, 31 October 2001.

2 'Expert Witness', *4 Corners*, television program, ABC TV, 22 October 2001. <http://www.abc.net.au/4corners/stories/s397448.htm>
During 2002 and the first six months of 2003, the Channel 7 *Today Tonight* television program (Adelaide) broadcast a series of eight programs dealing with these issues.

3 'Expert Witness', *4 Corners*, television program, ABC TV, 22 October 2001.

4 'Senior pathologist appeals over job', *The Advertiser*, 23 March 1978.

5 Trial transcript, *CH Manock v. State of South Australia and the Institute of Medical and Veterinary Science*, South Australian Supreme Court, 2355 of 1978, pp. 117–125.

6 'Judge rules on status of forensic director', *The Advertiser*, 8 June 1979.

7 'Forensic scientist claims "on call" pay', *The Advertiser*, 28 September 1979.

8 The details of this case are derived from *The Queen v. Van Beelen*, Supreme Court Appeal (1973) vol. 4 SASR 353 (in Banco) Bray CJ, Mitchell and Zelling JJ, and from Hawkins G, *Beyond Reasonable Doubt*, The Australian Broadcasting Commission, Sydney, 1977 pp. 79–104.

9 Transcript, first trial, p. 476. The judge also stated in his summing up at the second trial, that the only injury was the tear to the vagina caused after her death. (Transcript, second trial, p. 2816.)

10 See *The Queen v. Van Beelen,* ref. 8, at pp. 353–64.

11 For example, Dr Pocock, who gave evidence for the defence, made the following claims (references are to the second trial transcript pages):
With regard to the diatoms, Dr Manock should have checked for their presence in the liver, kidney and bone marrow, not just in the lungs, as they can get there without drowning, p. 2529.
Dr Manock was incorrect when he said that salt water makes the lungs contract. There is no evidence for this in the textbooks, p. 2530. The protein fluid in the lungs could have been caused by heart failure; therefore Dr Manock should have tested for drugs as a cause of death, which he did not do. If sea water had been there, the protein would not have been, p. 2531.
The body temperature and air and water temperature should always be taken when arriving at the scene and Dr Manock did not do that. The only exception is when the body is decomposed. A thermometer is quite cheap to buy, p. 2532.
The stomach contents had been frozen before detailed examination by Dr Manock, and this would have affected their composition, p. 2540.
While Dr Manock said that rigor mortis was consistent with death having occurred between 3.30 pm and 4.30 pm, he should have explained that it was also consistent with death occurring between 11 am and 11 pm, p. 2541.
Dr Manock said that hypostasis (lividity) showed that the body had not been moved, but it could have been moved before the hypostasis became established, which can take up to one to two hours after death, not 30 minutes as Dr Manock said, p. 2542.
Dr Manock said he had examined the internal organs microscopically, and had excluded other causes of death, but I don't see how he could exclude epilepsy, for example, p. 2554.

12 B Hailstone & B Whitington, 'The Taperoo Beach murder case 1: court was scientific battleground', *The Advertiser*, 18 February 1974.

13 Transcript, second trial, p. 2541.

14 'Expert Witness', *4 Corners*, television program, ABC TV, 22 October 2001.

15 M Horowitz & DJ Pounder, 'Gastric emptying: forensic implications of current concepts', *Medicine, Science and the Law*, vol. 25, 1985, pp. 201–214.
DJ Pounder, Report, 'Re opinions expressed by Dr Colin Manock in the Van Beelen case', 5 December 1986, 8 pages, plus CV in brief. Sent to Peter Womersley, Shelley & Partners, Solicitors, Adelaide.

16 Cross-examination at the trial concerning the death of Mrs Cooke (arising from an autopsy conducted on 14 April 1984), transcript p. 829.
See also Jessica Snyder Sachs, *The Time of Death*, Arrow Books, London 2003, p. 45. It was said in relation to experts called for the prosecution and defence in regard to the time of death of Nicole Brown Simpson (the OJ Simpson case) that, '… both experts had to admit that the quantity and quality of stomach contents had long ago been dismissed as the most unreliable of all post-mortem time scales. Such grasping at straws would continue to be part of medical expert testimony when all else failed.'
Sachs also quotes Dr Bernard Knight, from Claus Henssge, Bernard Knight, Thomas Krompecher, Burkhard Madea and Leonard Nokes, *The Estimation of the Time Since Death in the Early Postmortem Period*, Edward Arnold, London 1995, p. 27. 'Unfortunately, it is often the least experienced medical witness who tends to offer the most accurate estimates, not having seen enough cases to appreciate the many pitfalls and fallacies in the process.'
17 See Pocock, ref. 11.
18 'Juror claims "pressure"', *The Advertiser*, 18 February 1974.
19 RRStC Chamberlain, 'A former judge and the Van Beelen case', (letter), *The Advertiser*, 21 February 1974.
20 DJM Bevan, PY Dyer, HWJ Harding, GE Rogers & WB Taylor, 'Scientific evidence at Van Beelen trial', (letter), *The Advertiser*, 26 February 1974.
21 As related in the Opinion by EP Mullighan QC, 25 July 1988, Legal Services Commission, South Australia.

Chapter 6

1 The discussion of the Stevenson case is based on the appeal report, *The Queen v. Szach* (1980) 23 SASR (in Banco) King CJ, Legoe and Mohr JJ, 504–594, Dr Manock's autopsy report dated 27 July 1979. Also the following newspaper reports: 'Adelaide lawyer found murdered', *The Advertiser*, 6 June 1979; 'Lawyer, miner "were lovers"', *The Advertiser*, 7 August 1979; 'Bullet wound only injury: pathologist', *The Advertiser*, 9 August 1979; 'Miner, lawyer "fell for each other quickly"', *The Advertiser*, 10 August 1979; 'Man cried for his best friend, court is told', *The Advertiser*, 4 October 1979; 'Szach guilty: life imprisonment', *The Advertiser*, 20 December 1979; 'New probe into lawyer's murder', *Sunday Mail*, 25 August 1991.

2   The discussion of the Warren case is based on the autopsy report of Dr Manock dated 14 May 1985, the transcript of *R v. Stefan Niewdach and Alan Ellis* (1992), Dr Manock's evidence (pp. 122–144) and the summing up of the judge presiding at the trial.
3   Report of Dr Byron Collins to AD Dudek, Barristers and Solicitors, Adelaide, 5 August 1994.
4   RE Mittleman & CV Wetli, 'The threaded bolt injury pattern', *Journal of Forensic Sciences*, vol. 27 1982, pp. 567–71.

Chapter 7
1   The discussion of the Perry case is taken from *Perry v. The Queen* (1982) 150 CLR 580 (judgment dated 16 December 1982).
2   The details of the other cases are set out in the judgment of Gibbs CJ in the above judgment.
3   'Expert Witness', *4 Corners*, television program, ABC TV, 22 October 2001. <http://www.abc.net.au/4corners/stories/s397448.htm>
4   *Perry v. The Queen* (1982) 150 CLR 580 (judgment dated 16 December 1982).
5   Ibid., at 599.
6   Ibid., at 599.
7   Ibid., at 590.
8   Ibid., at 596.
9   Ibid., at 596.
10 Ibid., at 603.
11 Ibid., at 594.
12 Ibid., at 612.
13 Ibid., at 608.

Chapter 8
1   Royal Commission into Aboriginal Deaths in Custody: *Report of the Inquiry into the death of John Highfold,* 25 January 1989, (JH Muirhead, Commissioner).
2   *The Advertiser*, 19 April 1988.
3   Ibid.
4   See Royal Commission *Report* (Highfold), at 8.3.
5   Ibid. See also *The Advertiser*, 20 April and 21 April 1988.
6   See Royal Commission *Report* (Highfold), at 8.3.
7   *The Advertiser*, 21 April 1988.
8   *The Advertiser*, 16 August 1988. See also Royal Commission *Report* (Highfold), at 8.1.

9. *The Advertiser*, 15 April 1988.
10. See Royal Commission *Report* (Highfold), at 8.3.
11. Royal Commission into Aboriginal Deaths in Custody: *Report of the Inquiry into the death of Kingsley Dixon*, 2 February 1989, (JH Muirhead, Commissioner).
    The Advertiser, 30 September 1987, 19 February 1988 and 3 February 1989.
12. *The Advertiser*, 15 April 1988.
13. See Royal Commission *Report* (Kingsley Dixon), at 5.1.
14. Ibid.

Chapter 9

1. The information on this case is taken from the transcript of evidence before the Coronial Inquest which commenced on 23 April 1990, and the Finding of Inquest concerning the death of Elefterios Akritidis, 22 June 1990.
2. The pathology information is taken from the Forensic Science Centre autopsy report dated 7 August 1987, and from the transcript of Dr Manock's evidence to the Coronial Inquest.
3. Such as, for example, UKDA Goonetilleke, 'Injuries caused by falls from heights', *Medicine, Science and the Law*, vol. 20, 1980, pp. 262–75.
4. 'Intruder theory in shooting' and 'Bungle over shooting victim', *The Advertiser*, 7 February 1992.

Chapter 10

1. Mr Wayne Chivell, Coroner for South Australia, *Finding of Inquest into the Deaths of Storm Don Ernie Deane, William Anthony Barnard, Joshua Clive Nottle*, 25 August 1995.
   Report of Dr AC Thomas on the Deaths of Storm Don Ernie Deane, William Anthony Barnard, Joshua Clive Nottle, 11 February 1994.
   Dr CH Manock, Autopsy Report on Storm Don Ernie Deane, 27 October 1992.
   Dr CH Manock, Autopsy Report on Joshua Clive Nottle, 24 August 1993.
   Dr CH Manock, Autopsy Report on William Anthony Barnard, 15 September 1993.
   'Expert Witness', *4 Corners*, television program, ABC TV, 22 October 2001. <http://www.abc.net.au/4corners/stories/s397448.htm>
2. See Chivell, *Finding*, ref. 1, pp. 3, 9.
3. Address by Mr Moss (Counsel Assisting the Coroner), transcript, p. 979.

4 See Chivell, *Finding*, ref. 1, pp. 8, 27.
5 Ibid., p. 10.
6 Ibid., p. 25.
7 Ibid., p. 26.
8 Ibid., p. 88.
9 Ibid., p. 27. (Emphasis added)
10 Ibid., p. 52.
11 Ibid., p. 77.
12 Ibid., p. 72.
13 Ibid., p. 59.
14 Ibid., pp. 60–5.
15 Ibid., p. 82.
16 Ibid, p. 82.
17 Interview by Rohan Wenn, *Today Tonight,* television program, Channel 7 (Adelaide), recorded 27 June 2002.
18 The information in this section is taken from Dr Thomas's 'Anatomical Pathology Report'.

Chapter 11

1 The information for Chapters 11 and 12 is taken from the trial transcripts and evidence, witness statements, police and coronial running sheets and the law reports which resulted from the appeals in this case.
2 These matters are detailed in the Coronial Office running sheet.
3 *Today Tonight,* television program, Channel 7 (Adelaide), 30 July 2002.
4 Committal proceedings, Adelaide Magistrates Court, transcript, pp. 25–26.
5 SM Cordner, 'Further opinion in the case of Anna Cheney (deceased)', to Sykes Bidstrup, Adelaide, 16 December 1996.
6 Trial transcript, *R v. Henry Vincent Keogh,* (1995) p. 1019.
7 Ibid., p. 1022.
8 Ibid., p. 1062.
9 Interview by Rohan Wenn, *Today Tonight*, television program, Channel 7 (Adelaide), recorded 27 June 2002.
10 Ibid.
11 Ibid.
12 Ibid.
13 *Today Tonight*, television program, Channel 7 (Adelaide), 17 March 2003.
14 Attorney-General (Hon. Michael Atkinson), House of Assembly, South Australian Parliament, on 1 April 2003.

15 Baby Deaths Inquest, Coroner for South Australia, transcript, 25 November 1994, p. 601.
16 *Today Tonight,* television program, Channel 7 (Adelaide), 9 June 2003.
17 See interview by Rohan Wenn, *Today Tonight,* ref. 9.
18 See Cordner, ref. 5.
19 Ibid.

Chapter 12

1 SM Cordner, 'Further opinion in the case of Anna Cheney (deceased)', to Sykes Bidstrup, Adelaide, 16 December 1996.
2 'Expert Witness', *4 Corners,* television program, ABC TV, 22 October 2001. <http://www.abc.net.au/4corners/stories/s397448.htm>
3 Trial transcript, *R v. Henry Vincent Keogh* (1995), second trial, p. 1022.
4 Affidavit of Dr Tony Thomas to the Medical Board of South Australia and to the Solicitor-General of South Australia, paragraphs 144–147.
5 Trial transcript, *R v. Henry Vincent Keogh* (1995), first trial, p. 457. Examination of Dr Manock by Michael David QC, (emphasis added).
6 Trial transcript, second trial, p. 206. Examination of Dr Ross James by the prosecutor Mr Rofe QC, (emphasis added).
7 See Thomas, ref. 4, paragraph 151.
8 Trial transcript, second trial, p. 167.
9 Interview by Rohan Wenn, *Today Tonight,* television program, Channel 7 (Adelaide), recorded 27 June 2002.
10 *Today Tonight,* television program, Channel 7 (Adelaide), 9 June 2003.
11 See interview by Rohan Wenn, *Today Tonight,* ref. 9.
12 Affidavit of Michael Sykes, solicitor, dated 7 November 1996.
13 Statement by the Hon. Nick Xenophon to the South Australian Legislative Council, 31 October 2001.
14 *Today Tonight,* television program, Channel 7 (Adelaide), 24 December 2002.
15 'Atkinson attacks TV show ethics', *The Advertiser,* 2 April 2003, p. 2.
16 R Chamberlain, *The Stuart Affair,* Rigby, Adelaide, 1973, pp. 20–21.

Chapter 13

1 The details of Mr Penney's case have been taken from the committal proceedings transcript; the trial transcript; *The Queen v.*

Michael Ross Penney SCCRM No 194 of 1996; the Court of Criminal Appeal judgment [1997] South Australian Supreme Court 6071 (21 March 1997); and the report of *Penney v. The Queen* [1998] High Court of Australia 51 (13 August 1998).
2. Trial transcript, p. 240.
3. Trial transcript, p. 182.
4. Trial transcript, p. 154.
5. Trial transcript, p. 192.
6. Trial transcript, p. 197.
7. Trial transcript, pp. 205–6.
8. Trial transcript, p. 207.
9. Committal proceedings transcript, p. 82.
10. Trial transcript, p. 289.
11. Trial transcript, p. 293.
12. [1997] South Australian Supreme Court 6071 (21 March 1997)
13. *Penney v. The Queen* [1998] High Court of Australia 51 (13 August 1998).

Chapter 14

1. V Oakley, 'Settling for less', *The Advertiser*, 10 July 2003, p. 19.
2. G Kelton, 'DPP plea: just give us a fair hearing', *The Advertiser*, 2 August 2003, p. 9.
3. See Oakley, ref. 1.
4. G Kelton, 'Barrister calls for public plea input', *The Advertiser*, 2 August 2003, p. 8.
5. *Today Tonight*, television program, Channel 7 (Adelaide), 17 March 2003.
6. Ibid.
7. Mr Wayne Chivell, (Coroner for South Australia), *Finding of inquest in the matter of Lauren Kady and Callum Macdonald Aitken*, 6 November 2003.
8. *Today Tonight,* television program, Channel 7 (Adelaide), 17 March 2003, 27 April 2004 and 28 April 2004.
9. See Oakley, ref. 1.
10. Ibid.
    Today Tonight, television program, Channel 7 (Adelaide), 15 July 2003.
11. S Fewster, 'An eye for $100: justice on the cheap', *The Advertiser*, 26 July 2003, p. 1.
12. Sentencing remarks of Justice Sulan in the case of *R v. Paul Habib Nemer and K.* 25 July 2003, No. 146/2002.

13 C Hockley, 'Power of the people', *The Advertiser*, 31 July 2003, p. 1.
    C Hockley, 'Daughter's crusade to put shooter behind bars', *The Advertiser*, 1 August 2003, p. 4.
14 C Hockley, 'What judge wasn't told', *The Advertiser*, 7 August 2003, p. 1.
15 J Pengelley, 'Different barrel used in shooting', *The Advertiser*, 7 August 2003, p. 3.
16 S Fewster, 'After two years, Nemer appeal thrown out in 20 minutes', *The Advertiser*, 14 February 2004, p. 5.
    Nemer v. Holloway & Ors; Nemer v. The Queen [2004] HCA Trans 24 (13 February 2004, at pp. 6, 7.
17 G Kelton, 'Government "vindicated" on Nemer case', *The Advertiser*, 17 February 2004, p. 12.
18 *Re: Request to advise on matter of Paul Nemer and associated issues.* Report to the Attorney-General, by Mr Chris Kourakis QC, Solicitor-General of South Australia, 7 April 2004.
19 C Bildstien, 'Atkinson stops short of delivering Rofe verdict', *The Advertiser*, 24 April 2004, p. 34.
20 G Kelton, 'Get on your bike, Mr DPP', *The Advertiser*, 4 May 2004, pp. 1, 4.
21 Attorney-General Michael Atkinson, 'The case is closed', (statement to Parliament), *The Advertiser*, 4 May 2004, p. 19.
22 G Kelton, 'In search of our own Eliot Ness', *The Advertiser*, 6 May 2004, p. 11.

Chapter 15

1 G Samuels, 'Is this the best we can do?', *Australian Journal of Forensic Sciences*, vol. 25, 1993, pp. 3–9.
2 Ibid.
3 Mick Hamer, 'How a forensic scientist fell foul of the law', *New Scientist*, 3 September 1981, pp. 575–6.
4 Cited in Hamer, ref. 3.
5 Cited in 'Prisoner cleared of murder after serving 8 years', *The Times* (London), 20 June 1981, p. 1.
6 Ibid.
7 AR Brownlie, 'Expert evidence in the light of *Preece v. H. M. Advocate*', *Medicine, Science and the Law*, vol. 22, 1982, pp. 237–44.
8 'Cot death mothers: the witch hunt', *4 Corners*, television program, ABC TV, (program from the BBC), 5 August 2003.
9 Downloaded from <http://www.gmc-uk.org/news/current/Meadows%20Statement.htm> on 12 February 2004.

10 See 'Cot death mothers', *4 Corners*, ref. 8.
11 The information in this section has been compiled from the materials which are available through the Criminal Cases Review Commission website, <www.ccrc.gov.uk>
12 D Napley, 'Trial at law', *Medicine, Science and the Law*, vol. 8, 1968, pp. 227–42.
13 See, for example, the references to Havard (ref. 15), Kennedy (ref. 17) and Brownlie (ref. 21) which follow.
14 See for example, IF Sheppard, 'The issue of the inquisitorial system of justice', *Australian Journal of Forensic Sciences*, vol. 31 1999, pp. 19–28.
15 JDJ Havard, 'Expert scientific evidence under the adversarial system. A travesty of justice?', *Journal of the Forensic Science Society*, vol. 32, 1992, pp. 225–35.
16 See Napley, ref. 12.
17 L Kennedy, *Thirty-six murders and two immoral earnings,* Profile Books, London, 2003.
18 Ibid.
19 The Innocence Project at Benjamin N Cardozo School of Law, founded by Barry Scheck and Peter Neufeld. <www.innocenceproject.com>
20 T Simon, 'It wasn't me', *The Weekend Australian Magazine*, 26–27 July, 2003, pp. 28–31.
21 AR Brownlie, 'The presentation of scientific evidence in court: Great Britain', *Journal of the Forensic Science Society*, vol. 14, 1974, pp. 183–90.
    D Kinley & A Rose, 'The quest for the truth: a comparative analysis of the role of experts in litigation', *Australian Journal of Forensic Sciences*, vol. 31, 1999, pp. 5–18.
    See also Kennedy, ref. 17.
22 SM Cordner, 'Further opinion in the case of Anna Cheney (deceased)', to Sykes Bidstrup, Adelaide, 16 December 1996.
23 Interview by Rohan Wenn, *Today Tonight*, television program, Channel 7 (Adelaide), recorded 27 June 2002.
24 *Today Tonight*, television program, Channel 7, (Adelaide), 17 March 2003.
25 See interview by Rohan Wenn, *Today Tonight*, ref. 23.

Chapter 16

1 J Robertson, 'Integrity issues impacting on the provision of forensic services', *Australian Journal of Forensic Sciences*, vol. 31, 1999, pp. 87–97 at p. 89.

2. 'Premier right to criticise justice system' (editorial), *The Advertiser*, 1 August 2003, p. 16.
3. 'An injustice in our system of justice' (editorial), *The Advertiser*, 30 July 2003, p. 16.
4. 'Kourakis gets to heart of flawed case' (editorial), *The Advertiser*, 7 August 2003, p. 16.
5. Sean Fewster, 'Concern over number of dropped prosecutions', *The Advertiser*, 16 June 2003, p. 11.
6. Interview by Rohan Wenn, *Today Tonight*, television program, Channel 7 (Adelaide), recorded 27 June 2002.
7. *Today Tonight*, television program, Channel 7 (Adelaide), 30 July 2002.
8. JF Keefe, 'Forensic science services and the criminal justice system as viewed by the defense', *Journal of Forensic Sciences*, vol. 24, 1979, pp. 673–80.
9. *Boucher v. The Queen* (1955), pp. 110 CCC 263 (SCC). Quoted in Robertson, ref. 1.
10. Christmas Humphries, in Crim LL 739, 1955. Quoted in Crispin, ref. 29.
11. *Re: Request to advise on matter of Paul Nemer and associated issues.* Report to the Attorney-General, by Mr Chris Kourakis QC, Solicitor-General of South Australia, 7 April 2004, p. 4.
12. Justice Wood, 'Forensic sciences from the judicial perspective', *Australian Journal of Forensic Sciences*, vol. 35, 2003, pp. 115–32. C Porter, 'The evidence of experts', *Australian Journal of Forensic Sciences*, vol. 27 1995, pp. 53–8.
13. G Samuels, 'Is this the best we can do?', *Australian Journal of Forensic Sciences*, vol. 25, 1993, pp. 3–9.
14. See Justice Wood, ref. 12.
15. R Amlot, '4. Leave the jury alone', *Medicine, Science and the Law*, vol. 38, 1998, pp. 123–5.
16. See Justice Wood, ref. 12.
17. D Patterson, 'What can science do for the law?', *Journal of the Forensic Science Society*, vol. 15, 1975, pp. 3–6.
18. DS Bell, 'The expert misleads. The court follows', *Australian Journal of Forensic Sciences*, vol. 27, 1995, pp. 59–64.
19. C Porter & RWR Parker, 'The demeanour of expert witnesses', *Australian Journal of Forensic Sciences*, vol. 33, 2001, pp. 45–50.
20. JD Jackson, '3. Trying criminal cases without juries', *Medicine, Science and the Law*, vol. 38, 1998, pp. 112–22.

21 John Doyle, (Chief Justice of South Australia), 'Jurors cannot investigate details of crimes', *The Advertiser*, 29 May 2004, p. 28.
22 Stewart Cockburn, 'The jurors: some serious doubts', *The Advertiser*, 4 May 1981, p. 4.
23 S Cordner, 'Outcomes for society: forensic pathology', *Australian Journal of Forensic Sciences*, vol. 35, 2003, pp. 133–40.
24 See Porter, ref. 12.
25 RFG Ormrod, 'Evidence and proof: scientific and legal', *Medicine, Science and the Law*, vol. 12, 1972, pp. 9–20.
26 See Porter, ref. 12.
27 See Porter & Parker, ref. 19.
28 AA Moenssens, RE Moses & FE Inbau, *Scientific evidence in criminal cases*, Foundation Press, New York, 1973, p. 13.
29 KJ Crispin, 'Coping with complexity', *Australian Journal of Forensic Sciences*, vol. 24 1992, pp. 74–81.
30 DS Bell, 'Whose accountability, judges or experts?', *Australian Journal of Forensic Sciences*, vol. 26, 1994, pp. 74–6.
31 See Samuels, ref. 13.
32 JB Weinstein, 'Enhancing the relationship of science and the courts', *Journal of Forensic Sciences*, vol. 43, 1998, pp. 242–5.
33 See Cordner, ref. 23.
34 Greg Kelton, 'Special appeals court ruled out', *The Advertiser*, 7 April 2004, p. 25.
35 Sean Fewster, 'Judge joins "elite" on the bench', *The Advertiser*, 15 May 2004, p. 19.
36 Andrew Goode, 'Impartial judiciary a must, however selected', *The Advertiser*, 18 January 2003, p. 28.
37 IF Shepherd, 'The issue of the inquisitorial system of justice', *Australian Journal of Forensic Sciences*, vol. 31, 1999, pp. 19–28.
38 See Samuels, ref. 13.
39 Andrew Goode, 'Panel to place a focus on issues of law', *The Advertiser*, 25 August 2003, p. 18.
40 'Expert Witness', *4 Corners*, television program, ABC TV, 22 October 2001. <http://www.abc.net.au/4corners/stories/s397448.htm>
41 B Manarin, 'Assessing the expert: a call for reciprocal disclosure in Canada', *Medicine, Science and the Law*, vol. 39, 1999, pp. 17–22.
42 KE Melson, 'President's editorial — The journey to justice', *Journal of Forensic Sciences*, vol. 48, 2003, pp. 705–7.

INDEX

ABC *4 Corners* 'Expert Witness'
    program xxii, 258
  Baby Deaths 143, 149, 152
  Frits Van Beelen 82, 90
  Henry Keogh 190
accountability xxiii, 259
acquittal 5
actus reus (element of a crime) 4
  Henry Keogh 158, 161
Adelaide *Advertiser* 3, 241
  report of drowning case,
    Sydney 170
admissibility of evidence 15
adversarial system 11, 246–9
Ahern, Mr (Coroner) 122
airway 63
Aitken, Hayley, Hayden, Callum
    and Lauren 211
Aitken, Scott (plea-bargain) 210
algor mortis (cooling of body —
    timing of death) 72
allergies 66–70; *see also*
    anaphylactic shock
alliances of convenience xxiii,
    259
American Society of Crime
    Laboratory Directors 226
anaphylactic shock 68–71
  Henry Keogh 170–2
anatomy (role of) 27

aorta (blood vessel coming from
    heart)
  explained 57
  Henry Keogh 170
  Terry Akritidis 129, 133–4
appeals 19–20
  limitations of 23
  Henry Keogh 187
  reform of 252–5
Archer, Graham (Producer
    Channel 7 *Today Tonight*) 236
artifactual bleeding 53
asphyxiation 60
Association in Aid of the
    Wrongly Convicted 234
assumptions (danger of) 240
  John Highfold 122
  Terry Akritidis 137
Atkinson, Michael
  Henry Keogh 162, 190–1
  Parliamentary statement 173
  Paul Nemer 215
  see also Attorney-General
Attorney-General (powers of)
    6–7, 21
asystolic (or straightline) 66
autopsy 40
  hospital/forensic distinguished
    40
  report 55

Barnard, William (Billy) 145; *see* Baby Deaths chapter
Bevan, Dr (professor of chemistry) 88
beyond reasonable doubt (onus of proof in criminal cases) xx
Birmingham Six (UK terrorist case) 8, 24
black and white photos (Henry Keogh) 174
bleeding 57
bleeding post mortem
    Frits Van Beelen 91–2
    Terry Akritidis 135
blood pressure and bleeding 134
blowfly activity 74
    Stefan Niewdach & Alan Ellis 107
    see also entomology
Blumbergs, Dr (neuropathologist) 147
blunt force injuries 58
    Stefan Niewdach & Alan Ellis 104
body chart
    (reliance upon) Henry Keogh case 179
    (utility of) Terry Akritidis case 137
body cooling (David Szach) 100
body temperature
    (not taken) Baby Deaths 150
    (not taken) Frits Van Beelen 85, 89
    (not taken) Terry Akritidis 135
bond (for good behaviour) 214
Borick, Kevin QC xxii, 241, 243
    Frits Van Beelen 90
    Henry Keogh 161, 163, 190
    Michael Penney 197, 199

botany and geology 28
brain (at autopsy) 50
    Baby Deaths 142, 147, 150
    Henry Keogh 175–6
    in drowning 59
    John Highfold 121
    Terry Akritidis 133
breathing and oxygen absorption 59
'Brides in the bath' (R v Smith) 116
bronchopneumonia 139; *see* Baby Deaths chapter
bronchospasm (not detectable at autopsy) 149–50
Brown, Stacey (victim of Darren Schmidt) 212
bruising 52, 183
Byard, Dr Roger (paediatric pathologist) 143, 149

case management 38
cause of death (investigate all reasonable possibilities) 121
CCRC (Criminal Cases Review Commission) UK 24, 228–35
chain-of-evidence 34
Chamberlain, Lindy (Australian 'dingo' case) 8, 24, 234
Chamberlain, Sir Roderic 94, 192
chemistry 28
Cheney, Anna-Jane 155, 180; *see* Henry Keogh chapters
Cheney, family 191
circulatory system 56
circumstantial evidence
    Emily Perry 117
    Frits Van Beelen 87
    Henry Keogh 155, 180

circumstantial evidence (*cont.*)
  Michael Penney 196, 207
  Stefan Niewdach & Alan Ellis 105
Clark, Sally (UK babies case) 227
Clift, Dr Alan (biologist UK) 223–6
coaching a witness (not allowed) 17
Cockburn, Stewart (journalist) 3
Collins, Dr Byron (pathologist)
  David Szach 100–2
  John Highfold 121
colour photographs
  policy, Henry Keogh/Baby Deaths 173
  taken in Kingsley Dixon case 123
committal proceedings 10–11
communication strategies 39
contamination of crime scenes 30, 36, 39
  Henry Keogh 165
cooling of body, timing of death (algor mortis) 72–3
Cordner, Professor Stephen (pathologist) 161, 181
coroner 26
Coronial findings
  Baby deaths cases 151, 154
  Henry Keogh case 188
  Terry Akritidis case 137
cost of pathology tests
  John Highfold 120–1
course of conduct
  Emily Perry 110–14
Court of Criminal Appeal 19
  Emily Perry case 110, 239
  Henry Keogh case 188–9
  reform of 252–4

CPR (cardio pulmonary resuscitation) 163
crime scene investigations 31–9
Criminal Cases Review Commission; *see* CCRC
criminal offence (elements of) 4
cross-examination 9, 16–17, 250–1
critical evaluation essential xix, 259

David, Michael QC
David Szach case 102
  Henry Keogh case 158, 181
Deane, Storm Don Ernie 140; *see* Baby Deaths chapters
defence counsel 8
diatoms (diagnosis of drowning) 64
  Frits Van Beelen 92
Dietrich principle (unable to afford a lawyer) 12
Donald, Dr Terry (Child Protection) 143, 146, 149–52
DPP (Director of Public Prosecutions) 7, 240
drowning 58, 65
  see also Henry Keogh chapters
Duncan, Jim 112; *see* Emily Perry chapter

electrocardiogram 66
entomology 28, 74
epilepsy 71–2
  John Highfold 120
evidence-in-chief 16
evidence
  latent 35
  options for accused in court 18
  preservation/destruction of 35

exculpatory (favourable to the
    accused) 244
experts
    accountable to the public xix
    publication of evidence 251
    role of 14, 22, 249–52
    Terry Akritidis 132
    testing of 8–9
eye-witness evidence
    (unreliability) 13

fall from a height 132
fibrillation of heart 66
footprints 38
    Terry Akritidis 130
forensic 25
Forensic Science Centre
    (Adelaide) 26, 226–7
forensic science services 26–7,
    246
    in UK 223–6, 246
    range of 27–9
fractures
    (of arm) Baby deaths 146
    (of ribs) Baby deaths 142, 148
    (of vertebrae) Terry Akritidis
    133
frothing of mouth in drowning
    63

General Medical Council UK
    228
geology and botany 28
Guildford Four (UK terrorist
    case) 8, 24

Haag, Albert 111; *see* Emily
    Perry chapter
haemolysis (bursting of red blood
    cells) 62
    Henry Keogh 170

hairs and fibres
    Frits Van Beelen 87–8
hanging (Kingsley Dixon) 123
heart at autopsy 50–1
    Baby deaths 141
    Henry Keogh 175–6
    John Highfold 121
    schoolboy death 153
heart attack 47
heart defect (schoolboy death)
    153
heart failure in drowning 62
heatstroke (schoolboy death) 153
Henneberg, Professor Maciej
    (anatomy) 184
High Court of Australia 19
    Emily Perry 110, 114
    Henry Keogh 188
    Paul Nemer 216
histology 47–9
    samples in Keogh 175
histamine in allergic reactions 67
hypostasis (settling of blood for
    timing of death) 73; *see also*
    lividity

Institute of Medical and
    Veterinary Science, Adelaide
    (IMVS) 81, 83
Innocence projects 235
inquisitorial system 11, 233–4
insects (timing of death) 74; *see
    also* entomology
insurance (as motive for murder)
    Emily Perry 110
    Henry Keogh 159

James, Dr Ross (pathologist)
    178–9, 183, 217
Jessel, David (UK journalist) 230
Judicial review system 255

jury xviii, 11, 246–8
   selection 12

Keogh, Susan (former wife of Henry Keogh) 160
Kourakis, Chris QC (Attorney-General SA) 244

lawyer
   obligations as officer of the court 9, 17
   role of 23
Leach, Deborah (murdered) 84
leading question (not usually allowed) 16
leave to appeal 20
lividity (settling of blood) for timing of death 73
   Terry Akritidis 135
   see also hypostasis
Locard principle (of transference) 30
   Frits Van Beelen 88
Lunn, Robert M, *Criminal Law in South Australia* 15

Manock, Dr Colin (background) 80–4
mast cells (in allergic reactions) 67
Meadow, Professor Sir Roy UK 227
medical records (John Highfold) 120–1
Medicare records 54
   Henry Keogh 169
mens rea (element of a crime) 4
   Henry Keogh 158–61
miscarriages of justice 23
   examples in UK 231–3
   frequency in UK 24
molecular biology 28

Montgomerie, Francis 111; *see* Emily Perry chapter
motive, Henry Keogh 159
mucous plugging (anaphylactic response) 171
Mullighan QC (in Van Beelen case) 96

National Association of Testing Authorities (NATA) 48
natural justice 247
Neighbour, Sally (reporter ABC *4 Corners*) 258
   Baby Deaths 152
   Colin Manock 82
   Frits Van Beelen 90
Nemer, Paul (plea-bargain) 213–16
neutrophils (to age bruising) 53, 57
no case to answer (at criminal trial) 196–7
no suspicious circumstances
   Henry Keogh 156, 168
   John Highfold 121
   Peter Marshall 138
   Terry Akritidis 127
not proven verdict (benefits of) 249
Nottle, Joshua Clive (*see* Baby Deaths chapter) 148
NSAID (non-steroidal anti-inflammatory drug) 177

odontology (teeth) 29
oedema (causes swelling) explained 61
Ormrod, Sir Roger (British judge) 250
overdose of drugs
   John Highfold 120

Parliamentary accountability 216
parole board
   David Szach 102
   Frits Van Beelen 97
pathologist (forensic) explained 25–6
Penney, Julie 193; *see* Michael Penney chapter
peer review 39, 226, 257
   Henry Keogh 178
Pereira, Margaret (forensic scientist UK) 223–4
Perry, Ken 109; *see* Emily Perry chapter
petition to the Governor 20
   Henry Keogh 189–91
photographs 37
   bruising 52
   Henry Keogh 178
   (not developed) Michael Penney 201
   (not taken) Terry Akritidis 127, 134
physics 29
plea-bargaining 9–10, 209–10
poisoning 109; *see* Emily Perry chapter
   John Highfold 120, 123
Police Forensic Procedures Manual
   crime scene investigation 31, 242
   General Orders 31
   Henry Keogh 174
   Paul Rofe (DPP) 241–2
   Terry Akritidis 131, 136
Porter case (US miscarriage of justice) 24
post mortem bleeding
   Frits Van Beelen 85

Pounder, Derrick (professor of pathology UK) 90, 174
Preece (Scottish miscarriage of justice case) 224
prejudice xx
preliminary hearing 10–11
prerogative power 20
presumption of innocence xx, 5–6
   (brushed aside) Emily Perry 117
   Frits Van Beelen 96
Priestly, Andrew (plea-bargain) 212
prima facie (on the face of it) 10
Privy Council (Frits Van Beelen appeal) 94
prosecutions (reform of) 245
public prosecutor 6–7, 244

Rann, Mike (Premier South Australia) 241
   Paul Nemer 216, 218
re-enactment
   Henry Keogh 183
   Michael Penney 205
   Scott Aitken 212
reflection (peeling back) of scalp 174
re-opening appeal (in Henry Keogh) 188
rigor mortis (stiffening of muscles) for timing of death 74
   Terry Akritidis case 136
Rofe, Paul QC (DPP) 241–3
   Baby Deaths 153
   Henry Keogh 162, 165, 169
   Michael Penney 199
   Paul Nemer 215–8
   police procedures manual 174
   Scott Aitken 211

Royal College of Pathology of
    Australasia 83
Royal Commission 21, 237
    Aboriginal deaths in custody
        119–20
    Runciman, UK 228
    see also Splatt
running sheets 38
    Henry Keogh 177

Samuels, Gordon QC 221–2
Schmidt, Darren (plea-bargain)
    212, 217
search strategies 36
scientific evidence
    David Szach 101
    Emily Perry 114–18
    Frits Van Beelen 86
secretor (explained) 224
shaking babies 150
Shannon, Judge (in Splatt
    Commission) 22
skull fractures (Terry Akritidis
    case) 133
Solicitor-General 244
    Henry Keogh 191–2
    Paul Nemer 215–8
specialist examination of body
    50
    Henry Keogh 175
Splatt, Edward (Royal
    Commission) xxii, 3, 21–2,
    177, 226–7, 234, 250
Stevenson, Derrance 98; *see*
    David Szach chapter
stomach contents (for timing of
    death) 75
    (unreliable) Frits Van Beelen
        case 89–91
sudden death in adults 169

summing up
    by judge 18
    by prosecutor (Henry Keogh
        case) 161–2
Supreme Court trial 12, 19
suspicious deaths (investigations)
    32, 41

temperatures and timing of death
    34
Thomas, Dr Tony
    Baby Deaths 236
    Henry Keogh 169, 182
    schoolboy death 154
timing of death 72–6
    David Szach 99
    Frits Van Beelen 89
    Stefan Niewdach & Alan Ellis
        108,
Today Tonight (Channel 7) 242
    Henry Keogh 160, 162, 169,
        190
    Scott Aitken 212
    virtual re-enactment, Keogh
        case 186
topic-by-topic jury trials 247
toxicology 49
    Henry Keogh 176
    John Highfold 120
trace evidence 38
transference (principle of) 29–31
trial procedures 16–18
tyremarks 38
    Terry Akritidis 130

UK forensic science services
    27
UK miscarriage of justice cases
    231–33
US Supreme Court 244

verdict 5, 13
virtopsy (virtual autopsy) 54
voir dire (trial within a trial) 15

Warren, Gerald 102; *see* Stefan Niewdach & Alan Ellis chapter

Wenn, Rohan (reporter Channel 7 *Today Tonight*) 160, 236, 242
Williams, Dr Alan (UK pathologist) 227
Williams, Mr (victim of Paul Nemer) 213
witnesses 13, 22, 226